Race and Ethnic Relations in Today's America

GREG OSWALD
Former Principal Teacher of History/Modern Studies,
Lockerbie Academy, Dumfries and Galloway, Scotland

Ashgate

Aldershot • Burlington USA • Singapore • Sydney

Published by
Ashgate Publishing Limited
Gower House
Croft Road
Aldershot
Hampshire GU11 3HR
England

Ashgate Publishing Company
131 Main Street
Burlington, VT 05401-5600 USA

Ashgate website: http://www.ashgate.com

British Library Cataloguing in Publication Data
Oswald, Greg
　　　　Race and ethnic relations in today's America. -
　　　　(Interdisciplinary research series in ethnic, gender and
　　　　class relations)
　　　　1. United States - Ethnic relations 2. United States - Race
　　　　relations
　　　　I.Title
　　　　305.8'0073

Library of Congress Control Number:　　00-111416

ISBN 0 7546 1584 7

Printed and bound by Athenaeum Press, Ltd.,
Gateshead, Tyne & Wear.

Contents

List of Figures and Tables

Figures

Tables

Preface

In writing this book, my aim is to accomplish two goals: first, to acquaint undergraduate students with the main developments in the field of U.S. race and ethnic relations in the past decade, and second, to challenge misconceptions, especially those held abroad. Both objectives are the result of personal experience. Although an American citizen, I have spent a good portion of my life – upwards of thirty years – either in higher academic study or teaching social subjects in the UK. Throughout that long time I have come across innumerable students who, while well grounded in American history and culture, often have done little formal study of contemporary U.S. public policy issues. An exception to this in Britain are those Scots fortunate enough to have taken the race relations option in 'Higher' and 'Advanced Higher' Modern Studies courses. But these scholars are relatively few in the broader realm of academia, and this work, while it assumes no prior knowledge of the subject at hand, does try to take the reader some way beyond what he or she learned at the senior secondary level.

The preconceived notions that foreigners and, indeed, some Americans themselves have about racial matters in the United States are numerous and, alas, often ill founded. Stereotypes abound about such matters as African American political views and social leanings, non-white indigence and the lack of a work ethic on the part of many racial and ethnic minorities. Without trying to be iconoclastic, this book asserts among other things that poverty is a native born white as well as a black and immigrant problem, that desegregation rather than integration is a goal of many African Americans, and that for better or worse a conservative political, social and economic outlook can be found in plenty of Asian, Hispanic and even black households.

Although a white male author, I feel I have no particular ideological axe to grind and so have endeavoured to present the subject matter and various arguments in what I think is an objective manner without sacrificing intellectual rigour. This book presents, occasionally through extracts, attitudes to relevant current public policy issues from a number of perspectives – Left and Right, black and white, immigrant and native born –

while drawing attention to nuances of opinion. It uses statistics to discern group socioeconomic trends and performances while urging readers to exercise caution in interpretation. It analyses in an evenhanded way both sides of the debate presently going on in learned circles in the US about the nature and extent of minority progress in 1990s America. And while it offers conclusions, it does so primarily as springboards for further discussion rather than as pronouncements from on high.

Given its public policy orientation, this book focuses on those issues that have preoccupied social scientists and politicians the most. It generally neglects popular culture, even though African Americans and other minorities have played and continue to exert a big role in sports, entertainment and the arts in the U.S. As regards presentation, I have organised the chapters to be read consecutively, with some of the more thorny issues like affirmative action and immigration saved till later in the work following earlier discussions of jobs, education, the status of non-black minorities and the like. Furthermore, many opening paragraphs refer to previously mentioned issues. Nonetheless, I have tried to make each chapter a relatively free standing and independent essay capable of being read on its own, if the student so wishes.

One keynote of the book is that semantics is at the root of much of the current racial and ethnic divide. Blacks and whites either tend to define certain practices in quite different ways or argue as to whether some of these practices can be subdivided into acceptable and unacceptable forms of behaviour. 'Racism' is an example of the former; 'rational' and 'irrational' discrimination are cases of the latter. Even more fundamentally, perhaps, 'race' means something quite other to Hispanics than what it does to Caucasians, just as Latino notions of 'assimilation' (in the sense of gaining majority white acceptance) are often at odds with those of African Americans. How these differences arise and the difficulties they can cause are themes that the work visits time and again.

Indeed, phrasing can be a rather thorny matter when considering some rather less abstract terms in an area such as this. Defining just what 'race' and 'ethnic' mean has long been fraught with difficulties, and never moreso than today when travel and intermarriage have brought about an unprecedented mixing of peoples. In the United States the former word is as much a social construct as a scientific reality, as is explained in Chapter 1, while the latter is a complex concept capable of being interpreted in either a broad cultural or more narrow geographic sense. For the sake of simplicity, this book generally treats race as a biological classification based largely on skin colour and ethnicity as a cultural one, in which a group of people share and act out a common tradition of some sort. In the pages that follow, 'race' refers to blacks, whites, Native- and even Asian Americans and treats them, as does the U.S. Bureau of the Census, as though they are in pigmentation terms distinct single groups, even though this clearly is by no means always the case. By contrast, the word 'ethnic' has been incorporated into the title of the book almost by default chiefly to denote Hispanics, who because they include whites, blacks and others in their ranks cannot be classified as a race. Only to a lesser extent does 'ethnic' refer here to specific nationality groups that have emigrated to the USA and then primarily to the less assimilated ones like Cuban-, Mexican- and Vietnamese Americans rather than to the subsets of peoples from 19th and early 20th century Europe usually included in this category.

Although race and ethnicity are usually defined quite differently, this is not to say that the two classifications are mutually exclusive. Many would contend that everyone has both a racial and an ethnic identity, sometimes multiple layers of them because of generations of marriage outside a grouping. In the case of U.S. blacks, however, the claiming of a particular ethnic affiliation has often been very hard, if not impossible, to achieve, largely because so many of their ancestors were captured centuries ago in unrecorded circumstances in various parts of Africa and then transported as slaves to the New World, where cultural heritage was denied them. Unlike most American Indians, for instance, a U.S. black almost never can know for certain the tribe(s) from which he or she is descended, and part of the great popularity of the 1976 book and subsequent TV miniseries *Roots* was the fact that author Alex Haley was able to achieve this in a credible way through a fictionalised version of actual events concerning his family. Other U.S. blacks have not been so lucky in their endeavours, and to offset this lack of information and to assert that they, too, have a cultural heritage of their own, many people now commonly called 'black' prefer to describe themselves as 'African American'. However, others belonging to this category remain quite happy with the former term, seeing it as a succinct and clear counterpoint to 'white', the word most commonly used to describe those of European ancestry. This book seeks to draw no distinction between the two and uses them interchangeably when discussing America's biggest racial minority.

A similar approach has been adopted with regard to those who are of Caribbean, Mexican, Central and South American origin. 'Latino' and 'Hispanic' are the two most widely used terms to label this group of people. The latter is strictly speaking a bit less correct than the former inasmuch as it describes a language that not all people from this part of the world speak. (Brazilians, for instance, have Portuguese, not Spanish for their native tongue.) Furthermore, in some circles 'Hispanic' carries with it a connotation of affluence while 'Latino' is associated with poverty and injustice. In California, America's biggest state and the one with the largest such population, 'Latino' is favoured regardless of socioeconomic circumstances. However, as 'Hispanic' was the only term that until the year 2000 was employed on census and other forms in connection with this group and continues to be used in everyday conversation in Texas and Florida and other parts of the country with large Spanish speaking populations, it has been decided here to treat the one as being fully synonymous with the other.

Considerations of style rather than anything else have been the main factor in the decision to use two or more terms to describe most of the other leading groups mentioned in this book. Thus to prevent the overuse of one word, 'Caucasian', though rather awkward sounding and cumbersome (not to mention historically incorrect), has been placed on a par with 'white'. Likewise, 'American Indian', 'Native American' and 'Red Indian', all of which seem to have no different nuances of meaning attached to them, are freely used back and forth in the pages that follow when talking about the tribesmen and women on the reservations. By contrast, in general only 'Asian' has been employed to label en masse America's immigrants and their descendants from across the Pacific. This is in many ways unsatisfactory because it is an extremely vague expression applying to hundreds of different ethnic and racial groups who sometimes have little in common except that they happen to come from the same huge continent. 'Asian' is also the category to which the U.S. Bureau of the Census assigns the Pacific Islander peoples of Hawaii. But in the absence of any other single all embracing politically correct term – 'Oriental' is now thought to contain an offensive Western bias and, like 'Negro' or 'coloured' in connection with blacks, is seen as antiquated – it has been decided here to adhere to the one expression. It is to be hoped that the reader does not find all this inadequate and/or confusing.

Greg Oswald

Alexandria, Virginia
August 2000

Series Editor's Preface

Any book on race and ethnic relations anywhere in the world is bound to be controversial and this one by Greg Oswald on the volatile relations in America is no exception. The key question the author tries to answer is why, in spite of policy initiatives to end racism, the problem still persists?

According to Oswald, the majority of white Americans who believed that O.J. Simpson was guilty would blame affirmative action and the welfare state (as if O.J. was on welfare) for encouraging single parenthood among African Americans (with 70% of children born out of wedlock) compared to Caucasians (22%) and Hispanics (44%). On the other hand, the majority of African Americans who believed that O.J. was innocent would blame institutionalised racism and direct discrimination for the disproportionate poverty rate among African Americans who are more likely to be racially profiled by law enforcement agents and the general public alike. As Oswald put it:

> If the main source of income for black females according to popular perception is the welfare cheque, the main source of income for black males in the minds of many is crime. A national survey in 1990 showed that over half of non-black people questioned thought African Americans were more violent than whites, and that African American men were especially dangerous (p.83).

Oswald suggests that individual prejudice remains part of the problems facing even middle class African Americans who frequently find their qualifications being doubted by colleagues and who find themselves being assigned predominantly to public relations departments that would be the first to be down-sized in times of recession.

The author is most controversial when he argues that white Americans tend to overestimate the number of African Americans in the total population due to prejudice against them. The author adds that African Americans are also prejudiced against immigrants and that anti-Semitism is widespread among them, disputing the claim by some that the relatively powerless cannot, by definition, be racist.

Some readers could question claims like this in the book especially because the author provoked many of the thoughts without exhausting the discussion in this slim volume. To suggest that black and white of all classes are fleeing the inner cities to the suburbs and smaller towns in the south for the same (racist) reason of prejudice against immigrants (who presumably take away jobs from the underclass and scare the rich with violent crimes) is certainly controversial. A sceptical reader might suggest that the reason why the poorer people are migrating down to the south is different from the reasons of the richer migrants because the cost of living on minimum wage is lower down there compared to the expensive cities up north.

Overall, Oswald plays the role of the school teacher well by presenting different sides to the controversies. History teachers will find this book useful because of the way arguments on different sides of the issues are carefully outlined without taking a dogmatic position. Also, dating the origin of *Race and Ethnic Relations in Today's America* back to the European genocide against Native Americans and the enslavement of African Americans is a welcome departure from texts that start discussions of race relations with the civil rights movement.

Biko Agozino

Associate Professor of Criminology
Indiana University of Pennsylvania

Acknowledgements

I am grateful to the following for their help in providing material:

The Free Press division of Simon and Schuster and the Sagalyn Literary Agency for the quote from *The End of Racism: Principles for a Multiracial Society* by Dinesh D'Souza;

James K. Glassman for the quote from his article 'Is America Finally Going Colour-Blind?' in the *Washington Post*, 3 June 1997;

The Milton S. Eisenhower Foundation for the quote from *The Millennium Breach: Richer and Poorer in America*;

The Nation for the quote from 'Discrimination in Favour of Minorities Is Necessary' by E. Foner in the Greehhaven Press anthology, *Interracial America: Opposing Viewpoints*;

The Washington Post, Inc. for the quote from 'Trashed by the Welfare Bill' by C.I. King, 27 July 1996;

The World and I for the G. Bikales quote in 'Immigrants Take Jobs from Blacks' by J. Miles in the Greenhaven Press anthology, *Race Relations: Opposing Viewpoints*.

List of Abbreviations

ABC   American Broadcasting Corporation

AFDC   Aid to Families with Dependent Children

AIM   American Indian Movement

CBS   Columbia Broadcasting System

FBI   Federal Bureau of Investigation

HBO   Home Box Office

INS   Immigration and Naturalisation Service

KKK   Ku Klux Klan

MIT   Massachusetts Institute of Technology

NAACP   National Association for the Advancement of Coloured People

NAFTA   North American Free Trade Association

NBC   National Broadcasting Corporation

PBS   Public Broadcasting System

UPN   United Paramount Network

WASPs   White Anglo-Saxon Protestants

WB   Warner Brothers

1 Introduction

'The problem of the twentieth century is the problem of the colour line.'

Thus remarked the African American scholar W.E.B. DuBois in 1903, and as regards the United States the comment has proved to be quite prescient. There have been more intense and more immediately frightening problems facing America since the above remark was made. The two world wars with Germany are obvious examples, as are the economic swings involving boom and bust in the Twenties and Thirties and the more recent nuclear rivalry with Russia, to name but a few. But for sheer intractability and pervasiveness nothing has come close to matching the problems surrounding race relations and the differing ways in which whites and blacks see matters.

Anyone who doubts this need look no further than the 1994-5 trial of O.J. Simpson, the African American celebrity and former National Football League player accused of murdering his white ex-wife and her white male companion. Most Caucasians believed Simpson was guilty; most blacks believed him to be innocent and a victim of a biased criminal justice system. When the verdict of innocence was announced, whites were dismayed that two deaths had, as they saw it, gone unpunished, while blacks cheered that one of their own had overcome the odds and been allowed to walk away a free man. Bitterness rose between the two groups. The Simpson trial involved a nationally known personality, but in America cleavages can occur over the most mundane matters. In 1999, a furore erupted when a white fiscal aide to the black mayor of Washington, D.C., urged colleagues to be 'niggardly' with their resources. Many African Americans claimed that the word was too close in sound to a racial slur to be acceptable; Caucasians insisted that it was perfectly valid, standard English usage and wondered at black touchiness. The fact is that race is an ongoing issue at many levels in the U.S., and while feelings currently are not as explosive as they have at times been in the past, they nonetheless are real and are often found not far beneath the surface.

Not that highly placed attempts have not been made over the years to bridge the racial divide. In the 1950s, the Supreme Court ruled that segregated public schools were unlawful. In the 1960s, various pieces of civil rights legislation were passed outlawing discrimination in jobs and public places, at polling stations and in housing. In the 1970s, affirmative action, or the policy of giving minorities and women preferences in hiring and college admissions over white males, got underway. By the 1980s, this policy had come to incorporate a whole raft of goals, timetables and virtual quotas. In the late 1990s, President Clinton launched his 'Initiative on Race', a national dialogue in which whites, blacks and others were to speak their mind on the subject in town halls across the country. It was hoped that in so doing they would not only clear the air somewhat but also come to terms with the nation's fast changing racial and ethnic reality.

Why has the problem not withered away, despite all the efforts at healing and reform? This is, needless to say, the central question about the 'colour line' and in many ways has become so precisely because it cannot be answered easily. To some extent shortcomings in each of the above steps provide an explanation. Whites, for instance, cite affirmative action as a culprit. By granting preferential treatment in some areas to African Americans and others over Caucasians, the policy is in their minds little more than a form of reverse discrimination that draws attention to rather than away from skin colour. Blacks, while applauding the courage of President Clinton in starting his national dialogue at a time when there was no immediately pressing need to do so, thought the endeavour a bit vague and woolly minded and so largely a waste of time.

A more fundamental reason, however, is that blacks and whites continue to have strikingly different perceptions of the social condition of modern day America. African Americans believe that racism not only exists but is alive and well. Caucasians, by contrast, think the beast is virtually dead. That the two can come to conclusions so widely at variance with each other is the result of their defining the word in entirely different ways. Whites see racism as a matter of personal attitudes and actions. For them, it is defined in terms of segregation, lynching and explicitly supremacist beliefs. Because these practices are now largely a thing of the past, they regard racism as a peripheral issue in present day USA that becomes key only on exceptional occasions like in 1991 when Rodney King, a black motorist, was badly beaten by white Los Angeles policemen for all to see on videotape or in 1998 when a disabled African American hitchhiker was dragged to death by three Caucasians in a pickup truck in Texas. And even in cases such as these whites insist that racism does not remain long to the fore because such behaviour is met with near universal revulsion and outrage.

Blacks, on the other hand, are inclined to see racism nowadays in institutional terms. They acknowledge that overt, official discrimination and persecution of the sort that once thrived in the Old South have gone. But in their place have remained – indeed, grown - structures of power to which one group has more access than others or that cater to one set of people's cultural distinctions more than others and so in their view are racist. Included in this category can be anything from school systems whose buildings might be integrated but whose curricula incorporate European but no African history to, say, drug companies that devote much research to curing melanoma (largely a white person's disease) but nothing to sickle cell anaemia (largely a black person's disease). Whereas Caucasians see racism as something that goes on in people's heads, African Americans see it more in terms of what is actually happening in the world. The difference in definition can perhaps best be understood by looking at a handful of individuals in different but highly publicised walks of life. Whites wonder how anyone can say there is racism in a country where perhaps the most respected national political figure is General Colin Powell, the most worshipped athlete is Michael Jordan, and the most honoured and rewarded entertainers are Oprah Winfrey and Bill Cosby. African Americans wonder how anyone can deny there is racism in a country where no black has come remotely close to being president, owning a major sporting franchise or running a mainstream media network; this despite blacks having been in the country ever since it got started.

U.S. Distinctiveness

Whichever of the above two interpretations is correct, there can be no doubt that in the United States issues of race and racism have often been identified with Caucasian supremacy. The condition is not always a black-white one. The first European settlers commonly regarded Red Indians as savages, as did later homesteaders further west, and it was not until 1924 that citizenship was finally bestowed on Native Americans. Furthermore, some minorities in the U.S. have in more recent times been known to exhibit a racism of their own and focus it on other minorities. Black anti-Semitism, especially in urban areas, is a notable example of this. But in the main American racism has come to be associated with white beliefs of superiority and attempts on the part of Caucasians to keep blacks in particular in place.

    The United States has not been altogether alone in this. Other multiracial societies have produced social, political and economic pyramids topped by whites. Where America has been unique, however, is in her rigid categorisation of people by skin colour type. Notions of whiteness and blackness are very much fixed, with the traditional definition of what constitutes the latter now giving rise to all sorts of anomalies, as is explained in Chapter 2. Unlike South Africa or the Latin American countries, there is no legal recognition of a racial category somewhere between white and black, and one cannot belong to more than one race. Whereas Brazil acknowledges at least forty skin colour shadings, the USA claims only to have a handful. In America, words like 'mulatto', 'quadroon' and 'octoroon', once part of almost everyday language, have now for all intents and purposes disappeared.

The United States is also different inasmuch as there is no legal or official social mechanism for changing one's race. From Mexico to Chile, those of Red Indian ancestry can often switch to mestizo (mixed race) with relative ease, if they so desire. For better or for worse, throughout Central and South America people of darker hues are construed as being more Caucasian by virtue of their education and professional achievements. Money especially whitens in parts of the Caribbean and southern hemisphere. Even South Africa at the height of the apartheid regime had a government board that every year reassigned hundreds of individuals to a different racial category. In America, however, neither wealth nor career accomplishments nor bureaucracy can really alter one's racial identity. The lightest coloured and most racially ambiguous looking African Americans have sometimes been known to indulge in 'passing', or masquerading as whites in order to get certain perceived benefits. This was particularly true in the earlier part of the twentieth century before black pride and pro-minority race based policies existed. But 'passing' is an individual decision that U.S. society as a whole refuses to endorse.

This treatment of race as an absolute is important. It not only marks out the United States from other countries but in the opinion of many helps to explain the traditional inability of blacks to be absorbed easily into an otherwise open society. Unlike Irish Catholics, who in some instances were treated almost as subhumans in the nineteenth century, and Jews, who were feared and reviled in much of the twentieth, African Americans have found it very hard to overcome barriers because they are regarded as an autonomous social group. This latter is a stereotyped view that is a holdover from the days when significant parts of the United States did have a closed society, but it still has some force.

Indeed, the existence of a longstanding closed society in the Old South has caused questions of responsibility to permeate race relations in the United States in ways unknown elsewhere. America is the only modern country to have a history of official oppression by skin colour that lasted in some form or other within part of her confines for three and a half centuries. Slavery is the best known but by no means the only example of this, and the controversies surrounding the practice have given rise to what the African American social scientist Shelby Steele sees as competing claims of innocence that do not exist abroad. Blacks insist that they are innocent victims of the aftermath of slavery and its legislated successor in the South. From their point of view, the central task of race relations today is the achievement of equality for people who collectively have been disadvantaged through no fault of their own. Some have gone so far as to demand reparations for their group's loss of civil rights and unpaid labour that did so much to turn the USA into a wealthy country. Yet present-day Caucasians also claim to be innocent. They acknowledge the evils of slavery but insist they are personally blameless on the grounds of not having been around when the South's 'peculiar institution' was in place. In the United States, the past has thus produced a special kind of group assertiveness and denial that other societies containing large numbers of blacks and whites do not possess. The spawning by early 2000 of a number of books with titles like *The Debt – What America Owes to Blacks*, *Paying the Social Debt* and *The Dream and the Nightmare* provides testimony as to just how much this controversy has come to the fore in U.S. academic circles of late.

Yet demands for compensation are but one controversy to arise in the U.S. in connection with the legacy of slavery. Other issues that continue to vex academics include whether racism was the cause or the result of America's system of human bondage, whether slavery strengthened or weakened social institutions like the African American family, and whether other circumstances that slavery foisted on blacks like geographic concentration in the southeastern region of the U.S. have been a boon or hindrance to the development of African American political power. Given that the impact of history has been the subject of so much debate, it is worth looking at the past a little more closely.

The Historical Backdrop – African Americans

Blacks alone of America's various racial and ethnic groups for the most part came unwillingly to the country. Native Americans were already in it when Europeans arrived, as was to happen to many Mexicans when they were absorbed into the U.S. in the late 1840s. Members of these two groups were by no means always happy in their transformed circumstances, but they had not been brought forcibly to the New World.

The first blacks reached America in 1619. They strictly speaking came to the Jamestown settlement in Virginia as indentured servants rather than as slaves, and in theory they were entitled to become free men once their indentures expired at the end of five years. However, very few did so, as in practice they almost always fell into debt and had their periods of service extended to pay it off. Most ended up being legally bound to their employers for the rest of their working lives. Meanwhile, the sheer size of the colonies together with the need to cultivate intensively tobacco and other cash crops soon meant that many more labourers were required than indentured servitude could supply. Landowners in Virginia and the Carolinas were once again buying men, this time those who had been captured and imported from West Africa as chattel.

Contrary to popular impression, not all southern whites, or even a majority of them, were slaveowners. By the mid-nineteenth century, only about one Caucasian in four from Maryland and Delaware in the Mid-Atlantic region to Alabama and Mississippi in the Deep South possessed black workers, and they were not the only racial group that did so. A number of Native Americans held African immigrants and their descendants in bondage, as indeed did some blacks who had got their freedom upon completing indentured servitude and later acquired a bit of land. Nonetheless, the existence of slavery in the U.S. is almost universally associated with southern whites, the great majority of whom felt they benefited from it in some way. Plantation owners had a large supply of free labour. Small farmers hoped to become rich through not having to pay the one or two workers in their possession. Businessmen often thrived on the custom of these two groups. Working class whites did not have to fear significant job competition if African Americans were enslaved, and in the class conscious South the poorest Caucasians could claim one-upmanship on blacks because of it.

Similar misconceptions have abounded about the treatment of slaves. Life for blacks was by no means as idyllic as southern apologists long made out, but equally it was not as bestial as northern abolitionist propaganda portrayed it. Much depended on a black's workstation, with field hands experiencing quite a different set of conditions from household workers. Estate owners in the South in some ways did have more of a vested interest in seeing to it that their labourers were better clothed and fed than did northern factory magnates. Moreover, many of the slaves became quite adept at avoiding excessive work, though admittedly only at the risk of incurring the wrath of their overseers. Most endured a subsistence life, eating and sleeping in primitive cabins and, when supervised, toiling long hours in the open or at their master's whim indoors. But however varied the conditions, slavery aroused moral qualms because it intrinsically involved the complete degradation of one category of humans by another and greatly qualified the assertion of Americans being endowed with 'inalienable rights', including 'life, liberty and the pursuit of happiness', as Thomas Jefferson, himself a slaveowner, put it in the Declaration of Independence.

Ethical reservations such as these were to a fair extent responsible for the growing divide in the first half of the 1800s between the South and the North, where slavery had been abolished shortly after independence from Britain. Officially, the cleft was about 'states' rights' – that is, whether such matters as chartering banks, building roads and setting voting requirements should be left up to each state, as the South wanted, or placed in the hands of the Federal Government, as many northerners desired. Unquestionably, however, the most important and controversial such right was to decide if a state could permit the continuance of slavery within its borders.

The relentless westward expansion of the United States added a new degree of urgency to the states' rights question. Peoples from both the South and the North were settling in territories beyond the Mississippi River, and there was debate as to whether slavery could be expanded into these areas and, if so, by how much. In 1820, a compromise had been reached excluding slavery north of a certain latitude and pairing a slave with a non-slave territory in their application for statehood so as not to upset the delicate political balance between the North and the South in the U.S. Congress. But amidst the flood of new westbound migrants, particularly following the discovery of gold in California in 1848, this arrangement was abandoned in favour of one allowing the settlers in each territory to decide for themselves whether they should have slavery. The upshot was violence. In the mid-1850s, 'Bleeding Kansas' became a testing ground for diehard northern and southern marksmen. Passions became further inflamed when in the 1857 case of the runaway African American Dred Scott the Supreme Court ruled that black slaves had no rights even when they escaped into 'free' territories. In 1860, northern Republicans nominated and got elected Abraham Lincoln, a man known for his strongly anti-expansionist views about slavery. Feeling increasingly cornered and isolated, the South seceded from the Union a year later, a move the North felt it could not accept, and so fighting between the states broke out.

The details of the Civil War (1861-5) need not concern us here, except to say that in the long run the North with its greater resources and more advanced industrialisation was almost bound to prevail. That it did not do so sooner owed a lot to the spirited fighting of the Confederate troops. Of more concern here is the post-war period, properly known as 'Reconstruction', which ostensibly brought gains for blacks. The Thirteenth Amendment to the Constitution, passed in 1865, accomplished in a fuller way what Lincoln's Emancipation Proclamation of two years earlier had set out to do, abolish slavery. The subsequent Fourteenth and Fifteenth Amendments entitled African Americans to complete citizenship rights. Congress created the Freedmen's Bureau to set up hospitals and schools for blacks and stationed federal troops in the South to enforce martial law. Because southern whites protested Reconstruction by refusing to take part in elections, hundreds of blacks got voted into office and dominated state legislatures in the Old Confederacy for part of this period.

Yet in many ways the gains were more apparent then real. African Americans may have got their freedom, but plantations and estates had not been broken up, with the result that the freed men had little choice but to work for their former masters as sharecroppers or tenant farmers. This state of economic dependence made blacks vulnerable to all sorts of pressures, and the formation at this time of the likes of the KKK, whose terrorist activities the North simply could not control over an area as large as the Old Confederacy, soon scared most African Americans into political submission. Meanwhile, Yankee enthusiasm for Reconstruction steadily declined as the costs of occupying the South mounted, and by 1877 the policy had come to an end.

By the 1890s, the threat of renewed northern intervention seemed sufficiently remote for southern whites to begin reasserting their authority in a more formal way. Devices like the poll tax and the literacy test were introduced to give an aura of legality to keeping the still largely poor and ill-educated blacks away from voting stations. An unofficial but elaborate system of etiquette was established to make sure that African Americans knew their place in their everyday dealings with Caucasians. The former could never enter the homes of the latter, for instance, except by the back door. Whites were allowed to be on a first name basis with blacks, but the reverse was not permitted. Handshaking across racial lines was deemed unacceptable. All this evolved in a society where people of one skin colour were dependent for their livelihood on those of another, thereby making private interaction inevitable.

But race conscious southern whites saw to it in the 1890s that the same did not apply in the public sphere. 'Jim Crow' laws, so called, it is believed, after an early 19th century minstrel of that name, were passed from Virginia to Texas to ensure that there was as little mixing in the open as possible. The races were kept rigidly apart on trams and trains, in classrooms and courtrooms, and in their use of anything from park benches to public toilets. Not all southern jurisdictions went as far as Mobile, Alabama, which enforced a curfew on blacks at night, even in the most peaceable of times, but the process was quite thoroughgoing and received the sanction of the highest authority. In the 1896 case *Plessy v. Ferguson*, which called into question the use of racially segregated railway cars in Louisiana, the U.S. Supreme Court employed the 'separate but equal' concept to say that Jim Crow laws were constitutional. Just because there was segregation, argued the Court, did not mean that one race was being treated in an inferior way to another.

Despite oppression at virtually level, most southern blacks at first opted to stay put. Their station in life was secure, however lowly. In contrast to the North, where hordes of European immigrants were arriving every year and competing for jobs, the South offered guaranteed employment. Furthermore, southern bosses, though by no means above criticism, were at least used to hiring African Americans. Much of this came to an end, however, with the outbreak of the First World War. Starting in 1914, immigration inflows were reduced to a trickle. Labour shortages began to appear in northern factories, and these intensified once the USA entered the conflict in 1917. Lured by higher wages and by a social structure that did not require deference, more and more African Americans went north. The 'Great Migration' was underway, and 1920s legislation drastically curtailing immigration from southern and eastern Europe ensured that the phenomenon continued at least to the end of that decade.

Yet life in the North turned out to be far removed from paradise for blacks. Urban jobs existed aplenty in the Twenties, but the best ones tended to go to whites. Much of this had to do with education. The quality of teaching in underfunded Jim Crow schools had been atrocious, and in a more practical sense recent arrivals from the rural South of whatever skin colour had much catching up to do in terms of learning northern city ways. Then there was the matter of union antipathy. Labour organisations saw the black newcomers as a threat to white workers' wages and so used what power they had in the Twenties to try to restrict African Americans to the more menial jobs. Northern neighbourhood associations employed all sorts of social and financial pressures to ensure that the colour line in the housing market was as well delineated as that in the workplace. Meanwhile, states like Indiana and Ohio saw the spread of a revived KKK into their borders. The Great Migration had turned daily black-white relations from a largely regional into a national question.

The stock market crash of 1929 and ensuing depression put an end for the time being to the Great Migration. There was little point in African Americans heading north to places where jobs were nonexistent, and at least black sharecroppers and tenant farmers in the South could grow their own food. The vast bulk of African Americans in the 1930s were stuck with either no work or with eking out a living in agriculture or domestic service. Yet this is not to say that there was no black mobility during this decade. In politics, African Americans switched their loyalty from the Republicans, the party of Lincoln, to the Democrats. It was a transfer of allegiance that almost certainly owed as much to personalities as to policies. The 'New Deal', designed to help society's most vulnerable through state intervention, in some ways left southern blacks worse off than they had been before, and the new Democratic president, Franklin Delano Roosevelt, refused to sign an anti-lynching bill going through Congress for fear of alienating powerful southern politicians in his own party. But 'FDR', unlike his opponents, exuded charm and charisma. His cabinet members were not averse to giving minorities, including blacks, more federal government jobs, and Roosevelt's wife, Eleanor, was a genuine civil rights supporter who did not care if she upset Washington, D.C., society by dining out or attending functions with African Americans. Of all the disparate groups that made up the new Democratic coalition forged by Roosevelt, none changed its backing from America's party of the Right to that of the Left in proportionally greater numbers than did blacks. And none has been more steadfast in its fidelity. Even today the overwhelming majority of those blacks who do cast a ballot vote Democrat.

The Second World War as much as anything put an end to the Great Depression, and America's entry into that conflict as much as anything got going the forces that eventually would put an end to Jim Crow. Blacks were once again physically on the move, this time not only from the rural South to the North but from rural to urban 'Dixie'. Between 1941 and 1945 even southern cities experienced labour shortages, and the decision of the owners of the steel mills in Birmingham, Alabama, for example, to hire blacks at relatively good wages was not unusual. African Americans still were not earning as much as whites, even for comparable work, but differentials were narrowing, and the pay was certainly much better than that in tenant farming.

There was another difference between the First and the Second World Wars as far as African Americans were concerned. The struggle against the Kaiser had basically been a military one; that against Hitler was also ideological. The inconsistency of fighting for freedom abroad while there was precious little of it for many blacks at home was not lost on organisations like the NAACP, and numerous African Americans detected what they regarded as a strong similarity between Nazi racial theories and those of white supremacists in the Deep South. Although prejudice and mistreatment did not come to an end and race riots broke out in Detroit and Harlem, the black area of New York City, white America did begin to reconsider its attitudes towards skin colour. In 1941, President Roosevelt issued an executive order banning discrimination in plants with federal government defence contracts. Unlike in 1917-8, African Americans were now allowed to hold somewhat more responsible positions in the armed forces. The trend continued in the post-1945 period when racial intolerance in society as a whole was providing the USSR, America's ideological opponent in the Cold War, a valuable propaganda weapon, particularly in the eyes of the newly emergent nations in Asia and Africa. Worries about the USA's reputation abroad were one factor in President Truman's decision to end racial segregation in the armed forces in 1948. Meanwhile, on another plane and for entirely different reasons, African American athletes began breaking through the colour line in sports at about this time, the most celebrated instance being the signing of Jackie Robinson into major league baseball in 1947.

All the same, there were still many hurdles to overcome in mid-20th century America. Jim Crowism was entrenched in the South; de facto segregation was a fact of life in much of the North; and fear of communism, culminating in the excesses of the right-wing Senator Joseph McCarthy, caused a lot of Americans to view with suspicion civil rights campaigns of all stripes. Then in a 1954 NAACP-sponsored case, *Brown v. Topeka Board of Education*, the Supreme Court ruled that Linda Brown, an eight year old African American, could attend an all-white primary school just a few blocks away from her Kansas home rather than cross town. The 1896 ruling of 'separate but equal' was now dead in theory, if not in practice, and de jure segregation of public facilities began to be challenged across the South in a number of ways. In 1955-6, the blacks of Montgomery, Alabama, led by the young Baptist minister Dr Martin Luther King, Jnr, organised a boycott of their city's public transport system following the arrest of Rosa Parks for her refusal to give up her bus seat to a white man. In 1957, African American dignity in the face of Caucasian mob hostility got

President Eisenhower to despatch troops to protect nine blacks about to attend a hitherto all-white high school in Little Rock, Arkansas.

NAACP litigation, church led passive resistance, private example and appeals: these were the hallmarks of the civil rights struggle in the 1950s. The 1960s, however, saw the advent of a mass movement. Over 70,000 people took part in sit-ins across the South in 1960-1 to get restaurant and store lunch counters desegregated. Shortly afterwards white liberals organised 'freedom rides' to test the end of discrimination in interstate transportation in the Deep South. In the North, members of both races staged pickets and rent strikes against biased employers and landlords. The crowning achievement of the mass movement occurred in 1963 when civil rights campaigners organised an orderly 200,000 strong 'March on Washington' to demand equality and hear Martin Luther King, Jnr, deliver his 'I have a dream' speech.

The alliance between Caucasian liberals and blacks lasted long enough for Congress to pass in the mid-1960s legislation banning discrimination in public facilities and at polling stations. But the slow pace of reform along with growing black resentment at perceived white patronage was causing the coalition to crack. There had always been a strain of black nationalism in twentieth century African American consciousness, and it had been gaining strength during this period thanks to the efforts of the Black Muslim speaker and organiser Malcolm X. Soon after his death in 1965 at the hands of another black separatist, disaffected young African Americans coined the term 'Black Power' to denote their desire to go it alone. The militancy of some had its origins in the series of race riots that had already broken out in the long hot summers of the mid-Sixties. Following the assassination of Dr King by a white man in 1968, an event that provoked hundreds more disturbances across the country, the more extreme ones joined the two year old Black Panther party and collected weapons to fight the police.

Yet the worst did not come to pass. Despite some shootouts with law enforcement bodies in the early 1970s, the Black Panthers never amounted to much. They were always under close FBI scrutiny, and they became prey to internal wrangles. The group's gunslinging antics, such as they occurred, served to alienate African American public opinion, the bulk of which was finding itself somewhat pleasantly surprised at the moderacy of the new Republican administration in Washington. If Richard Nixon upset blacks by playing the race card in the 1968 election campaign, he subsequently soothed them somewhat by cajoling recalcitrant southern local education authorities into abandoning their dual school systems. Indeed, whites were the ones who in time would perhaps most come to dislike Nixon's racial policies; this on account of the new construction America's 37th president would place on affirmative action. It is a story that is taken up in Chapter 9.

The Historical Backdrop: Non-Black Minorities

Inspired by African American success, other groups, including women, students, gays and lesbians, the disabled and the elderly, started to advance their respective causes. America's non-black racial and ethnic minorities did the same. The 'Chicano' movement of Mexican Americans got a boost through the publicity that accompanied a 1965-70 grape boycott organised by the trade union leader Cesar Chavez on behalf of downtrodden Californian fruit pickers, the great majority of whom were from south of the border. Mexican Americans then went on more generally to try to improve their financial, political and social status. Native American activists in the late 1960s created the American Indian Movement (AIM), at first simply to protest police harassment. However, before too long AIM had become much more militant, with its leaders barricading themselves in federal government offices, seizing Alcatraz prison near San Francisco and occupying Wounded Knee, site of the 1890 massacre of Sioux tribesmen in South Dakota. It was also in the late 1960s that Asian Americans first began joining together. Militancy was a good deal slower to materialise amongst them than it was in the case of Chicanos and American Indians, owing in part to much greater ethnic diversity. But two incidents in the 1980s – the murder of a Chinese American in Detroit in the belief that he was Japanese and so somehow responsible for the recession then going on in the U.S. car industry, and the discovery of entry quotas against Asian Americans at the University of California at Berkeley – caused this group to become more assertive.

Each of these groups has over the years experienced some special victimisation. Fears of the 'yellow peril' on the West Coast induced the U.S. Government to exclude first Chinese and then Japanese immigrants decades before Caucasians from eastern and southern Europe were so restricted in the 1920s. Those Chinese and some other Asians already in the country were denied citizenship for decades. In the wake of Pearl Harbour (December 1941), Japanese Americans were placed in internment camps for the remainder of the Second World War. Mexican Americans, whose history has been closely linked to immigration, found themselves aliens in their own homeland when, following war with her southern neighbour, the U.S. annexed huge tracts of land from the Rio Grande to the Pacific. Throughout the nineteenth century Chicanos were looked upon as little more than a conquered people, and if Mexican immigrants were tolerated in the next hundred years it was essentially only during boom times such as World War Two. During the Great Depression of the Thirties, many were repatriated, including offspring that happened to be born in the USA.

But of these groups it is the Red Indians who have had the longest standing grievances. Their perceived heathenism made them targets of white racism in early colonial days. Some were captured and put to work almost from the start and would have remained enslaved but for their unmanageability and their tendency to escape readily into the wilderness. The tribes were forever being pushed westward by advancing European settlers, and the resulting warfare, together with lack of immunity to Caucasian epidemics and diseases, led to what some regard as a kind of white genocide. To prevent wholesale massacres in the West, Congress enacted a 'reservation policy', in which millions of acres were set aside for supposedly permanent Native American settlement. But broken treaties, remoteness and the denial of self-government kept reservation Indians among the poorest groups in the country.

Why have these wrongs not received as much attention as those inflicted on blacks? Basically it is a matter of extent. There is the view that the historical mistreatment of African Americans differed from that of the other minorities only in degree, not in kind. Some would go one step further and argue that at times the non-African American minorities found Caucasian injustices harder to overcome. When in the 1950s and 1960s Latinos copied blacks and brought forth civil rights cases, Texan courts ruled that the 1868 equal protection clause of the 14th Amendment to the Constitution, upon which the claims were made, applied only to blacks and whites. And since in the idiosyncratic U.S. definition of such matters Mexican Americans were white, they could not get relief; this despite the fact that Latinos in that state were required by custom to use toilets and other public facilities marked 'coloured'. The consensus opinion, however, is that because Jim Crow was systematically institutionalised into every aspect of life and because slavery was tantamount to a denial of humanity, what southern blacks had to endure was in a category of its own. Furthermore, to many the fact that Mexican colonisation, Red Indian resettlement and Asian exclusion, some of which were arguably the result of the irreversible force of history, all essentially went back only to the 19th century while slavery, which contributed to the outbreak of the Civil War, began in the 17th meant that black-white relations were bound to become more deeply etched in the nation's collective memory.

Whether the black-white framework will permanently remain in place is another matter. For the fact is that there is an additional consideration to be made: numbers. African Americans are the largest 'population of colour' in the United States and believe they deserve a kind of paramountcy on account of this. Traditional white perceptions of the next again biggest group, Latinos, as a rural and so less noteworthy people have bolstered these claims. If nothing else, modern day black riots, such as they have occurred, have taken place in major cities and so have been harder for Caucasians to ignore than Red Indian disturbances on faraway tribal lands or Mexican agitation in fruit picking areas. Yet circumstances are changing. For the past thirty years or so America has had strongly liberal immigration policies that have opened the door to millions of newcomers who are neither black nor white but brown and yellow. A great many of these more recent arrivals have opted to settle in urban settings. The 'colour line' problem has thus taken on new aspects, which W.E.B. DuBois could hardly have imagined all those years ago. Will the newcomers from Latin America and Asia and their offspring end up on the 'white' side of this line, thereby furthering the exclusion of blacks? Or will they finish on the 'black' side, meaning that they also will largely be left out of the mainstream? As their numbers grow and if they do move more into the realm of relative privilege, will they be tempted to create colour lines of their own, or will their coming spark a process of social change that obscures, possibly even erases, the old sharp division between African Americans and Caucasians? Indeed, is this division really as razor edged today as some people maintain? It is the purpose of this book to explore these and related issues. Definitive answers cannot always be found because in some instances events have only just begun to unfold. However, by summarising developments and by presenting data, attitudes and arguments, it is hoped that readers will be able to make informed and educated guesses.

2 Demographic Figures and Trends

Population and the Census

Equal numbers of people are not to be found on the two sides of America's longstanding racial divide. Far from it, in fact. Blacks account for only a little more than an eighth of the total population, and if because of the arrival and high birth rate of large numbers of other non-whites Caucasians do not comprise all of the remaining seven-eighths, they nonetheless do outnumber African Americans by about six to one. It is a statistic that does not match what most people in the United States think. White respondents to a 1995 survey, for instance, gave estimates of the black portion of the overall population that averaged 23.8%, a figure that is nearly twice as high as it actually is.[1] Misperceptions are understandable. Numerous cities in the eastern half of the USA have a large African American population, and the number of blacks residing in the inner suburbs around them is on the rise. People tend to talk about the number of black faces they see on their television screens or in advertising catalogues as a reason for thinking that there are more African Americans in the country than really is the case. Whatever the explanation, plenty of Americans have the racial headcount wrong, and the black population, which is undeniably big in the metropolitan areas of the North and East and upper Midwest and meets that of whites in the rural South, is rather thinly spread elsewhere.

The official figures can be found in the census. Every ten years, the U.S. Government takes a headcount of the American population. The first census was compiled in 1790, and one has been conducted regularly ever since. The one taken in 1990 showed the American population to be approaching a quarter billion people, broken down racially in the way shown in Table 2.1 on page 18.

It has been a constitutional requirement ever since the United States was founded in the late 18th century that there be a census every decade. Initially, this was insisted upon out of political considerations. Proper headcounts are periodically needed to record demographic shifts so that both representation in Congress among states and constituency boundaries within states can be changed to reflect reality, processes known respectively as 'reapportionment' and 'redistricting'. But over the years the census has been redirected to measure the economic and social circumstances of Americans in addition to these original purposes. It is now used to classify jobs, measure income and unemployment, establish numbers by race, religion, marital status and age as well as identify housing conditions, among other matters. Politicians, academic researchers and community leaders regularly urge the Census Bureau to provide still more and better data to suit their needs, and so its scope seems constantly to be expanding. Once published, the findings are used by policy makers not only to redraw seats and shift electoral votes but also to plan and evaluate programmes and allocate government funds. Lobbyists and interest group advocates use them to advance the goals of their constituents. Marketers find them invaluable in the promotion of commercial products. Last but not least, courts have used them to measure compliance with civil rights laws.

Table 2.1 Population of the USA by Race and Hispanic Ethnic Group, 1990

Race/Group Population	Numbers (in thousands)	% Total
Whites	188,160	75.6
Blacks	29,191	11.7
Hispanics	22,122	8.9
Asians, Pacific Islanders	7,345	3.0
American Indians, Eskimos	2,044	0.8

Source: Statistical Abstract of the United States, 1997, Table 20. Hispanics may be of any race and so were not given a category of their own on the 1990 U.S. census form. They were identified as such by surname and questions pertaining to place of birth and ancestry. Redistributing Hispanics among Americas two main races yielded the following results that year: whites – 208,376,000; blacks – 30,377,000.

Controversies

Recently, two highly contentious race related issues have emerged in connection with the official census: undercounting and racial categories. The 'undercount' is the difference between the number of people missed in the tally and those counted twice. Census officials have always found it harder to add up some groups than others. People without a settled residence like the homeless or with more than one dwelling cannot be contacted so easily, and in the U.S. such classifications tend to fall along racial and ethnic lines. Given that there are proportionately more destitute blacks than whites in urban America and that a significant body of Latino newcomers are migrant workers, it is almost always minority group members who do not get counted. Conversely, given that the great majority of two or more homeowners per household in the country are white, it is Caucasians who most often tend to get overcounted. The size of the two errors can be quite large when taken together and appears to be growing. The undercount in 1990 of African Americans and other minorities was reckoned to be the largest ever, both in absolute terms and relative to the white population. For blacks and Hispanics, the shortfall is quite serious. Not only does it mean less federal government financial assistance for their local areas and so fewer public works projects and social services than would otherwise be the case, but also a smaller claim on jobs and student placements at colleges through affirmative action programmes.

To rectify this discrepancy in numbers, the Census Bureau began in the second half of the 1990s to call for the use of statistical sampling techniques to try to reduce the undercount. Second surveys would be made of certain households in selected areas where undercounting is thought to be most serious. Based on the findings, the Bureau would then make projected adjustments rather than relying strictly on head counts. The proposal is, however, contentious. While social science experts, big-city mayors and civil rights leaders generally are in favour, others say that the method would amount to little more than conjecture and so be a violation of the Constitution, which calls for an 'actual renumeration' of the population. Congressional Republicans are especially hostile, as they fear sampling would be open to political manipulation by the Clinton administration to increase the power of the Democratic Party. This is because it is in cities in traditionally Democrat states where the undercount is thought to be greatest. An increase in the population there might add to the electoral vote of these states and so improve the chances of Democratic candidates becoming President. If Republicans see statistical sampling as a plot on the part of Democrats, the latter are convinced that the former are out to lower population counts in areas that vote Democrat. The Census Bureau's proposed new method of counting has thus become a highly charged partisan issue, as well as one with fairly strong racial and ethnic overtones.

So upset were some conservatives at the prospect of counting being done by guesswork, however educated, that they went all the way to the

Supreme Court for help. Yet rather than resolve the bitter debate, the highest judicial body in the country appears to have raised the possibility of there being still more fierce battles to come. In January 1999, it ruled that statistical estimates were against the law as far as determining the nation's total population and dividing congressional seats among the fifty states were concerned. But beyond this 'reapportionment' aspect of the census, the Court seemed to leave the door open as to whether sampling could be used for redrawing constituency boundaries within states and allocating federal government aid to specific areas. Certainly this is the way the Clinton administration interpreted the language of the Court's ruling, and it has indicated that it intends to go ahead with sampling for redistricting and funding purposes. Republicans, aware that redrawn congressional borders within states could affect many more election results than the shifting of a few seats among states every decade, are adamant that this must not happen and have threatened to sue once again. Thus little has been settled to date on this matter.

Equally controversial in recent years is the matter of racial categorisation. The United States has been counting, or not counting, by race ever since the country was founded more than two hundred years ago. For long spells the most spurious methods were used. From the time of the first census in 1790 to the Civil War of the 1860s a black, for instance, was only tallied as three-fifths of a person because of the existence of slavery. American Indians were not included in the figures at all till 1940 because the tribes were exempt from paying taxes. Throughout the years persons of mixed background have been counted but only in one of the four skin colour types officially recognised by the Government – white, black, red and yellow – and since 1980 multiracials have been campaigning for a category of their own in the census. Such a change, they believe, would give a more accurate portrait of the population. It would spare them having to pick between their parents' differing ancestries when declaring their race and so in effect deny half their heritage. The same benefit would accrue to mixed couples having to assign just one race to their children when completing the returns. The most such people could do on recent census forms was to tick a box marked 'Other Race' and have the Government decide the category to which they and their offspring belonged based on additional information given concerning their family backgrounds. Yet to multiracials the very act of pigeonholing people into a category they have avoided by choosing 'Other' is downright dishonest.

Displeasure at this state of affairs is reflected in the statistics. The number of people who ticked the 'Other Race' category on the official census forms increased 45% between the 1980 and the 1990 censuses to 9.8 million people, or about one in every 25 Americans at the time. Of that group, 98% claimed Hispanic origin on the ethnicity question, which means that more than forty per cent. of the nation's Latinos in 1990 were not willing to identify themselves as being simply black or white.[2] Since then, others have come to feel the same way. The golf celebrity 'Tiger' Woods is a case in point. His mother, from Southeast Asia, is half Thai, a quarter Chinese, and a quarter white. His father is half black, a quarter Chinese, and a quarter American Indian. African Americans have sought to claim him as one of their own, a classification he continually resists, preferring instead to label himself as 'Cablinasian' (Caucasian + black + Indian + Asian).

For their part, established civil rights organisations representing the leading minority groups, including Hispanics, have stoutly opposed the idea of a multiracial category. Their reasoning has been that its introduction would exacerbate what they regard as the already serious undercounting of non-whites and dilute further the perceived weight of minorities in politics and in the marketplace. Native American leaders are particularly worried because of the especially high rates of intermarriage of their people with those of other races and because much of the money the tribes get from the Federal Government for maintaining the reservations is based on their numbers. Still others find the proposed category uncomfortably reminiscent of the 'coloured' heading that South African governments gave to people they considered to be mixed in the days of apartheid. Comparisons have even been made with the *Mischlinge* category that Nazi Germany created for the children of Aryans and Jews. In view of the fact that so much is at stake and such stark images conjured up, it is little wonder that debates have often turned acrimonious, with remarks about insensitivity or group disloyalty being flung back and forth between mixed racials and more traditional 'people of colour'.

Yet arguably the group that in a sense has the most to lose by the introduction of a separate multiracial category on census forms is the African American community. Here the danger is not so much dwindling numbers and influence owing to interracial marriage, although that phenomenon is on the increase between blacks and others, but the theoretical possibility that African Americans one day will not constitute an officially recognised group. Despite claims to being distinct, the fact is that relatively few African Americans are pure black. Many have white blood in them going back to the days of the antebellum South when large numbers of slaveowners fathered illegitimate mulatto offspring. Some acquired it as a result of subsequent interracial liaisons. If enough people of mixed African and other ancestry chose to follow the path of Tiger Woods and classify themselves as belonging to some other category, 'black' Americans could conceivably become an extinct species.

In order to prevent such an outcome, however remote, the foremost African American civil rights organisations like the NAACP have become principal defenders of the 'one-drop rule'. Once devised by slaveowners and segregationists to create more human property and to deny kinship between groups, the 'one-drop rule' held that a trace of black blood in a family line, even if it went well back in time, made a person black. As blacks were regarded then as totally inferior, having even a little black blood was considered enough to sully a person in every way, rather as a single drop of ink taints an entire glass of milk. For decades, African American leaders denounced the 'one-drop rule' as a slur on the dignity of their people and a key instrument in their oppression. However, in recent years many came round to accept, indeed espouse, the concept to keep up entitlements in racial preference schemes. If by insisting that persons with even the most distant African ancestry were black one could maintain the black portion of the population in a given area at, say, 20% rather than see it fall to 10%, then African Americans should in theory be able to lay claim to roughly a fifth instead of a tenth of the jobs there. Critics see hypocrisy in such a changed stance, but others say that there is nothing wrong with it, arguing that since society as a whole sees the vast majority of black-white people as 'black', then they should be tallied as such or otherwise a social reality will be distorted.

Faced with conflicting demands and a welter of sensitivities, the Census Bureau in 1997 chose to compromise. It rejected a separate multiracial category, but starting with the 2000 census allowed individuals to tick more than one box to indicate a multiracial background. As with the Supreme Court decision on sampling, here too a new ruling has not ended the debate. Many multiracials are not satisfied, arguing that having a distinct separate category is necessary, if only as a means of affirming their identities in the same way as blacks and whites. Meanwhile, civil rights groups worry that the new option will make it harder for them to prove discrimination, not to mention also possibly serving to dilute the numbers of their people and so their influence. Others contend that it does not matter which method the Census Bureau chooses to employ, the multiracial category or the 'more than one box option', as either one can only be a temporary measure. According to them, the process of keeping data by skin pigmentation and ethnicity is already a bit of a pretence, failing to take into account how notoriously fickle some individuals can be on this matter, identifying themselves one way for one census and another on a subsequent tally so as to pay equal homage to differing parental lineages or for even more tenuous reasons. But more to the point, intermarriage is now proceeding at such a pace as sooner or later to render almost all attempts to categorise people by race or ethnic origin as irrelevant:

> Now, at last, things are changing. There's mounting evidence that the days of counting by race may now be numbered... more and more blacks are marrying whites, and the lines between the races are fading... In 1993 one in eight African American marriages included a white spouse, and since 1970 the number of children in homes with a mother and father of different races has quadrupled... The trend could lead... to the most pleasing result of all: the implosion of the identity of blackness – and, with it, of whiteness.[3]

Both history and demographic statistics lend some credence to this view. The collection of people Americans today call 'white' were once diverse groups of Europeans speaking a variety of languages, practising different religions and often disliking each other intensely. The notion that their progeny could eventually marry each other would have at one time been received with incredulity, yet this is precisely what has happened. Nowadays the great majority of younger U.S. born non-Hispanic whites are of mixed ethnic ancestry. They are far more likely to be part Swedish, part Italian or part Greek than wholly descended from just one of these nationalities. Indeed, it is because so many have become so thoroughly ancestrally mixed that Americans are now much more likely to refer to even those of entirely one ethnic background as 'white' rather than in double barrelled terms like German- or Irish American.

What has happened with whites is to a certain degree today taking place with the new immigrants and their offspring. By 1990, 30% of all marriages involving Asian Americans were to non-Asian Americans. Nearly one-fifth of Asian American births were to mixed race couples. Two-thirds of all Japanese Americans are now marrying someone of a different racial or ethnic background. The figures for Hispanics are similar. More than a quarter of the marriages involving Mexican Americans in 1990 included a non-Hispanic. For Puerto Ricans the rate was higher. All told, there are six times as many interracial marriages in the U.S. today as there were in 1960, and projections are that this trend will accelerate, particularly as immigrant families become second- and third generation Americans and lose more and more of the old country's influence.[4] So convinced was *Time* of the inevitability of this process that it devoted an entire special edition to the subject of multiethnicity in the autumn of 1993, on the cover of which was featured a woman whose image was created by a computer from a mix of several racial and ethnic backgrounds, including African. 'What you see', the periodical announced, 'is a remarkable preview of the new face of America.' But others beg to differ. Writing about the desirability of a black-Latino alliance to fight common causes, one inner city advocacy group has nonetheless warned:

> Whether or not this hope is realised may depend on the effects of racial intermarriage in coming decades, among other factors. Hispanics, as well as Asian Americans and Native Americans, are far more likely to marry outside their race than are African Americans. Conceivably...the result could be the replacement of the historic black-white dichotomy in America with a new black-beige dichotomy.[5]

Projections and Implications

In discussing the implications of such forecasts, it is important to remember that there is of course no certainty as to what the population will amount to in the future. Demographers can make guesses, but these are based on highly tenuous assumptions about fertility, immigration and other factors. No one knows what wars, epidemics or economic pressures will do to family size half a century hence. In the depths of the Great Depression, self-proclaimed experts predicted that the U.S. population would decline sharply as people married later, if at all, and had fewer children to save expenses. Instead, it more than doubled between 1930 and 1990.

That said, one should not ignore altogether the projections. Certainly the shorter term ones seem to have a good chance of being realised. Taking these first, one can say that the group most likely to be affected in the near future is African Americans. They are the ones whose numbers are about to be surpassed by Hispanics. To some black civil rights advocates, long concerned with the thought that other minorities are possible competitors for jobs and housing and that white employers supposedly prefer immigrant workers to native black ones, the forecasts portend a significant threat to the economic and social status of their people. Even more important perhaps is the direction the civil rights movement will take as the one group supplants the other as the nation's leading minority. African Americans and Latinos have traditionally shared a broadly common outlook on affirmative action programmes, but increased tension is possible as more and more Hispanics get job and university placements at black expense in preference schemes based on numbers. In these circumstances, some wonder if African American enthusiasm for affirmative action might wane in time. The two groups also sometimes have different views about how best to tackle underclass poverty and unemployment, as is explained in Chapter 8. These could widen as Hispanics claim paramountcy on the basis of their numbers, while blacks do so on historical grounds and having suffered greater past injustices.

As regards the longer term, the conventional view is that these trends will severely test the premise of the fabled 'melting pot', the idea that for nearly a hundred years has been central to the national identity – namely, that the U.S. can transform people of every colour and background into 'one America'. Just as likely, say many social scientists and demographers, is that the United States will fracture into many separate, disconnected communities with no shared sense of what it means to be an American. This is particularly true if the multiculturalists with their rejection of the dominance of the Anglo-Saxon traditions have their way. Others see the evolution of a pluralist society midway between these two positions in which all Americans will retain some basic beliefs in citizenship and capitalism, but with little meaningful interaction among the various groups. They regard fears of non-assimilation as being somewhat overblown inasmuch as the arrival of so many newcomers from such differing parts of the world – some 120 nationalities in the New York City borough of Queens alone[6] - is bound to assure the survival of English as the *lingua franca* of the country, despite the particularly large influx of Spanish speaking peoples. But ethnic enclaves and identities will remain in many ways intact, and domestic issues will be seen through several lenses rather than just one or two.

Concerning whites, the perceived wisdom is that their relative decline in numbers will mean a corresponding loss of political and economic power. In business, companies will devote more and more time to developing and advertising products geared to non-whites. Black, brown and yellow chief executive officers of corporations will become a commonplace as the minority market increases. In politics, whites will no longer hold such a disproportionate share of congressional seats. The fact that the newer racial and ethnic minorities are strong not just numerically- but also geographically speaking, as is explained in Chapter 8, will, it is thought, give them extra leverage in key electoral states and so a much bigger say in determining who becomes president. Many pundits expect them to insist and get the major parties to nominate candidates sympathetic to minority problems, and few rule out the prospect of an Asian American or a Hispanic, especially the latter, being in the White House by 2050, even though whites will in all probability still constitute a slender majority by then. Of course, not everyone concurs. Some say that it would take the sustained cooperation of all the non-white groups to curtail white power in any dramatic way, and this is unlikely given the rivalries and jealousies among the minority groups at many levels. But most see at least some diminution of Caucasian power and influence.

Then there is the matter of issues. That affirmative action might encounter growing scepticism from blacks has already been discussed. But other topics having at least a certain racial or ethnic tinge to them could also undergo change. Poverty, for instance, is apt to be discussed more in terms of the Latino notion of the working poor than in the black concept of those unemployed and on welfare. The immigration debate, already hotly contested in recent years, is likely to be further stoked as the inflows continue. Foreign policy might need to undergo some revision as public perceptions of good and bad countries and regional importance on the international stage change. The future of Social Security, the federally sponsored old age pension scheme that has been the subject of much funding debate in recent years, could be saved as younger members of the new minorities provide contributions that an ageing and relatively declining native born workforce cannot make. Alternatively, the entire scheme could be thrown into further doubt as these younger minorities increasingly resent having to support an ever larger number of retired white folk. Similarly, the native born elderly may hesitate to maintain out of their taxes bilingual education and job training schemes designed primarily for the former group. Many say that in a number of ways the Census Bureau estimates provide a glimpse into a possible future generational as well as racial and ethnic divide.

Migratory and Settlement Patterns

A 'majority minority' situation already exists in a number of places in the country and has done so for some time. According to the 1990 census, racial and ethnic minorities taken together comprised at least half the population in 12 of the 20 largest cities that year, up from previous censuses, and a trend that is expected to continue as immigration proceeds largely unchecked and as the birth rate of the newcomers tends to outstrip that of native born Americans.[7] Nor is it just a question of cities. Entire states like Hawaii and New Mexico are now 'majority minority'. California and Texas, the two most populous states in the Union, are expected to become so before too much longer, as is shown in Figure 2.1 below:

Figure 2.1   Non-Hispanic Whites as a Percentage of State Population

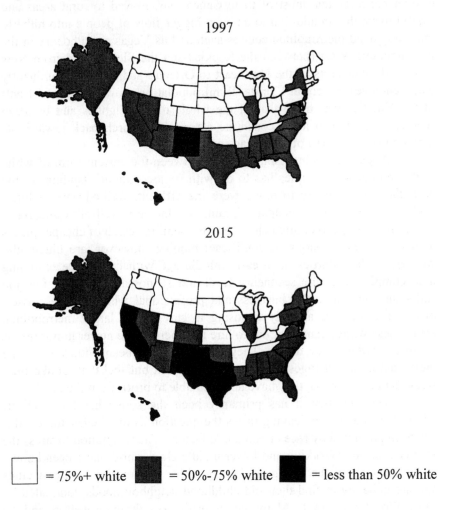

Source: K.O. and S. Morgan (eds), *State Rankings* (Lawrence, KS: Morgan Quinto Press,1999), pp 452-8, 462-8.

The exodus of a significant number of whites (and blacks) from urban areas is serving to accelerate this trend. There is nothing new in white migration to avoid other groups, but this latest movement appears to have one or two special characteristics. One is distance. Unlike thirty or forty years ago, those leaving the cities are not just going to the suburbs or even the exurbs but far beyond. Between 1990 and 1994 alone more than a million net migrants, most of them Caucasians, moved to rural areas and small towns; this in addition to an even bigger flow of people into hitherto middling sized metropolitan centres such as Las Vegas and Phoenix in the Intermountain West (between the Rockies and the Sierras) and from New York and other parts of the Northeast to Orlando and other predominantly white enclaves in central Florida. Rural population growth in the first half of the Nineties was triple that of the whole of the Eighties and by 1996 seemed so sustained as to constitute a veritable 'march back towards its hinterlands on the part of American society'.[8]

A second distinguishing feature between the current form of white flight and earlier examples has to do with socioeconomic standing. In the past, those most likely to move were the affluent, well-educated whites. Today, however, the principal migrants are the less well-off Caucasians. Some are older people, often close to retirement, in search of cheaper places to live on their pensions. A significant number, however, are blue-collar workers in their thirties or in early middle age with little more schooling than completion at the secondary level and so possessing rather few job skills. In contrast to the business and professional white middle classes, many of whom are actually choosing to stay in the larger metropolitan areas, these whites cannot afford to hire members of the newer minorities as nannies, gardeners or maids. They therefore have been witnesses of the racial and ethnic changes going on around them but feel that, unlike their wealthier counterparts, they have not been able to profit from them.

The fact that it has primarily been the somewhat less well-off whites who have been leaving raises the question as to whether the exodus has been prompted by race or economic factors. The temptation to stress the former is strong. Working and lower middle class whites have been known to be upset about the changing demographics of America's biggest cities and are unhappy to find their old childhood neighbourhoods dominated by Third World immigrants. Many see minorities as a drain on welfare and the social services, if not a threat to physical safety on the streets. On the other hand, there can be no denying that it is these less well educated people who are the most vulnerable of all whites to competition from barely literate immigrants for low skilled, low wage jobs when such employment becomes scarce, as was the case in the early to mid-1990s. California, the state with the most foreign arrivals, has led the way in white emigration for much of the past decade. But it also was the part of the country that was hardest hit by recession several years ago, and in the meantime midwestern 'Rustbelt' states like Ohio and Michigan, which have not drawn many immigrants, still have experienced a kind of white flight. A safe conclusion to make is that both race and jobs are involved, as are still other considerations like cleaner air, a warmer climate, less traffic congestion and lower property prices.

An internal migration of somewhat smaller magnitude but hardly less significance has involved African Americans. U.S. blacks have been on the move in recent years in two general respects: from the central cities to the suburbs, and from the various other parts of the country to the South. The former is the subject of some academic controversy and is dealt with in a fair amount of detail in Chapter 4 on housing. The latter is of greater historical interest, since it reverses one of the best known population shifts of this century, the massive exodus of blacks from the southern states to the North and Midwest between 1900 and 1970. The South was the only region of the U.S. in the early 1990s to have more African Americans move in than leave, and what began as a trickle in the mid-1970s has grown into a near flood some two decades later.[9]

Americans of all races and ethnicities have been moving from the Northeast and Midwest to the Sunbelt during the past few decades for many reasons, but the pull of the 'old South' has been stronger for blacks than for whites. For the African American middle class, the lure of high-tech jobs in cities with lower than average living expenses like Memphis and Dallas has been important. But more important still is the fact that the racial climate in the South has changed markedly during the past ten years, the occasional nasty incident or controversy notwithstanding. Atlanta's portrayal of itself as 'the city too busy to hate' might well apply to the region as a whole. In an odd turn of events given the official segregation there of the past, blacks and whites appear now to be generally more comfortable and relaxed in dealing with each other than in the North. Younger southerners in particular have markedly differing attitudes about skin colour than their elders. At the same time, older African Americans, many of whom were born in the South, have been returning to their more rural homes, drawn by relatives and a familiar cultural setting. Elsewhere, the dissemination of blacks into previously white areas has been happening in the suburbs and in a more limited way in the hinterland of the country, where it is often associated with an institution like a university or a military base.

There are some signs, too, of increasing internal migration on the part of Hispanics and Asians. At one time immigrants were almost totally concentrated in a handful of places. In the 1980s, more than three-quarters of the foreign born lived in just six states, and more than half of these resided in only eight metropolitan areas. Thus Miami was dominated by Cubans; New York became home to tens of thousands of Puerto Ricans and émigrés from the Dominican Republic; cities in Texas like Dallas, Houston and San Antonio took in droves of Mexicans; San Francisco and Seattle absorbed a great many Asians; while Los Angeles was the preferred choice of both those from across the Pacific and those south of the border. Today, however, the newcomers are not so confined and can be found in a good many parts of the nation, although admittedly by no means always in large numbers. Part of the drift is linked to employment. Latinos long involved in migratory agricultural labour up and down the plains states of the Midwest did their jobs so repeatedly that they became familiar enough with certain areas to settle in them. In Wisconsin alone their numbers have tripled since 1980 to 185,000, and in Milwaukee, easily the largest city in that state, they now constitute 4% of the population.[10] Meanwhile, highly educated Chinese- and Japanese Americans have moved to take advantage of the many new science laboratories in states like Texas and New Mexico.

As often as not, however, the internal migration is being done by newer types of Hispanics and Asians keen to strike out on their own in places where earlier waves of immigrants of different national origin do not predominate. In the Washington, D.C., area, for instance, Central and South Americans and not Mexicans, Cubans and Puerto Ricans, traditionally the largest Hispanic groups, account for more than half of the local Latino population. Vietnamese and Thais have set up communities throughout the Northeast. On balance, though, the hinterland of America is experiencing ethnic diversity only in modest numbers or not at all. Despite their increasing willingness to move, nearly nine in ten Hispanics still live in fewer than a dozen of the nation's fifty states. Close to half of all Asians and Pacific Islanders continue to reside in the far west of the country. For the more established members of both of these groups, migration, if it is being achieved at all, consists of doing what the general population does: leaving the central cities for the suburbs.

Thus it is tempting to say that what is emerging demographically speaking is two separate Americas: one native born, older, less urban and largely white, though including a portion of retired and more affluent blacks; and another that is immigrant, younger, intensely urban and multiethnic and multicultural. It is a view usually subscribed to by those who take Census Bureau forecasts about the future racial composition of the country more or less at face value and needs perhaps to be treated with some caution. The drift of whites to hitherto less populated parts of the country is a relatively recent phenomenon confined to a fairly small number of people. As yet it is too soon to say whether it is part of a major long term trend or merely a statistical blip of the 1990s. Equally, the movement of Asians and Latinos farther and farther beyond their original settlement areas, while small, might well gain momentum. The conventional wisdom at the time of the race riots of the 1960s was that the U.S. was moving towards two societies rooted in a growing gulf between white suburbs and black cities. Yet many would say that the reality turned out to be quite different. Perhaps as likely is that the same will happen here and that the new national segregation along foreign and native born lines will not be fully realised. Extrapolating from existing trends and assuming that they will continue indefinitely rarely provides a good glimpse of the future.

Conclusion

Why is information about such matters as patterns of racial migration and numbers of blacks, whites, Hispanics and Asians important? The answer, it seems, is manyfold and involves concrete claims on civil rights and affirmative action programmes and alerting Americans to future policy difficulties on a host of other issues. Yet part of the response should also be that such information sheds further light on the complex nature of racism in America, suggesting to us that neither of the two interpretations offered of that term in the Introduction to this work is wholly correct. If, as seems certain, the recent white flight to the outer suburbs, smaller towns and cities and the interior of the country has been prompted at least in part by fear or dislike of people of a different skin colour or ethnic origin, then racism in America is today something more than the minor phenomenon many Caucasians would have us believe. On the other hand, the emotions behind such flight point to racism being more a personal than the institutional affliction that many African Americans now see it as being. And the fact that there has in places been black as well as white flight from immigrants puts paid to the notion of some African Americans that blacks cannot be racist simply because they do not have power.

No less significant, the selective nature of this flight and of other types of discriminatory attitudes and behaviour suggests that racism in the USA is in all probability not the result of some kind of unconscious compulsion but is more likely to be based on numbers, real or imaginary. Thus the reason that many whites (and blacks) have left California but not, say, Tennessee in the past ten years or so owes at least something to the fact that the proportion of immigrants, especially poor immigrants, to the overall population is high in the former state but not in the latter. Likewise, the explanation for Chicago, which is forty per cent. black, having a greater degree of housing segregation than Tucson, which is less than 5% black, is not that white people in the Arizona city are more tolerant than their brethren in Illinois. Rather, it is because integration does not affect as many people in Tucson as in Chicago. Sociologists who believe in this 'group conflict theory' of racism argue that members of one group practise discrimination and bias in response to a perception of a political or social or economic threat from members of another and that the greater the perceived threat, the greater the response.[11]

In this connection, the findings of the 1995 survey given at the outset of this Chapter are telling. The fact that whites then regularly estimated the size of the nation's black population to be much larger than in reality it was speaks volumes about Caucasian concerns over the state of race relations at the time and perhaps more generally. Whether a newer poll would produce similar results now that the O.J. Simpson affair is over and earlier riots in Los Angeles, economic recession and some other causes of insecurity are more distant memories is difficult to judge. Even if it did not and it could be shown that Caucasians were able to make approximately correct guesses about the size of America's other racial and ethnic groups, many would say that continued record keeping of this sort is necessary, if only to counteract future misperceptions. The argument of conservatives that the maintenance of statistics to support affirmative action and other controversial programmes only serves to exacerbate social divisions is not entirely unfounded. But at the same time, the argument of liberals that such record keeping is a useful antidote to false impressions and paranoia has its merits too. The impact of official figures on the overall atmosphere among the various groups is potentially positive as well as negative.

Notes

1   M. Gladwell, 'Personal Experience, the Primary Gauge', *Washington Post*, 8 October 1995, p. A26.

2   C.Page, *Showing My Colour* (New York: Harper Collins, 1996), p. 290.

3   J.K. Glassman, 'Is America Finally Going Colour Blind?', *Washington Post*, 3 June 1997, p. A19. Some think biotechnological advances will lead to a further breakdown

of concepts of racial purity, with increasing numbers of Americans in the 21st century changing hair texture and skin colour through genetic manipulation. See O. Patterson, 'Race Over', *New Republic*, 10 January 2000, p. 6.

4   Rochelle L. Stanfield, 'The Blending of America', *National Journal*, 13 September 1997, pp. 1780-2.

5   The Milton S. Eisenhower Foundation and the Corporation for What Works, *The Millennium Breach* (Washington, D.C.: Executive Summary, 2nd edition, 1998), p. 36.

6   P. Waldmeir, 'Great Third Wave on No 7', *Financial Times*, 18/19 September 1999, Weekend Section, p. I.

7   The twelve cities, as ranked by racial and ethnic minority percentage of their population in 1990, are: Detroit (80%), Washington (73%), Los Angeles (64%), San Antonio (64%), Chicago (63%), Baltimore (61%), New York (60%), Houston (60%), Memphis (57%), San Francisco (54%), Dallas (53%) and San Jose (52%). A thirteenth city, Philadelphia, had a 49% such minority population that year. S. and A. Thernstrom, *America in Black and White* (New York: Simon & Schuster, 1997), p. 208.

8   J. Kotkin, 'White Flight to the Fringes', *Washington Post*, 10 March 1996, p. C1.

9   About 100,000 African Americans moved from other parts of the U.S. to the South in the years 1975-80. This grew to 368,000 between 1990 and 1995, 230,000 of whom came from the Northeast, 100,000 from the Midwest and 30,000 from the West. See B. Vobejda, 'In Turn Back, Blacks Moving to the South', *ibid.*, 29 January 1998, p. A3.

10   P. Thomas, 'In the Land of Bratwurst, a New Hispanic Boom', *Wall Street Journal*, 16 March 2000, p. B1.

11   Gladwell, *loc. cit.*

3 Black Middle Class, Black Underclass

The Middle Class

A major impression of foreigners, especially those who have never been to the United States, is that the country is economically divided between a comfortably off white population and a distinctly less well-placed black one. The image makes allowances for certain African American athletes and entertainers being super-rich and concedes that there are disadvantaged whites. Yet the belief is strong that prosperity is almost entirely linked to skin pigmentation. Even in the minds of many Americans themselves the words 'black' and 'poor' are regarded as synonymous and used interchangeably in conversation. The idea that a sizeable portion of African Americans live reasonably affluent lives tends to be either dismissed or regarded as an exaggeration.

Yet as with racial demographics, evidence shows that reality is somewhat different. Much of course depends on how one defines 'reasonable affluence'. The term is relative, since what is a lot of income to one person is a paltry sum to another, depending on personal circumstances and lifestyle. One method of delineation that some have used is to double the official poverty line as calculated by the U.S. Government every year. In 1997, that would have rendered an income of $26,000 p.a. for a family of three and about $33,000 a year for a family of four.[1] Such sums hardly constitute true wealth, but in most parts of the U.S. they would more than enable a household to buy the bare necessities, with at least some money to spare.

Using this definition, approximately half of all black families in the United States were at least reasonably affluent in the mid-1990s. The figure is significantly below the three-quarters of all white families that fit this description, but equally it is remarkably above the mere 1% of African American households that did so in 1940.[2] Needless to say, there are those who would protest that such an index is arbitrary and cannot determine social class, which is really indicated by employment, status, attitude and outlook. But even using these traditional criteria to judge matters, one can say that a significant number of U.S. blacks meet the description of being

35

middle class. About two-fifths of African Americans in 1990 were engaged in nonmanual, white-collar work usually associated with the bourgeoisie. Nearly three-fifths of black women were so employed. Nor is it simply a matter of type of work done. According to recent surveys, more than four out of ten U.S. black citizens consider themselves to be middle class, as compared with almost two-thirds of whites.[3] Of those who do not, many have not altogether abandoned hope that some day their children or grandchildren will be classified as such.

Why, despite evidence to the contrary, does the stereotype persist? In part, it is because the portrayal does bear at least a grain of truth. As liberals are quick to point out, a disproportionate number of people who are poor are black, and the poverty they endure and the conditions associated with it are sometimes horrendous. In part, though, it is the fault of the media. Drug related crime and gang warfare in the ghettos make better stories than do individual cases of quiet success. For much of the past century, some American journalists have seen themselves as patrons of the disadvantaged. In their zealous desire to do something about African American poverty, they have unintentionally created an unwarranted and unflattering perception of blacks in the U.S. as a pitiable race. As a result, the general public gets the impression that what they see on their television screens and read in their newspapers reflects the lifestyle of most African Americans. Conservatives, meanwhile, increasingly point an accusing finger at civil rights organisations and certain black activist groups, which are said to have a vested interest in maintaining the indigent image. By constantly dwelling on the hardships of the black underclass to the exclusion of virtually all else, these groups are alleged to be playing on white guilt and feeding black anger in the hope of keeping alive their own jobs and controversial race based policies like affirmative action.

A black bourgeoisie clearly does exist and is thriving. Yet it is a middle class with special characteristics. To begin with, it does not contain a particularly large number of upper middle class professionals. As can be seen in Table 3.1 on page 37, African American representation in the more elite occupations such as law, medicine, architecture and engineering is small, while that in less prestigious professions like nursing, teaching and social work roughly corresponds with the black presence in the total workforce, and at times is even higher.

Stronger still is African American showing in blue-collar fields requiring special training like police and fire work and bus driving, all of which, while strictly speaking not necessarily middle class positions, nonetheless pay well enough to provide quite a comfortable standard of living. The portion of clergymen with low earnings in the black male professional workforce has declined substantially in the past half century. In their place, however, have come men working as often as not in routine, less selective white-collar jobs where real pay is definitely better than that of their parents or grandparents but remains not overly rewarding. Moreso than is the case for whites, black households are dependent on two incomes to provide a truly affluent lifestyle, often defined as $50,000 a year or more for a family of four. Although both the actual and comparative numbers of African American professionals are growing, their earnings put most of them in the lower rather than the upper middle class.

Table 3.1 Per Cent. Black Occupational Representation in the Workforce, 1996*

Over-Represented		Proportionately Represented		Under-Represented	
Welfare Services	28.5	Firefighting	13.5	Sales	7.9
Social Work	22.6	Personnel	12.9	Computer Sc.	7.2
Guards	22.1	Admin., clerical	12.5	Finance	6.5
Postal Work	21.3	Lorry Driving	12.4	Medicine	4.5
Police	16.0	Clergy	11.2	Law	3.4
Machinists	15.2	Teaching	9.8	Architecture	2.7
Counsellors	14.0	Nursing	8.6	Dentistry	1.2

* Blacks constituted 11.3% of the total civilian workforce that year.

Source: Statistical Abstract of the United States, 1997, Table 645.

Second, the black middle class is strongly inclined to work in the public sector. In contrast to whites, Asians and Hispanics, African Americans seem particularly attracted to government service as a source of livelihood. Although they comprise only about eleven per cent. of the total civilian workforce, they make up more than 17% of all federal government workers. About a quarter of all African American workers are employed by federal, state and local departments and agencies compared to one in seven of all Caucasians. Half of all black male professionals and two-thirds of all black female ones are government employees of one sort or another, twice the proportion of their white equivalents. Certain government departments that service a poor and largely black clientele like public (council) housing and welfare have especially big numbers of African American employees.[4]

Corresponding to this overrepresentation of blacks in the public sector is their underrepresentation in the ranks of the self-employed. Today only about 4% of African Americans in the workforce are entrepreneurs, as against close to ten per cent. of whites and even higher figures for certain subsets of the Asian population like Korean Americans. The firms that blacks do run take in barely 1% of total gross receipts in the nation, a statistic that owes much to the fact that most are tiny 'mom and pop' organisations that tend to be concentrated either in intimate community services like hairdressing, bars, restaurants and funeral homes, free of competition from other racial and ethnic groups, or slightly larger concerns with guaranteed 'set-aside' contracts with government at some level.[5] Even the bigger African American entrepreneurships are not all that large. According to one recent finding, if the top one hundred black owned enterprises today joined together in one company, it would still only be the 83rd largest corporation in the U.S. as ranked by revenue.[6]

In a capitalist country like the United States where the self-employed are held in high esteem, such low figures have not gone unnoticed. Some regard this state of affairs as being part of black culture, which is said to be people- rather than money- or power oriented. Yet this overlooks how vigorous African American entrepreneurship was at one time, with blacks in the aftermath of the Civil War running their own railway, dock and canal companies in certain parts of the country. Others put it down to discrimination, citing how difficult it has been for African Americans to get start-up or expansion loans from banks or other institutions[7] and to get whites to do business with them once they have begun operations. But borrowing difficulties through mainstream institutions have also been true of Asians, who nevertheless have gone on to own several hundred thousand businesses worth billions of dollars. Jewish Americans overcame similar hurdles in the past. Still other observers, usually those on the political Right, see it all as an extension of reliance on government, which has induced blacks to avoid taking risks of just about any sort. Equally plausible, though, is a contention of the Left that they have not been given sufficient experience in corporate management to be confident enough to branch out on their own. The latest theory is that the civil rights movement of the 1950s and 1960s is to blame. By freeing African American consumers to shop in white-owned stores, integration unintentionally destroyed the black businessman's captive clientele, especially as the 'windfall only worked one way' because Caucasians 'did not storm across the same open border to spend money in black establishments'.[8] Whatever the cause, there can be no denying that blacks have thus far made only limited progress in one area that is both a source of jobs and social mobility.

Those middle class blacks who have taken up employment in the private sector have almost always done so at larger rather than smaller firms. A few theories have been put forward for this, too, and these will be explored in Chapter 4. For now it is enough to say that as a general rule the tinier the firm, the less the likelihood that African American professionals are going to be found working there. Far more common is to see them taken on board by corporate America, where big businesses are often eager not only to hire but also to promote blacks. Knowing this, bright and ambitious young African Americans are increasingly getting degrees in Business Administration rather than in the more traditional subjects, and the heads of the better black colleges and universities are forging closer links with major companies to make sure the latter know which of their graduates are particularly suitable for employment. Even well-known black public figures appear at times to be getting in on the act. In 1997, the Reverend Jesse Jackson, after years of political and social activism, decided to turn to economic salvation for his people. His 'Wall St. Project' of that year succeeded not only in gaining symbolic gestures from whites like the closure of the New York Stock Exchange on Martin Luther King Jnr's birthday but also corporate promises to delegate for minority-owned companies more service contracts. Chunks of equity have been bought in American multinationals to induce management at shareholder meetings to appoint more blacks as directors.[9]

Thus on the face of it, professional blacks have good reason to be satisfied. Their numbers are growing. If the bulk of them belong to the lower rather than the upper echelons of the middle class, their presence in the world of big business is being increasingly sought. Society has officially become more accommodating, and as will be seen, many are putting their disposable income to ends that their parents only dreamt of, like buying property in the suburbs. And yet, despite these trappings of outward success, there are signs that all is not well. Time and again research polls, buttressed by anecdotal evidence, indicate that the black middle class is disgruntled, often embittered and occasionally left feeling alienated from society.

Social and cultural pressures are undoubtedly a factor in this. Many African American professionals feel that they are constantly on display as representatives of their race and so have to work doubly hard to avoid confirming stereotypes of laziness or incompetence. When they win a competitive post, they are sometimes left wondering either by remarks of others or doubts in their own mind if the appointment owed more to race based affirmative action programmes than to merit. Genteel office surroundings often have a certain racial etiquette that inhibits true dialogue between blacks and whites, with the result that pent up resentments and frustrations can sometimes increase. Meanwhile, the very act of having almost daily to divide one's personality between a largely white world of work and a predominantly black home community is to many African Americans highly wearying. On account of social and economic pressures such as these, a good number of older black professionals counsel their more business minded juniors to pursue entrepreneurship rather than corporate work, if possible.

Paradoxically, some blacks would say, the real professional difficulties start with job advancement. Thousands of African American white-collar careerists move up a few rungs on the corporate ladder every year, but it has been said that the promotions they do get all too often tend to land them in positions whose titles sound impressive and whose pay is better than before but whose actual work is not particularly career enhancing. Black managers have not infrequently been known to refer to being shunted off to 'The Relations' when they get advanced: community relations, industrial relations, and public relations, all of which have a certain outward profile but are not especially vital to the success of the company. That, together with the 'buddy system', a kind of during- and after hours cronyism among their white colleagues, has the effect of excluding African Americans from important decisions. For some, it is all part of the 'glass ceiling' syndrome of invisible barriers inside a corporation that a government commission of a few years ago found prevents just about all blacks and women from rising even close to the top. If true, such windowdressing and sidetracking constitute not only a slight but an outright danger to the livelihoods of middle ranking African American managers. If and when 'downsizing' occurs, for whatever reason, they are the ones who are vulnerable to early retirement because of the comparative unimportance of their posts. Scarcely surprising, then, that black workers are said to be a good deal more dubious about mergers, the big corporate trend of the 1990s in the U.S., than are their white counterparts. They also fully admit to being more anxious about recession.

Underlying this insecurity is perhaps the awareness of those in the black middle class that should redundancy occur they are much more apt than their white counterparts to wind up in poverty. This is because they have so little cushion against adversity. All things being equal, African Americans are as a matter of course entitled to the same unemployment and welfare benefits as other U.S. citizens. Studies show that young blacks are closing the savings gap between the races and tend to be more cautious than others about where they invest their nest eggs, preferring property and life insurance to stocks and bonds.[10] But in terms of overall *wealth* as distinct from *income* they lag far behind whites. Being late entrants to the bourgeoisie and having usually inherited little, if anything, from their poorer parents, black professionals have accumulated far fewer securities and physical assets than their white equivalents. The result is that they have not so much to fall back upon in the event of protracted difficulties. A single mishap could reduce them to a hand-to-mouth existence much more quickly than members of many other groups, and their awareness of this is said to be another explanation for their lingering malaise.[11]

One African American journalist, however, insists that it is not so much financial uncertainties as feelings of breach of faith that are at the root of the discontent. In his 1993 polemic *The Rage of a Privileged Class*, Ellis Cose, the current editor of *Newsweek*, attributed the bulk of black bourgeois frustrations and anxieties not to money but to 'the problem of the broken covenant'. Despite having gone through life having done and performed well everything whites demanded of them, African American professionals continued to be pigeonholed in 'black jobs'. Black middle class fury is said to arise not only out of being shunted into dead end employment but also out of enduring a certain amount of social isolation, self-censorship, silence at work and even of being damned with faint praise by bosses.[12]

Why should America care? Are these not the sort of difficulties that most poor people, black and white alike, would not mind having to suffer? Do not the problems of the black bourgeoisie pale in comparison with those of the underclass? To these and similar questions Cose stresses the negative impact of African American professionals' disappointments on underclass youths who do aspire to something better than life on the streets, adding that whichever of the two African American social classes has the bigger complaint, 'clearly the troubles of the one do not cancel out the concerns of the other'.[13] It is to 'the troubles of the one' that we now turn our attention.

Working and Underclass Poverty

Just as a surprisingly large percentage of African Americans fall under the heading 'middle class', so an unexpectedly large number of poor people in the United States are white. In 1997, non-Hispanic Caucasians accounted for close to half of all the people living below the poverty line. Non-Hispanic blacks comprised about a quarter of the nation's poor in that year, while Latinos, made up a little less than that figure.[14] And yet in the public mind poverty and deprivation are conditions associated primarily with black lifestyles. Whites are generally perceived as being affluent, with Hispanics vaguely thought to be in a financial state somewhat between that of America's two largest racial groups.

Undoubtedly not only ignorance but also prejudice plays a large part in these misperceptions. There is, of course, a white underclass whose members drift from one job and shelter to the next and who have spent many years receiving food stamps and cash assistance. Yet few think or speak of such people as a distinct class because of society's tendency to regard white poverty as an aberration, while that of blacks is seen as an extension of their history and culture. Geography lends a helping hand. Some two-thirds of the white poor are dispersed in the many suburbs and throughout the huge rural hinterland of America.[15] Even those who are to be found in the cities are not congregated in one or two areas but scattered throughout many neighbourhoods. By contrast, while there are poor rural blacks, especially in the South, a great many deprived African Americans live in concentrated urban ghettos, thereby being more visible and encouraging the impression of a single social stratum. Disadvantaged Latinos and other ethnic minority groups also tend to be clustered in the central cities, but as many are relative newcomers the general public until recently has not taken as much notice.

At the same time, it has to be admitted that there is at least something to be said for the stereotype that equates poverty with blacks. African Americans may account for only about a fourth of the poor in the USA and are outnumbered by the white poor by nearly two to one, but they amount to just 13% of the total population and in the country at large there are more than six non-Hispanic Caucasians for every black person. Thus African Americans represent a disproportionate number of the poor. Equally dismaying is the persistently high rate of African American poverty. In 1997, 26.5% of all African American families were below the poverty line. Although this is something of an improvement on earlier years, the fact remains that the poverty rate of black households has been more or less stuck at the 30% level or thereabouts since the early 1970s.[16]

Adding to this association of poverty with blacks in the public mind is the fact that African Americans have figured even more disproportionately in the nation's welfare rolls. Although blacks routinely account for about 25% of the poor, they were, in the early 1990s at any rate, three to four times as likely as whites to be receiving food stamps, Medicaid and public housing assistance. In the case of AFDC, a particularly controversial programme because it was aimed at single mothers, African Americans were almost five times as likely as Caucasians to be claimants; this despite comprising only about an eighth of the population.[17] The publicity that some politicians and certain parts of the media accorded these programmes reinforced the age old image of blacks being not only poor but also work shy and a drain on tax revenues. So widespread was the portrayal of supposed black indolence and spongeing on the public coffers that for a while a number of observers wondered if welfare might not replace crime as the leading offender of racial sensitivities. It is a fear that has since abated somewhat now that a booming economy and reformist legislation converting welfare into workfare have caused the number of African Americans seeking public assistance to drop. But the danger remains, especially if the number of whites claiming benefits continues to fall even faster than that of blacks, as has been happening recently, thereby increasing the relative African American share of the rolls.[18]

Whatever the perceptions of whites about the extent of a black dependency culture, the fact remains that sizeable numbers of African Americans have been mired in poverty for decades. That such a relatively large percentage of blacks should be poor over such a lengthy period of time has for a number of people basically one explanation, racism. White employers, full of stereotyped images and prejudices of lazy, incompetent or hostile blacks, simply prefer to hire and promote their own kind whenever possible. White police officers and judges are quicker to arrest and sentence black offenders than those of their own skin colour. The resulting criminal record makes finding steady employment upon release that much more elusive for African Americans. Meanwhile, white governing elites are said to be indifferent to black family daily problems.

There is room for all of these allegations, not least the last. It can be of little doubt that a laissez-faire Republican Congress and a politically centrist President Clinton, eager for much of his spell in office to transfer the Democratic Party's attention from the poor to the middle class, have between them done next to nothing about housing and education, two of the biggest problems for the urban segregated black underclass. But right-wingers are quick to point out that in 1996 welfare was reformed to get the poor, black and white alike, off the dole and back into the world of work. And left-wingers would add that twice in the 1990s minimum wages have been raised to help all of the working poor, regardless of skin colour. Both of these steps have arguably gone some way towards achieving their goals. At the same time, it has to be said that many of the cities with the worst statistics have long been run by black mayors, as have the social service departments set up to assist the poor. Add to this the fact that not all African Americans are suffering equally and that the disparity between upper and lower income blacks is if anything greater than that between the best- and worst-off whites,[19] and it is not unreasonable in the opinion of many to conclude that forces other than discrimination and bigotry are also at work here.

Poverty by Gender

It would appear that urban African American poverty springs in the immediate sense from two distinct sources, one for men and one for women. In the case of men, unemployment, especially the long term sort, is the primary origin. Government figures make for depressing reading. In the past few decades, black male unemployment rates have been on average about double those of white males. Thus in 1995, 7.2% of all African American men aged 25-64 were out of work, compared with only 3.8% of their Caucasian counterparts.[20] Even in the best of times, black male unemployment rates are higher than those for whites during recessions. The jobless picture is particularly grim for young African American males. Eighteen per cent. of black men aged 20 to 24 were out of work in 1998, a boom year, and in the case of black male teenagers the figure came to 30%. All this refers to official unemployment, which counts only those who are registered as being out of work and who are actively looking for employment. If one adds discouraged job seekers and those in prison to the official statistics, the rate of unemployment and underemployment (those working only part time or intermittently) for inner city African American youths rises by some estimates to 50%, the same as during the recessions of the 1970s and 1980s, though better than during the slump of the early 1990s.[21] How young black males have got into this appalling predicament is a matter to be discussed elsewhere; suffice it to say here that one can advance a spate of reasons and that black male poverty can be traced in the first instance to difficulties in getting more fully integrated into the world of work.

By contrast, the main source of poverty for African American females, especially those in urban areas, has to do with family structure. For much of the past thirty years, more and more black women of childbearing age have been starting families without getting married. It is a trend that applies to females of other racial and ethnic groups, but not in such a pronounced way as for blacks when considered over a period of time. In 1994, for instance, only a quarter of all African American women in the United States aged 15-44 were married and had a spouse living with them. The rest either never had a husband or were divorced, separated or widowed. The comparable figure for whites was 53% married.[22] Women in this type of situation almost always have a hard time making ends meet, but what makes matters worse for black single mothers is the fact that as a group nearly a third of them are teenagers - in effect, children having children. Without a high school diploma, still less a university degree, these girls have an extremely limited earnings capacity. Today the median income of African American families headed by women of all age groups is about $15,000 p.a., a figure that is not high in the U.S.[23] For single black teenage mothers it is considerably lower, indeed, little more than that received in welfare payments.

Relatively fewer African American women are getting married, and yet they continue to have children. Statistics compiled by the U.S. National Centre for Health show that while the birth rate for single black women in recent years has been declining from 90.7 per 1,000 in 1989 to 74.4 per 1,000 in 1996, the proportion of black births taking place out of wedlock rose dramatically during those years, as Table 3.2 shows:

Table 3.2 Per Cent. of Births out of Wedlock, by Race and Ethnic Group, 1960-1996

	Black	White	Hispanic
1960	22	2	NA*
1970	38	6	NA
1980	55	11	NA
1994	70	25	NA
1996	70	22	41

*NA = Not Available

Sources: S. and A. Thernstrom, *America in Black and White* (New York: Simon & Schuster, 1997), p. 240 and S.A. Holmes, 'Birth Rate Falls to Forty Year Low Among Unwed Black Women', *New York Times*, 1 July 1998, p. A1.

In 1997, the black illegitimacy ratio did in fact drop slightly to 69%, but this is still inordinately high. That it remains so is because there has been a simultaneous decrease in the fertility of all black women, married and unmarried alike.[24] Indeed, since the late 1980s, the birth rate of the former has been below that of the latter, a pattern unprecedented among America's various racial and ethnic groups. It is to many almost as if for much of the black population in the U.S. there is no real link between marital status and having offspring.

Precisely what is causing this apparent trend towards African American family disintegration is the subject of much debate. There are those who put it down to economic factors. Young black males are thought to be marrying less than before and in comparison with other groups because their unemployment rate is higher. Without a fairly reliable income, so the theory goes, they feel that they cannot assume family responsibilities. At the same time, the absence of a regular payslip makes them less appealing to women. Some observers, however, adopt a more sociological approach, arguing that the existence of extended family caring in many black households makes retaining the bonds of fatherhood less important. Others resort to blatant stereotyping, citing figures showing the historically higher rates of illegitimacy among African Americans as 'evidence' that they are a people with looser morals.[25] Still others note the rapidly rising incidence of white births out of wedlock to claim that it is all part of a broader cultural phenomenon that merely happened to occur in lower income black families first.

More and more, however, white America has been coming to the conclusion that welfare has been at least in part to blame. By according benefits, the generosity of which hinged on a young mother staying single, welfare was said to be discouraging marriage and so keeping people in poverty. It was partly in response to such beliefs that both President Clinton and the Republican Congress agreed in 1996 to a radical overhaul of the system, transferring much of the supervision from the Federal Government to each of the fifty states, some of which have in turn cut off benefits to teenage mothers and capped payments to older single women after a certain number of births. At the same time, the new Act placed time limits on just about all other forms of welfare assistance and required individuals to have completed two consecutive years of work before being able to claim aid.

For a while, it seemed that these changes might trigger a marked deterioration in black-white relations. The Left in general took the view that the 1996 legislation imposed an unfair burden on the poor and that children, the most innocent party in this situation, were being particularly victimised.

But given the disproportionate numbers of African Americans living in poverty, civil rights groups were inclined to think the impact would be more than doubly felt in black neighbourhoods. Moreso than their white counterparts, black businesses, especially as there were relatively fewer of them, along with the black churches would have to carry a very heavy load in providing work and charity. African American liberals were also more upset than their Caucasian peers at Washington's handover of welfare administration to the nation's governors and their elected assemblies. Both groups feared that the payments under the new system would be less generous, but to the former the transfer was an ominous portent of a resurrected states-rights movement of the sort that had done so much to hold back racial equality earlier in the century. Some could not help but notice that the states of the Old Confederacy, where the biggest percentage of African American welfare recipients lived, were among the most enthusiastic sponsors of the changes. For these onlookers, it was all part of a deliberate attempt not merely to save taxpayers' money but also to turn back the clock, even at the risk of racial confrontation:

> Congress pulled the rug out from under two million poor African American families and their four million children... Nearly 40% of African American children rely on Aid to Families with Dependent Children... And don't think for one moment that the folks on Capitol Hill don't know it, too. No, this was our fight.[26]

Yet to date black anger has been rather muted since the passage of the Act, and even awkward public encounters between the legislation's white supporters and black detractors have been few. In part this is because of economic health. So tight had labour markets become by the end of the 1990s that bosses were seeking even the least skilled members of the population for employment. Thus those cut from the rolls often had little difficulty in getting work, however low paying. In part, however, the doomsday predictions about black rebellion have failed to materialise because of loopholes in the law and a more lenient outlook on the part of the states themselves. Children not in the custody of their parents are in a number of instances exempt from the restrictions, and there is evidence that some mothers may be turning them over to relatives so that entitlements can still be collected. States with plummeting caseloads believe they can afford to turn a blind eye to these 'child only' cases, some 20% of the total, as they have with others involving special factors, thereby reducing the chances of strife.[27]

Black Solidarity

Ever widening differences in income and status between the African American middle class and underclass raise questions about black solidarity. These apply mainly to the feelings of the former group, as the latter has too few connections outside inner cities to feel much common cause with poor whites. Certainly it has long been the hope of mainstream America that as blacks enter the middle class they would start being middle class and stop being black.

Many would say that this has not turned out to be the case. Despite varying levels of economic and educational attainment, almost all blacks – middle, working and underclass alike – continue to share highly similar sentiments and values. Across all class lines, there is anger at the perceived continuance of racism, with blacks being upset not only at whatever slights or offences that have happened to them personally but to African Americans in general. More than 80% of those blacks who do vote regularly cast their ballot for the Democrats, and belief in the role of government as a force for good in society remains strong among African Americans of just about all walks of life. Those who have materially advanced often feel the emotional pull of their working class origins and admit to being socially more at ease with those of their own skin colour than with middle class whites. It has been said that they are aware of a certain lack of authenticity in their own existence and regard street culture of the inner city like rap music as being much more genuinely black than most anything they can produce. Indeed, some observers contend that in these days of affirmative action programmes and racial preference schemes the reason that many of them are in the middle class is because of their skin colour.

On the other hand, for all their professions of moral kinship and nostalgic reflections, middle class blacks have been willing in a physical sense to leave others of their own race behind. Feelings of guilt notwithstanding, affluent blacks have not hesitated to flee the central cities in record numbers for the suburbs. Housing, the subject of much of the next Chapter, is arguably an issue every bit as much about class as race. Education, also discussed in the next Chapter, is more a black-white bone of contention, but social class is not entirely absent from it either.

Notes

1   In 1997, the U.S. Government classified a family of four as poor if it had a cash income of less than $16,400 p.a. The threshold for a family of three was $12,802. See R. Pear,

'Black and Hispanic Poverty Rate Falls, Reducing Overall Rate for Nation', *New York Times*, 25 September 1998, p. A1.

2   S. and A. Thernstrom, *America in Black and White* (New York: Simon & Schuster, 1997), p. 196.

3   *Ibid.*, pp. 183, 185.

4   M.A. Fletcher, 'Worker Bias Lawsuits Flood Agriculture Department', *Washington Post*, 20 April 1999, p. A1; also D. D'Souza, *The End of Racism* (New York: Free Press, 1995), pp. 495-6.

5   D'Souza, *loc. cit.*

6   D. Masci, 'The Black Middle Class: Is Its Cup Half-Full or Half-Empty?, *CQ Researcher*, 23 January 1998, pp. 63-4.

7   Roughly 2/3 of all small business loan applications by blacks but only about a quarter of those made by whites are turned down, according to the National Bureau of Economic Research. Yet the survey that produced these findings was thought to be too broadly based to determine intentional discrimination. See J.A. Tannenbaum, 'Small-Business Lenders Rebuff Blacks', *Wall Street Journal*, 7 July 1999, p. A2.

8   R. Rymer, *American Beach* (New York: Harper Collins, 1998), pp. 219-220.

9   J. Kahn, 'Jackson Challenges "Capital of Capital" ', *New York Times*, 16 January 1999, p. C3.

10   M. Atasor, 'How Wall Street Is Bungling an Opportunity to Sell to High-Saving Young Blacks', *Fortune*, 6 July 1998, p. 226. Mistrust of white owned brokerage firms is said to be one reason for this conservatism with personal finances, as is a dislike of 'putting money into something you can't feel and touch'. See T. Mabry, 'Black Investors Shy Away from Stocks', *Wall Street Journal*, 14 May 1999, p. A2.

11   The median net worth of middle class white families in the mid-1990s came to $44,000. For the corresponding group of African Americans it was $15,000. 'Middle class' in this instance is defined as those earning between $25,000 and $50,000 a year. But the gap between blacks and whites in general was much bigger. The median net worth of all black families at this time was $3,700; for white ones it was $43,800. See D.K. Shipler, *A Country of Strangers* (New York: Alfred A. Knopf, 1997), pp. 17-8.

12   E. Cose, *The Rage of a Privileged Class* (New York: Harper Collins, 1993), pp. 1, 56-68. A recent study tracking the careers of thousands of black and white students who first matriculated in 1976 at 28 of the nation's most prestigious colleges and universities found similar dissatisfaction. Of more than a dozen job attributes, the one that the biggest percentage of African Americans in this cohort rated as 'very important', treatment of women and minorities, had one of the biggest gaps in racial perceptions in terms of accomplishment. 54% of white but only 31% of black respondents thought that employer dealings with non-male, non-white staff were being performed in a highly satisfactory manner. Likewise, more than twice as many Caucasian as African American workers in this group (48% versus 23%) regarded promotion opportunities as being good. See W.G. Bowen and D. Bok, *The Shape of the River* (Princeton, N.J.: Princeton University Press, 1998), p. 152.

13   Cose, p. 8.

14   See Pear, *loc. cit.*, in which it is stated that according to Census Bureau estimates there were 16.5 million whites, 9.1 million blacks and 8.3 million Hispanics living in poverty in 1997. No figures were given for either Asian- or Native Americans, though in 1995 Asian Americans accounted for 2.9% and Native Americans 1.3% of the 12.9 million people receiving federal welfare benefits. See R. Pear, 'Governors' Plans on Welfare Attacked', *New York Times*, 14 February 1996, p. A12.

15   A. Hacker, *Two Nations* (New York: Chas. Scribner's Sons, 1992), p. 99.

16   Pear, 'Black and Hispanic Poverty Rate Falls...', *loc. cit.*

17   *Statistical Abstract of the United States, 1997*, Table 584.

18   Between 1994 and early 1997, the number of white families receiving federal cash assistance declined 25%, while that of blacks went down by 17%. See J. DeParle, 'Shrinking Welfare Rolls Leave Record High Share of Minorities', *New York Times*, 27 July 1998, p. A1.

19   According to the U.S. Department of Commerce, the median income of the top fifth of black families by earnings was virtually nine times greater than that of the lowest fifth of African American families in 1996. The ratio between corresponding white family groups that year was 6:1. See *World Almanac and Book of Facts, 1998*, p. 388.

20   Thernstrom, p. 246.

21   G. Burkins, 'Strong Economy Leaves Young Blacks Behind', *Wall Street Journal*, 9 March 1999, p. A2.

22   Thernstrom, p. 239.

23   *Ibid.*, p. 197.

24   C. Murray, 'And Now for the Bad News', *Wall Street Journal*, 2 February 1999, p. A22.

25   Historians have long disputed the impact of slavery here. Liberal scholars see it as having had a debilitating effect with a lasting legacy. By contrast, conservative white southern academics for the longest time maintained that it served as a stabilising force on blacks, whose family life only began to deteriorate with emancipation. Still others in more recent times have claimed that the 'peculiar institution' did cause damage but not enough to destroy husband-wife relationships, an argument that a few latter day black intellectuals use to support their view that something more sinister than mere economics is the cause of present day problems. If the African American family could survive the ravages of the 19th century South, the argument goes, then whatever difficulties it encounters today can only be the result of white racism.

26   C.I. King, 'Trashed by the Welfare Bill', *Washington Post*, 27 July 1996, p. A23.

27   B. Vobejda and J. Havemann, 'Child-Only Cases Rise on Welfare Rolls', *ibid.*, 2 January 1999, p. A1; also same authors, 'The Welfare Alarm That Didn't Go Off', *ibid.*, 1 October 1998, p. A1.

4 Housing and Education

For all the talk about a new national segregation between the native- and foreign born in America, as discussed towards the end of Chapter 2, there are those who believe the 'old' type between blacks and whites never really disappeared. Housing was the last major area to be covered by civil rights legislation in the 1960s, and then only half-heartedly in the opinion of many. Education was dealt with earlier, but there is evidence that school integration peaked in 1967 and according to some has been going into reverse ever since. As a big percentage of whites still live in metropolitan areas and so fairly close to large numbers of African Americans, the recent drift to the hinterlands notwithstanding, such allegations are serious and cast doubt on the USA's claim to have made racial progress.

Housing

Since 1968, residential integration between the races has occurred but at a relatively slow pace. While schools, offices and factories often have become thoroughly racially mixed, entire blocks of neighbourhoods, indeed whole areas, remain all black or all white. The typical American metropolis has some kind of visible 'Black Belt' – largely black neighbourhoods that serve as home to a big percentage of their African American population. Meanwhile, a number of suburbs, in particular the newer ones on the outlying edges of urban areas, the 'exurbs', are lily white. Different explanations have been put forward for this state of affairs. Some have cited legislative shortcomings as being most responsible. The Fair Housing Act of 1968 lacked enforcement. According to its terms, the Government could conciliate between disputing parties but could not readily take a private offender to court as it could in cases of job or school discrimination. The Act was so worded as to outlaw only blatant refusal to sell or to rent to minorities. More subtle forms of exclusion, which in any event were harder to prove, seemed to be exempt. Thus 'Whites Only' for sale signs might have been removed, but people in the trade were said to be employing all sorts of ruses and deceptions against blacks, Hispanics and other minorities. Particularly guilty were estate agents, who were alleged to have 'steered' non-white clients, especially African Americans, towards those areas in which many of their own kind already lived, while neglecting to inform them of equally or even more suitable housing units elsewhere. Apartment managers were not unknown to have indulged in similar tricks. Yet it is the lending institutions that in the opinion of many have been most suspect.

Financial Discrimination

Banks and savings and loan associations, the U.S. equivalent of building societies, have had one main accusation repeatedly levelled against them in the area of racial housing: bias in deciding whether to lend. Studies show that blacks are about twice as likely as whites to be rejected when applying for a mortgage, with Latinos falling somewhere in the middle of these two groups. A 1996 investigation of nearly fifteen million home loan bids across the country revealed that financial institutions turned down nearly half (48.8%) of all those made by blacks but only about a quarter (24.1%) of those from whites. Even when the applicants had similar incomes, and high incomes at that, the gap in the approval rate was significant.[1] Minorities contend that such disparities are indicative of discrimination, and they are not alone in this view. In 1992, it was the opinion of the august Federal Reserve Bank of Boston that 'race plays a role, perhaps an unconscious and unintended role, but a role nonetheless in mortgage lending decisions'.[2] Others, however, are sceptical and wonder why banks would be willing to forego activity in one of the few growth areas in the U.S. property market in the past decade unless they had proper reason to do so. They think the analysis is flawed:

> The problem with most of the studies [of the early 1990s] was that they focused mainly on differences in rejection rates between black and white applicants, taking into account their levels of income but without considering other factors such as net worth, existing level of debt, credit history, job stability, and size of downpayment. Lenders consider all these factors, not just earnings...[3]

In the opinion of some of these observers, it is extra cost as much as anything else that is nowadays keeping neighbourhoods divided by skin colour. Information recently compiled in a Harvard University study claims to have evidence that whites are willing to pay a premium of nearly 15%

above the going rate for house prices to be able to live in a segregated neighbourhood. Oddly enough, the premium is higher in northern cities than in southern ones, where anti-black sentiment has historically been much greater. Yet it is a pattern that is said to be occurring more or less across the country, with regions containing not all that many African Americans like the Pacific Northwest not exempt from it. According to this view, segregation has not changed so much as the environment around it. Whereas in the 1950s and 1960s, the residential separation of the races was backed either by state law or by the collective actions of whites, today it is sustained by market forces. The laissez-faire economy set in motion by Presidents Reagan and Bush in the 1980s, and with which President Clinton is said not to have interfered much in the 1990s, has made equal opportunity in this area harder to achieve for minorities.[4]

Residential Segregation

Underlying at least some of the foregoing is the notion that irrational white prejudice is a continuing reality. There unquestionably remains an association in most people's thinking between blacks and a variety of anti-social behaviour threatening the character of a neighbourhood: noise, dirtiness, neglect and crime, with the latter seen as being especially worrisome. Some go so far as to say that the link between African Americans and crime is so strong in the public mind as to be the greatest single explanation for white resistance to integration. Caucasians might no longer panic and sell immediately at the prospect of a single black family moving into their area, causing property values there to fall dramatically as happened in the 1960s. But their tolerance threshold of having African Americans as neighbours is limited, and they tend to move before too long, paying over the odds to live in segregated areas as they do so. Overt, violent 'hate crimes' against darker skinned newcomers are rare, but anecdotal evidence suggests that exclusionary practices like cold shouldering are not.

To a certain extent, research bears this out. Several studies have been made in recent years referring to the 'tipping point', or the theoretical number of new black arrivals that prompts whites to leave for fear that the quality of their neighbourhood is on a downward path. Time and again, the results indicate a tipping point of 8%. In other words, whites are generally willing to remain in a racially mixed area, provided that blacks comprise no more than about one household in twelve. Beyond that, they start to leave.[5] Yet although this sounds like a low tolerance level, surveys show that it is higher than that which most whites were willing to put up with in years past. And in those neighbourhoods where the African Americans are of the same social class as the whites, the tipping point is said to rise to between 10% and 15%, or more or less in line with the portion of blacks in the overall population of the country.[6]

Meanwhile, the broader picture is perhaps revealing. Whereas in 1964 twenty per cent. of whites reported that they had blacks living in their neighbourhood, in 1994 more than sixty per cent. did so. The corresponding figures for blacks with whites living nearby were 66% and 83% respectively. Given that certain parts of the U.S. like a majority of the Rocky Mountain states and the northernmost parts of New England have virtually no blacks and that there are more than six times as many whites in the total population as African Americans, the absence of any black neighbours for two-fifths of the Caucasian population is perhaps not all that remarkable. Along with earlier data about changes in 'tipping points', such figures have led one pair of writers to conclude that whatever way one looks at it, residential integration has been on the increase since the 1970s, if not always at the fastest of paces.[7] There is room for this belief, but it must be added that the mixing is in many instances very slight, with both blacks and whites having hardly any members of the other race in their neighbourhood – indeed, on occasion only one. Certainly it is not comparable to that which takes place in many workplaces. What is more, 'neighbourhoods' in such surveys are often equated with census blocks consisting of two or three streets rather than just one. Statistical information almost invariably needs at least some qualification.

Many discussions about housing and race focus almost exclusively on the attitudes and behaviour of whites. This is because it is often simply assumed that blacks desire integration on just about any terms. Yet research indicates that this is almost never so. Surveys show that while most African Americans do not object to integration in principle, they like Caucasians do not see it as the main aim of race relations.[8] Nor do they particularly want mixing if it means having to live in those areas where whites greatly predominate. Sometimes this latter feeling emanates from an inkling that white neighbourhoods are apt to be hostile to them; sometimes it arises out of purely practical considerations. Among the many groups opposed to an early plan of the Clinton administration to rehouse some poor African Americans into surrounding suburbs were the inner city residents themselves who wanted to remain close not only to their families and friends but also to convenient buses leading to central city shops. Whatever the reason, polls show that for a majority of African Americans the ideal form of integration is to have neighbourhoods containing roughly equal numbers of each group. Some observers argue that these findings raise the possibility of there being another explanation for the slow development of racially mixed neighbourhoods in America – namely, the fact that whites and blacks define integration in quite different ways. African Americans prefer living in areas that are about 50% black, 50% white. Whites, if they are to have integration at all, prefer to reside in areas reflecting more the proportion of the two races in the country as a whole – that is, half a dozen white households, if not more, for every black one. Finding a mutually acceptable compromise is apparently hard to achieve.[9]

Indeed, it has been said that some African Americans are not really interested in integration at all. Even if the number of whites in a particular neighbourhood was so restricted as to pose no threat to their sense of feeling welcome, certain blacks would still not want to live among them. 'Integration fatigue', or the tiredness many blacks feel at having to conform all day long to white ways at the workplace is said to be one factor behind this. Another is wounded black pride, with many African Americans feeling insulted at the notion implicit in integration that they somehow would be better off if they lived alongside or in close proximity to white people. It was long the view of the 1950s and 1960s African American novelist James Baldwin, for instance, that black people never wanted integration in the first place. Rather, what they sought was 'desegregation', or the right to go to the same places as whites but not necessarily together with whites. That they have in some measure done so is because of insensitive liberals who rode roughshod over African American feelings in the wake of the civil rights revolution of a few decades ago. If true, then this is yet another reason, albeit a secondary one, for the continued existence of overwhelmingly black and overwhelmingly white neighbourhoods in numerous parts of the country. Equally, it along with the poll findings on black residential preferences casts doubt in the minds of some on the 'steerage' theory of racial segregation. White estate agents do not necessarily need to direct African Americans away from certain neighbourhoods or avoid showing them certain house listings. Many blacks are only too willing to steer themselves away from these places.

Black Suburbanisation

For decades, housing issues involving blacks have been discussed in the context of African Americans suffering at the hands of white injustices. Yet a second debate has surfaced in recent years that in its own way has become every bit as controversial as the first. This concerns black suburbanisation, the process in which hundreds of thousands of African Americans have been leaving the central cities for the outlying areas. That urban African Americans have been migrating to more leafy surroundings is beyond dispute. It is a process that has been taking place at an ever accelerating rate for the past half century, so that today about one African American in three lives in the suburbs.[10]

As might be imagined, the rate at which African Americans have been leaving the central cities for the suburbs has not been uniform across the country, and the general figures conceal all sorts of variations. Some urban centres such as Detroit, Indianapolis and Milwaukee have had comparatively little 'black flight' beyond their boundaries. Elsewhere it is an indisputable fact of modern day American life and in places has been so great as to create new African American majorities. In Prince George's County, Maryland, just outside Washington, D.C., five-eighths of the population is now black. Sometimes the suburban majority is within the black community itself. Three-quarters of all African Americans in greater Miami reside beyond the city's borders. The corresponding figure for the Los Angeles conurbation is 58%. Meanwhile, cities as economically varied and geographically scattered as Cleveland, Dallas, San Diego and Seattle have all seen the portion of black suburbanites in their metropolitan areas at least double between 1970 and 1990.[11]

What is in dispute, however, is whether such a process should be halted and whether at least some of those who have moved should return. Contrary to what might be expected, the debate is not taking place between blacks and whites but between blacks and blacks. Certain urban leaders and community activists contend that African American migration to the suburbs has removed a layer of social support that kept inner cities generally safe and hospitable, if poor. Mainstays of civilised communities like shops, small businesses and sometimes even churches have long since disappeared, and what has resulted is 'hypersegregation', the intense racial concentration of those left behind in neighbourhoods characterised by high crime and hopelessness. Such leaders want the most successful black professionals and entrepreneurs to return to serve as role models for younger members of the underclass and to increase economic opportunities by living and shopping in these areas and reopening businesses. It is also argued that the presence of more affluent residents would give the inner cities more voice in local politics and secure better cleansing, sanitation and other amenities. Not surprisingly, most suburban African Americans disagree. They regard the purchase of a home in more spacious surroundings as a quintessential right of passage for all middle class

Americans, including themselves, and they add that for many of them it is a dream that has only recently come true. At the same time, they are inclined to think that the sort of assistance necessary to revitalise the ghettos is more a function of government or big business than small private help and philanthropy.

Recent initiatives show how wide the chasm between the two classes is on this matter. To lure African American, indeed other white-collar, workers back to the worst off urban areas, certain cities have offered a number of incentives. In the early 1990s Philadelphia promised tax rebates to those willing to make the move. At about the same time Cleveland began selling property lots in rundown areas for as little as a hundred dollars. Yet neither has been a spectacular success, with only a few thousand people in each city taking up the offers. In 1994, President Clinton's Housing Secretary, alarmed at the downward spiral of the inner cities, proposed a move in the opposite direction. With government money, residents of public housing projects in the most blighted areas were to be relocated in subsidised flats in middle class suburbs where they would supposedly live an improved existence amidst better surroundings. Predictably the scheme was denounced by conservatives as yet another example of liberal social engineering that was doomed to fail. More interesting was the reaction of middle class blacks who joined their white counterparts in not wanting an influx of poor people because of the imagined adverse impact on schools, unprotected property, street safety and tidiness. Some threatened to leave if it was introduced, and a year later the scheme was dropped.

Thus what was once from an African American perspective a relatively straightforward issue of race has today evolved into one also involving class. Recriminations that used to be invoked almost exclusively across the colour line are now commonly made by blacks divided by social and economic standing. Possibly at jeopardy is not only the quality of everyday life for those left behind in the inner cities but also the ability of urban blacks to wield political power as more and more of their people disperse elsewhere. Small wonder, then, that the controversy has at times become especially sharp among African Americans. Of course, it is important not to overstate the matter. Some black professionals, taking the view that cultural assimilation pressures are apt to be too great in the still white dominated suburbs, never leave the city. Others have been enticed back now that crime rates are falling. But these middle class African Americans are more the exception than the rule, and their move is usually to older blue-collar neighbourhoods rather than the abandoned rundown areas where some say they are most needed. The more spacious parts of Harlem, the black area of New York City with a fabled place in African American consciousness, have for some time now been able to lure their share of well-to-do people. Equally important is to recognise that traditional housing discrimination against blacks is not dead. But with white tolerance having generally increased over the years and with segregation now sometimes being the result of black rather than other people's choice, this aspect of the question no longer always has the spotlight to itself. In this rather narrow sense progress has been made.

Education

It would seem that 'tipping points' exist with regard to education as well as to housing. Public opinion polls conducted over the years demonstrate that if Caucasian avoidance of integrated classrooms is not as pronounced as it was twenty or thirty years ago, it is still strong. According to one study, nearly two-fifths of whites in 1994 were opposed to sending their children to schools where blacks would comprise more than half the total pupil intake.[12] As will be seen below, black people also show something of a disinclination to attend places of learning with members of the other race. Much of the reluctance has to do with poor results and dissatisfaction with the quality of education in general in U.S. schools. Part of it, however, is cultural and driven by beliefs in differences in curriculum interests, ways of thinking and, indeed, fundamental abilities between the two races.

By one yardstick, at any rate, the education of American blacks has clearly changed for the better. This is in high school graduation rates. Whereas in 1960 the percentage of African American pupils completing four or more years of senior secondary schooling was only half as high as that of whites, today it is almost the same. But while blacks now receive high school diplomas at more or less the same rate as Caucasians, reservations have been expressed about how meaningful this is. Standardised tests conducted across the country reveal that in the mid-1990s 17-year old blacks could in mean score terms read scarcely any better than 13-year old whites. A five-year gap existed in science ability. True, the disparities by this time were not as great as they had been two decades earlier, but they remained wide and showed some signs of going into reverse after the improvement of the 1980s.[13]

Various explanations have been put forward for the persistently lagging performance of blacks in American schools. By far and away the most controversial one was enunciated by a pair of educationalists in a best selling work called *The Bell Curve*, in which it was stated that genetics was the cause. Some groups are simply more adept at academic learning than others, but blacks are not among them. The book created a storm of controversy when it was published in 1994 and still arouses indignation, even though it dealt only peripherally with race.

More mainstream groups see less extreme explanations. Conservatives of both races cite low expectations set by teachers and the conviction among black youths that education is a 'white thing' and so to be treated with contempt. Liberals, on the other hand, are inclined to see white rather than black cultural standards as being a main culprit. Vocabulary used in English exams draws on middle class suburban life experiences with which many blacks cannot identify. National exams in general measure the wrong kind of brainpower. Many test only a particular, static kind of intelligence said to be more suitable to Caucasians and their deductive type of thinking than to those of other groups. Timed essays are said to work to the advantage of whites, who are brought up to relay events in linear fashion and not the 'spiral', digressive style of blacks.[14]

So convinced were a number of black educationalists of the racial bias of the American public education system that they set about persuading school districts containing large numbers of African American pupils to overhaul much of the curriculum. Their efforts were not in vain. During the early to mid-1990s, local education authorities in such regionally diverse places as Atlanta, Detroit and Philadelphia, among others, agreed to make lessons more 'Afrocentric' in the hope that black pupils would be better able to identify with what was being taught. In some cases the reforms were mild, incorporating respectable teaching on African history and cultural practices as well as those of the West. In other districts, however, the changes were seen by many as excessive and based on dubious scholarship. The most stridently Afrocentric teachers often had their pupils reading only black authors and counting in Swahili. The history and religious education lessons portrayed ancient Egypt as a black civilisation from which the Greeks and Romans got all their ideas. Not only were the Pharaohs black, but so were Jesus, Moses and most of the leading figures of the Bible. No less controversial, certain city school boards have granted permission for 'Ebonics', the street talk of many inner city African Americans, to be used as a valid language of communication in the classroom and for exams.

School Busing and Integration

Implicit in the above discussion is a recognition of the fact that many blacks no longer necessarily see integration as a remedy for their educational problems. There was a time when African Americans almost unanimously saw racially mixed schools as desirable and put a lot of effort into securing them, but no longer. Even many of those who are not Afrocentric in their outlook have come to have misgivings about integration. They are not implacably opposed to it, but they do think that there are other, equally good, if not better, ways of improving the education of their sons and daughters.

What more than anything has contributed to this revised opinion is school busing. Often introduced under court order in the 1970s, busing was originally seen as a solution to both social and educational difficulties. The transporting of African American pupils to white area public schools and of some whites to black area ones would achieve a racial balance within districts. Both groups would have equal access to resources; tolerance would be increased; and the more eager blacks would supposedly be stimulated into performing better when placed in a largely white academic environment. If nothing else, the ensuing integration would help those African Americans less sure of themselves develop at least some of the confidence in predominately white settings needed to succeed in later life.

Yet the idea did not work all that well in practice. There was a widespread feeling in the African American community that blacks had borne the brunt of busing inasmuch as it was more of their children who usually had to do the travelling and over longer distances. The system broke up neighbourhoods and made it more difficult for mothers and fathers to get involved in their children's progress because the schools were so far away. As often as not tensions were stoked rather than eased. Convinced that racially mixed public schools were dangerous, violent places, many Caucasian parents put their sons and daughters either into private academies or moved to more outlying areas. Whereas public schools in Boston, for instance, were 60% Caucasian in 1972, by 1990 only about one pupil in five was white. In Milwaukee the drop was almost as precipitous.[15] Many African Americans came to the conclusion that in a number of school districts 'white flight' was so pronounced as to make busing an irrelevance. Even in those schools with significant mixing, there often was segregation behind closed doors thanks to 'tracking', or the grouping of pupils by supposed ability into separate classes.

The movement to end forced school busing got underway in earnest in the early 1990s when many ordinary people came to the conclusion that it was an obsolete policy. Whites usually led the way in seeking to put an end to it, but increasingly blacks were to be found not all that far behind, and in the case of a few cities like Denver, Minneapolis and St. Louis, it was actually they who spearheaded the campaign for repeal.[16] Aiding and abetting them were the federal courts, which by now had plenty of conservative justices serving on their benches thanks to numerous appointees by Presidents Reagan and Bush in the 1980s. Fighting a rearguard action was the NAACP, the country's oldest and largest civil rights organisation and one that clung to the tenets and methods of the 1960s. Despite a fair bit of evidence to the contrary, it believed that African American parents were still solidly behind integration. At first, it sought to reduce white flight by agitating for metropolitan wide desegregation plans. Then it tried turning to state rather than federal courts to break down racial separation. Both efforts came to naught. By the late 1990s, the majority of U.S. cities with a large African American population had ended forced school busing.

Having lost a number of courtroom battles, pro-integrationist blacks have now been concentrating on voluntary plans to get racial mixing. One idea has been to introduce 'magnet schools'. These are secondary level institutions designed to draw whites back to the cities by offering advanced courses and state of the art technology in racially balanced programmes. In some places they have brought the races together, but in at least as many they have not. Resentment has built up among some African Americans at the long list of blacks waiting to gain entry but who cannot because of spaces reserved for uninterested whites. Another idea is school vouchers. These are public funds set aside to help poor parents pay for private school tuition. They are a favourite cause of Republican Party conservatives and have deep support among younger inner city minority parents disillusioned with public schools but lacking the money to do anything about them. However, leading African American organisations see them as draining the best black pupils from the already beleaguered public schools and so are opposed. The fate of vouchers is thus as yet uncertain.

Higher Education

If racial affairs in primary and secondary schools have at times been tense, on the campuses of America's colleges and universities they have on occasion come close to being explosive. At issue for much of the early and mid-1990s was the alleged clannishness of many African American students. Rather than mix with whites, it appeared that black undergraduates increasingly wanted to live, eat and play and so ultimately grow apart from others in university life. They often demanded and got 'ethnic theme' halls of residence, their own social and service clubs and their own 'black studies' courses. University cafeterias quickly came to have unofficial black and white dining tables. The media bandied such phrases as 'racial balkanisation' and 'campus culture wars' as whites, resentful at perceived special treatment accorded to minorities, occasionally lashed out and made physical attacks. When university administrators imposed speech codes and 'sensitivity sessions' on undergraduates, whites complained that 'political correctness' was running amok. Since the mid-1990s, accusations and counter-accusations of this type have abated somewhat as university authorities decided to adopt a more laissez-faire approach and generally let undergraduates sort out problems by themselves. But at some institutions of higher learning race relations remain reserved.

What has gone wrong? Is it simply a question of a greater black presence leading to increased tensions? Most people would disagree, but there are some who think the difficulties symptomatic of a deeper problem concerning inequality caused by affirmative action. Not only were blacks being treated differently on campuses but arriving there in different circumstances. By granting admission to many black and some other minority high school graduates with lower results on entrance exams, colleges and universities are thought to be practising double standards in the name of diversity. The upshot is, in the opinion of many, the worst of all possible worlds. Certain whites (and Asians, many of whom do very well academically) are denied the education of their choice, while blacks (and Hispanics, who also tend to perform less well on entrance exams) are not only allowed entry but are left to struggle in courses for which they have been inadequately prepared. Caucasians are bitter that many of their own kind with very good paper qualifications are denied entrance, while African Americans, especially the more able ones, strongly resent having their own academic credentials constantly being questioned.

Viewed from a strictly numerical perspective, there appears to be much evidence to support this assessment. In the mid-1990s, blacks were entering California's Stanford University, one of the most prestigious learning institutions in the country, with test scores on average only about 90% as high as those of whites. Elsewhere the figure was often 80%, occasionally less. At the University of California at Berkeley, another institution of considerable repute, African American first degree students were dropping out at a rate two and a half times that of whites and Asian Americans. Their withdrawal rate from law degree courses across the country was about double that of members of the other two groups.[17] Yet except in those so far few instances where the public have voted otherwise in state referenda, university officials continue their race- and ethnic based policies. Some insist on the long term social value of diversity. Others cast doubt on the predictive value of entrance exams for ultimate success. High school achievers have become disappointments in college, while others with lower entrance results have gone on to get respectable degrees. Still others say racial tensions on campus have been overblown. As evidence, they point to a huge study published in 1998 of tens of thousands of undergraduates showing a majority having significant social interaction with classmates of another race and favouring the continuation, even the extension, of diversity programmes in higher education.[18] Sorting out who is right and who is wrong on this issue is difficult and is a matter that is explored more fully in a subsequent chapter on affirmative action. Suffice it to say here that whatever the state of campus relations and the merits of preferences, one can only feel that racial difficulties in America's higher education will not be solved until the real problem is tackled lower down in the system. Not until state public schools do a more adequate job in preparing blacks for college will there be a happier environment. On that there is almost universal agreement.

Conclusion

On the basis of all the above, one might be forgiven for thinking that in racial terms housing and education are heading in two diverging directions in the U.S. With regard to the first category, blacks and whites are coming together, however slowly; in the case of the second they are not. Yet not everyone accepts this verdict. Some see the findings of the aforementioned large study of elite colleges as proof that the integrationist spirit is alive and well. Others come completely to the opposite conclusion. 'America is resegregating', argues the Milton S. Eisenhower Foundation, and in saying this the inner city advocacy group is referring to both residential and schooling patterns.[19]

How can such starkly contrasting views plausibly exist side by side? The answer, it seems, has to do with definitions. When discussing this topic, the optimists focus strictly on residential trends to conclude that integration is gradually but steadily taking place. The pessimists incorporate other data. They take into account, for instance, the increased imprisonment rate of blacks in the 1990s, especially young African American males convicted of certain kinds of drug offences, as part of their thesis that segregation is on the increase. The greater the number of blacks behind bars, the fewer that can mingle in a predominantly white society. They cite changes in the structure of the economy, especially the fact that work has to some extent disappeared in the central cities, to bolster their claim that blacks have become more isolated.[20] Yet while there is something to be said for this approach, it must be added that what the naysayers are really talking about is a rather different kind of segregation. Optimists in their discussion refer to the traditional type based purely on skin colour. By contrast, the pessimists' view of segregation is one of social class as much as of race. For the fact remains that it is basically the poorer blacks who have been left behind by economic change, not the more affluent ones, as the 'hypersegregation' debate within the African American community only too readily testifies. And the poverty and physical isolation poor blacks endure is often as much related to richer blacks as to whites and applies with equal force to less advantaged Hispanics and impoverished members of other groups dwelling in the ghettos. Whether, therefore, segregation is on the increase in present-day America is a matter of semantics as much as of anything else, and it is important for students to bear this in mind when exploring such matters.

Notes

1   'Mortgage Rejections Stay High for Blacks', *New York Times*, 5 August 1997, p. A16.
2   C.C. Clark, 'Housing Discrimination: Are Minorities Still Treated Unfairly?, *CQ Researcher*, 24 February 1995, p. 185.
3   See, for instance, D. D'Souza, *The End of Racism* (New York: The Free Press, 1995), p. 280. There is evidence that African Americans in general have worse credit ratings than Caucasians, even when those members of the two groups with similar incomes are compared. A study launched by Freddie Mac, a federally chartered corporation that provides mortgage lending, discovered that in 1999 48% of the former but only 27% of the latter fell behind in paying off bills. The aforementioned black-white wealth gap, 'cultural attitudes' and underlying racism, with black workers said to be often the first to be let go from jobs, were all speculated as reasons for the poorer repayment records. See C. Loose, 'Racial Disparity Found in Credit Rating', *Washington Post*, 21 September 1999, p. A1.
4   R. Morin, 'The Price of Segregation', *ibid.*, 28 December 1997, p. C5.
5   Clark, p. 186.
6   S. and A. Thernstrom, *America in Black and White* (New York: Simon & Schuster, 1997), p. 224.
7   *Ibid.*, p. 219.

8   A Wall Street Journal/NBC poll conducted in early 2000, for instance, found that about 60% of Caucasian, African American and Hispanic respondents alike thought equal opportunity more important than racial mixing and that of the remainder interviewed a majority expressed a preference for equal results rather than integration as a primary social goal. See A.R. Hunt, 'Blacks, Whites Find Common Ground on Attitudes Towards Race', *Wall Street Journal*, 9 March 2000, p. A19.

9   Thernstrom, p. 226.

10   D. Masci, 'The Black Middle Class: Is Its Cup Half-full or Half-empty?', *CQ Researcher*, 23 January 1998, p. 56.

11   L. Frazier, 'Prince George's Is 62% Black, Study Finds', *Washington Post*, 7 December 1997, p. A1; also Thernstrom, p. 212.

12   D.K. Shipler, *A Country of Strangers* (New York: Alfred A. Knopf, 1997), p. 64.

13   Thernstrom, p. 355.

14   A. Hacker, *Two Nations* (New York: Chas. Scribner's Sons, 1992), pp. 212-3.

15   J. Taylor, *Paved With Good Intentions* (New York: Carroll & Graf, 1992), p. 204; J. Coleman, *Long Way To Go* (New York: Atlantic Monthly Press, 1997), p. 22.

16   Thernstrom, p. 345; D. Johnson, 'Then the Colour of Classmates. Now the Colour of Money', *New York Times*, 26 September 1999, IV, p. 3.

17   A. Thernstrom, 'Who's Afraid to Debate Affirmative Action?', *New York Times*, 22 November 1997, p. A15.

18   56% of white and 88% of black undergraduates who first entered higher education in 1989 at certain select institutions claimed to have got to 'know well' two or more classmates of the other race while on campus. See W.G. Bowen and D. Bok, *The Shape of the River* (Princeton, N.J.: Princeton University Press, 1998), p. 232. Further data can be found on pp. 241-8. Yet critics remain unimpressed with such findings as a justification of affirmative action. The authors of this investigation, claims one such opponent, 'explore a ridiculously closed universe' because they ignore the experiences of ordinary whites and blacks, who surveys show nowadays also report much higher interracial friendship rates than before. See A. Thernstrom, 'A Flawed Defence of Preferences', *Wall Street Journal*, 2 October 1998, p. A14.

19   The Milton S. Eisenhower Foundation and the Corporation for What Works, *The Millennium Breach* (Washington, D.C.: First Edition and Printing, 1998), p. 10.

20   *Ibid.*, pp. 9, 11, 32-3.

5 Unemployment and Income Disparities

Whatever the nature and extent of segregation in the USA today, there are those believe its effects are not confined to the home and the classroom. For them, the 'steerage' of African Americans towards certain types of housing restricts black access to good schools, which in turn leads to skills differentials and a significant earnings gap by race. The accusation is serious, for few pieces of data about the races in the U.S. are quoted so regularly as the official ones pertaining to jobs and incomes. To some, such statistics provide hard evidence of the amount of racial discrimination purported to be taking place in the country. Others say that figures of this sort prove nothing. For them, data showing blacks persistently trailing whites might represent real facts about the relative economic standing of the two races, but they insist that the interpretation of these facts is wide open to debate. This Chapter seeks to explore both sides of the argument.

Unemployment

One of the greatest areas of controversy is joblessness. Even throughout most of the prosperous 1990s, African American redundancy rates came to fully double those of whites, sometimes two and a half times as great. The year that provided the one exception was 1991 when recession in many white-collar sectors hit Caucasian employees rather hard, and that proved to be fairly short lived. By the latter part of the decade, African American unemployment rates were beginning to fall noticeably amidst a prolonged economic expansion, but white rates were falling about as fast, thereby keeping the overall racial ratio of those out of work more or less the same. Thus black joblessness dropped to 7.8 % in January 1999, while that for whites declined to 3.8 %.[1]

For a number of people, the first explanation that springs to mind for the persistent discrepancy in black-white unemployment rates is racism. Bosses, full of negative stereotyped images of African Americans as lazy, incompetent or hostile people, are reluctant to hire them. In most instances, affirmative action programmes all but require companies to employ a certain amount of blacks. But where there are loopholes in the law, employers are inclined to take on African Americans only as a final resort when there are no other workers available and dismiss them as soon as possible once the labour shortage has eased. Particularly guilty of participating in this 'last hired, first fired' syndrome are said to be those businesses with fewer than fifteen employees, which because of their tiny size are exempt from equal employment opportunity laws. Being very small, they are also less visible to the public, less prone to being charged in expensive 'class action' lawsuits and so less vulnerable to adverse media coverage. One study conducted over a three-year period in the 1990s of such firms found that they were only about half as likely as the large ones to hire blacks.[2]

Others, however, take a different view. While not denying that discrimination exists, they contend it is a charge that in some respects does not make sense. It does not, for instance, bear up to historical scrutiny. Studies have shown that the ratio of black men out of work to whites has been as high, if not higher, in recent years than it was half a century or so ago when blatant racial prejudice was commonplace and in the case of the South was formally encoded into law. The notion that African Americans are being treated less fairly today when attitudes have changed so markedly and when blacks have much greater legal protection is to these observers absurd. A much more plausible explanation according to some is the enormous structural change that the U.S. economy has undergone in the past few decades. Blue-collar jobs have disappeared as manufacturing has given way to information-gathering service employment and as the cheap labour 'global economy' has opened up. A great many black and white members of the working class were being made redundant, but proportionately more of the former, as it was countless numbers of their families who had migrated north over the years to seek such relatively unskilled 'smokestack' employment in the first place.

Meanwhile, the comparatively few blue-collar jobs that have been created or kept going in this post-industrial environment require problem solving abilities undreamt of before. Thus car manufacturers now insist that employees have a more than rudimentary reading ability to be able to cope with rather detailed training and assembly line manuals. Component firms regularly require floor workers to be able to chart and analyse data electronically to gauge both the quality and quantity of the parts they make. Even the likes of furniture and other more basic manufacturing firms increasingly expect written fluency from their staff to process reports and orders. Yet these are precisely the cognitive skills that some observers claim

African Americans have in general been failing to acquire during their schooling.

In the case of poor black residents of the central cities there is an additional reason for higher unemployment rates. This is the migration of businesses to the suburbs. Across virtually the whole of the United States thousands of companies have decided to take advantage of advances in transportation and communication and lower taxes, land prices and crime rates to move from the core to the fringes of metropolitan areas. High-tech computer companies have led the way by moving to specially created 'office parks', but more traditional enterprises like retailers have not been far behind, as can be seen by the proliferation of shopping malls at the periphery of most conurbations. The upshot for central city people is still less economic opportunity, as even those few with the requisite skills find it hard to commute on a daily basis.

'Spatial mismatch', as some social scientists have labelled this phenomenon, applies not only to the distribution of people and jobs within the metropolitan areas but also to entire regions of the United States. A large portion of African Americans is concentrated in the 'Rustbelt' cities of the Northeast and upper Midwest, but the fastest growing parts of the country have been in the West and Southwest, where most of the population is white. Las Vegas, San Diego and Phoenix have all experienced dynamic expansion but have not attracted many black newcomers. Some African Americans have been uprooting themselves from the more stagnant urban centres of the North to move to the South, as was mentioned in Chapter 2. But while southern cities like Atlanta and Memphis have economies a good deal more robust than those of Newark or Detroit, their growth rates have not been as rapid as those in many parts of the West. In any event, black mobility on the whole has not been as great as that of whites, leaving a good number of African Americans in the wrong place at the wrong time.

Most of the discussion has so far focused on less well off blacks with only secondary schooling and possessing relatively few skills. But what about those who have at least some tertiary education and are perhaps computer literate? Do they suffer from relatively higher unemployment rates than whites as well? Comprehensive evidence is hard to come by, but it would appear the better the level of educational attainment, the greater the likelihood of racial differentials being narrowed. A snapshot study of April 1995 found that 6% of all black male college graduates were without work, a little under double that of their white counterparts and so somewhat better than the performance of black men in general vis-à-vis white men. Three per cent. of African American graduates of the more elite institutions were unemployed that month, the same as for Caucasian men with first degrees from the same places of learning. And as regards women, the figures actually favoured blacks, especially those with 'Ivy League' credentials, over their white equivalents, though differences here were attributed primarily to a 'leisure gap', in which the latter were much more likely than the former to be married to a man earning a lot of money and so not needing always to be in the workforce, rather than any other factor.[3]

The question remains as to why blacks with degrees should have higher unemployment rates than their white equivalents at all. Some contend that employers have double standards regarding qualifications, with African American graduates being required to have much more impressive ones than Caucasians, even when competing for the same job. In the opinion of one writer, the situation regarding aspiring young African American professionals is comparable to that of black baseball players in the 1950s, years after teams first became integrated. Just as athletes like Hank Aaron and Willie Mays had to have superstar potential in order to gain entry to the major leagues while white ones could be mere 'journeymen', so today black partners at prestigious law firms are much more likely to have needed good degrees at Harvard or Yale than is the case for their Caucasian counterparts.[4]

There are, however, those who contest this view, if only on practical grounds. With the economy booming and the national unemployment rate for those with bachelor's degrees or better at less than two per cent., major companies are pursuing higher education students everywhere in the country. And they are courting African Americans and Hispanics with especial enthusiasm. As far as these observers are concerned, the difficulty is graduation rates. While blacks constitute about 13% of the total population, they receive only 7.5% of all B.A. and B.Sc. degrees and get comparatively fewer still higher awards. Thus there is a much smaller pool of talent from which to recruit African Americans, and to lure them the bigger companies often go to non-'Ivy League' campuses, where they make particularly lucrative offers.[5] Cynics contend that all this is for appearances' sake rather than reflecting a true belief in diversity. Nevertheless, the ardent pursuit of minorities from higher education institutions that do not 'do well in the national ratings'[6] is to some further evidence that racial bias is not widespread, at least not in the hiring practices of corporate America.

Then there is the matter of immigration. There can be little doubt that the large scale influx of people from abroad has had an impact on the African American workforce, but more at the lower rather than the upper end of the jobs scale. The willingness of many Third World newcomers to work for minimum wages, sometimes less, is regarded as a kind of unfair competition by many blacks who know that numerous Asians, Hispanics and others are only able to do so by living in overcrowded multiple earner dwellings. The argument that such people are keeping thousands of jobs in the United States that otherwise would go overseas is cold comfort to those used to better paid employment. There are some, however, who argue that blacks themselves are as much to blame as anyone else for this loss of share at the lower end of the labour market. The civil rights movement has for years been accused of spreading the false message that African Americans did not have to work their way up from the bottom rungs of the ladder. Many blacks are said to have believed it and looked down on entry level positions with disdain, even if they had little experience or few qualifications themselves. Meanwhile, employers are said to be impressed by immigrants' desire to please and by their especially strong work ethic.

And it cannot be denied that as the economy has become more service oriented, 'soft skills' such as projecting a good personality and attitude have come to count as much as traditional 'hard' ones like speed, efficiency and technical knowledge. Yet they are attributes that African American males are sometimes alleged not to possess. There has always been a tendency on the part of employers when hiring blacks to choose women in preference to men. The former are perceived to be less assertive and less tense about race. A recent study quoted in the *Wall Street Journal*, however, found that a significant number of employers across the nation ranked African American males poorly not only in terms of teamwork but also in their dealings with the public. When asked about how they arrived at these conclusions, some bosses did admit to stereotyping but others cited definite experience following complaints lodged by customers.[7] Answers such as these are inevitably subjective and so should be treated with caution. However, along with generally weaker academic qualifications they for some people do provide a clue to the fundamental reason for black males on the whole faring less well than black females in the jobs market.

Yet many would say that the most telling explanation for the dire employment figures of black urban males, especially the younger ones, is crime. An age-old tenet of liberals is that poverty causes crime, but some believe the reverse to be equally true. There can be no denying that the crime rate of black men is astonishingly high. In 1995, fully one-third of African American males in the country were either in jail or on parole or on probation, more than twice the rate for Latinos and several times that for whites and black women. The figures have declined somewhat since then but nevertheless remain well above those of other groups. Crime, especially the violent sort long so prevalent in the central cities, leads to unemployment in several ways. It increases costs to firms and so discourages business activity in the most troubled neighbourhoods, thereby aggravating the aforementioned 'spatial mismatch'. Criminal records damage job prospects upon release. The lucrative pay in certain types of crime, most notably drug dealing, decreases young black male interest in regular employment. Worst of all, it tars others with the same brush. Black males of all social classes tend to get stigmatised and consequently find it harder to land decent employment.

To blacks, however, much of the foregoing serves as evidence that racial prejudice is alive and well in the U.S. jobs market. If African American men get treated warily in interviews simply because they are black and male and so statistically speaking more likely to have a criminal record, then they are victims of a kind of discrimination in which judgements are made on the basis of cold data rather than personal history. Likewise, if bosses see 'black culture' as a main reason for African American men bringing few 'soft skills' to the workplace, then racial stereotyping is flourishing. Little wonder, some contend, that black unemployment rates are higher than those of whites, especially as it is the latter group that controls access to most jobs.

Others, mostly whites, counter that this conclusion is too facile. They do not deny that favouritism exists, but they have strong doubts that it is so widespread. Some bosses do discriminate, if only on the basis of a subconscious 'affinity impulse' that leads them to prefer their own kind. Some would discriminate a good deal more were it not for civil rights and equal opportunity laws. But to say that it is prevalent merely because certain blacks have lost out for having been judged by the behaviour of some of their brethren is wrong. Even when measurable factors like age, education and experience are taken into account, the final choice at the interview stage can be swayed by intangible considerations such as poise, confidence and attractiveness. In short, a myriad of criteria affect the outcome.

Income Inequality

Gathering information about unemployment is one way of trying to learn whether there is discrimination in the workplace. Perhaps another is by comparing income and earnings, or the amounts of money received over set periods of time, by race. Mention of income inequality in today's world of big business profits usually conjures up images of executives annually gaining millions of extra dollars through higher salaries and offerings of stock options while staff lower down the corporate ladder receive only modest pay increases, if that. Yet civil rights groups maintain that there long has been in the United States a second and recently rather less publicised form of disparity in this area along racial and ethnic lines. To them income inequality by skin colour might not be as glaring as that by job position, but they argue that it is as least as pernicious.

The traditional yardstick used to make comparisons of this sort are figures produced by the U.S. Bureau of the Census, like those below:

Table 5.1 Median Family Income, by Race

	Black	White	Black/White Ratio
1970	$6,279	$10,236	61
1980	12,674	21,904	58
1990	21,423	36,915	58
1995	25,970	42,646	61

Source: Statistical Abstract of the United States, 1997, Table 724.

As can be seen in the above Table, African American family incomes were stuck at approximately three-fifths the level of that of whites for about twenty five years. Since 1995, blacks have narrowed the gap somewhat, but the fact that the income differential has been so wide for so long is to many one of the most depressing socioeconomic facts of modern day life in the U.S. In 1995, the ratio of black/white family income was no better than it had been in 1970, the year in which the Nixon administration first gave the go ahead to racial preferences in hiring and promotion programmes.

Once again, the explanation most commonly given for the continuance of the gap is racism. It is argued that in the private sector at any rate African Americans not only face obstacles in trying to secure employment but also in gaining advancement once they are part of the workforce. Blacks are said to be taken on in many workplaces merely to avoid charges of bias and any accompanying unpleasant publicity, but all too often they are not put in positions of real responsibility because of prejudice about their abilities or, alternatively, because of worry that they could not then get the best performance out of resentful, if not actually resistant, white subordinates. According to data published by the Federal Glass Ceiling Commission in the mid-1990s, only six-tenths of one per cent. of senior management positions in the nation's largest companies were held by blacks.[8] If certain African Americans have since become president or chief executive officer of Disney, Maytag, Federal National Mortgage and one or two other prominent corporations, the racial promotion chasm is still felt to be very wide, not least in the increasingly important high-tech sector.

Others, however, contend that comparisons such as those made in Table 5.1 are inadequate. To begin with, most official data list 'income', a very broad heading and one that includes about a dozen or so categories of money received, ranging from pensions and unemployment benefits to dividends and interest got from stocks and bonds, as well as the usual wages and salaries. Given that proportionately more African Americans are out of work than whites and that the latter tend to have greater amounts of inherited wealth, some of which is invested in the financial markets, might not a good portion of the wide income gap between black and white families be attributable to these extraneous factors rather than discrimination in the workplace? In the opinion of some, a more accurate gauge of how well black workers are doing vis-a-vis whites is to study family income figures by subsets to compare better like with like. If one focuses on families of the same type, the picture improves as far as blacks are concerned, particularly in the case of two-parent families.

As can be seen in Table 5.2 on the next page, as many African American married couple families earned $40,000 p.a. or thereabouts in 1994 as did not, almost 90% of the figure for white married couples that year. A gap remained, to be sure, but much narrower than that shown in Table 5.1. Nor, according to some, should one presume that racism is necessarily the main explanation for the remaining 11% difference. As they see it, both geography and education must be factored into the equation. Today a little more than half of all blacks but barely a third of all whites reside in the South where the cost of living, and so incomes, are about 10% lower than the national average. Meanwhile, whites are relatively speaking twice as likely as African Americans to have graduated from college or university, which enhances earnings power. Make allowance for these regional and educational considerations, critics argue, and the reduced difference in married couple family income by race for all intents and purposes disappears.

Table 5.2 Median Income of Families, by Race and Family Type, mid-1990s

	Black	White	Black/White Ratio
All families	$24,698	$40,884	60[a]
Married Couple families	$40,432	$45,474	89[a]
Female headed family	$13,943	$20,795	67[a]
Female headed families as a % of the total	46.8	14.1	332[b]

[a] = 1994; [b] = 1996.

Source: Statistical Abstract of the United States, 1997, Tables 49 and 727.

What really has kept the gap unbridgeable in the minds of many is the changing structure of the African American family. Whereas in the 1950s and 1960s the great majority of households – black and white alike – consisted of two-parent families, today a large portion of the African American ones are headed by a single parent, usually the mother, as Table 5.2 indicates, and often a teenage mother at that. Of course, African Americans are not alone in this set of circumstances, but they tend to figure more prominently than do members of most other groups. In 1996, 81% of all white families still consisted of married couples.[9] As divorce and separation involve the creation of two domestic social units instead of one, black incomes had to rise particularly fast just to keep pace with the extra black households and so maintain median family income levels. The same was often true every time a woman had a child out of wedlock and went on welfare, an occurrence also generally more common to blacks. In recent decades, African American incomes have been rising, often at a faster rate than that of whites, but because their earnings have had to be spread over a great many more households, for whatever reason, the improvements do not show up in the more general statistics pertaining to families by race. Add to this the arrival of feminism in Middle America and the acceptance of working motherhood, making two earners more of a norm in suburban households than in the past, and the failure of blacks to close the gap with whites becomes still more understandable.

Critics contend that in discussions of racial income the need to compare like with like not only applies to studies by family types but also by educational attainment. Indeed, if anything, one needs perhaps to add extra caveats here, given that there are more types and levels of schooling than there are of families and that education in America is decentralised and so tremendously varying in quality from one district to the next. Sceptics maintain that the likes of Table 5.3, which appears to be quite detailed and is the sort of source often cited, still do not present the whole picture.

As a case in point, critics think the categories pertaining to tertiary education are far too imprecise. They fail to take into consideration areas of study. The jobs market values certain subject qualifications more than others. Degrees in Accountancy, Computer Studies and Engineering are all more remunerative than those awarded in Education, a subject that usually only leads to careers in teaching and one in which a rather high percentage of African American undergraduates have traditionally specialised. Then there is the aforementioned matter of quality or, perhaps more accurately, prestige. Degrees in Business Administration from world-renowned universities like Harvard and MIT are more prized than those from small state institutions. Yet the Government in its racial income statistics lumps them together in the same broad categories, which also fail to distinguish honours from other graduates.

Table 5.3 Black Incomes as a Percentage of White Incomes, by Sex and Education, Persons Aged 18 or Over, 1997

	Men	Women
Not a high school graduate	85	100
High school graduate	78	95
Some college	83	125
Bachelor's degree	74	102
Master's degree	64	98

Source: Statistical Abstract of the United States, 1998, Table 263.

The same logic applies to official data concerning those with lesser qualifications. Numbers of years spent in a high school classroom do not necessarily reveal how skilled an individual is. The time may have been spent productively for one but not another. Critics say that it is not so much a matter of whether whites and blacks with high school diplomas have the same incomes that is important as whether those with the same numeracy and literacy abilities at the end of their secondary schooling are faring roughly the same. In view of the fact that African American high school seniors on average perform less well than members of other racial and ethnic groups in national standardised tests, as was noted in Chapter 4, the omens generally do not augur well for them in the workforce.

For those who see little or no racial discrimination in the world of work in America, the most revealing figures in Table 5.3 are those pertaining to black women. That the income of African American females more or less matches that of white women with approximately the same amount of education is, they say, largely unknown to the general public. That black women with at least some college education often earn a good deal more than their white counterparts and, indeed, have done so for about forty years is, according to some, one of the best kept social studies secrets and a fact usually ignored by civil rights groups and their alleged sympathisers in the mainstream media. If skin colour is such an important factor in the hiring and promotion practices of white employers, conservatives ask, how is it that African American women, who are vulnerable to sexism as well as racism and who attend the same spectrum of colleges and universities as African American men, do so well? The answer, they maintain, has not so much to do with white bosses or black females as with black males and their presumed cognitive and 'soft skills' deficiencies, leaving the latter only about two-thirds as well represented as black women in the professional and managerial sectors of the workforce and holding only three-eighths of all technical positions held by blacks.[10]

Others, however, are not so certain. Quite apart from suspecting that African American men are more likely to be denied opportunities rather than fail to seize them, they contend that black women are not doing as well as at first appears. The approximate parity among women stems from the fact that few females of either colour rise very high in the earnings tables. The relative progress of African American women can therefore only produce restrained applause: achieving equality is easier among an underpaid group. Furthermore, necessity dictates that black women earn as much as possible. More of them must manage on their own, since they are not so likely as their white counterparts to have a partner who brings in a second income. Thus they generally work longer hours and have fewer protracted breaks from their careers for child rearing or other reasons, giving them in the first instance more overtime and in the second lengthier work experience.

In fact, the list of variables influencing racial gaps in earnings can be quite long and extend far beyond gender, family structure and education. Already we have discussed the impact of geography depressing median earnings of African Americans. Age is arguably another such factor. According to the 1990 census, blacks in the United States have a median age of just over twenty eight, and for both Hispanics and Native Americans the figures are lower still. Meanwhile, the median age for whites is about thirty five, and for some subsets of Caucasian population like American Jews it is as high as forty.[11] Since most people's earnings increase as they get older and their careers mature, some contend that age differences are definitely part of the disparity in wages and salaries by race. Consideration, too, must be given to health. Black women may be steadier workers and on the job longer than white women, but medical factors alone make it harder for black men to achieve the same feat with regard to white men. A study published in the *Wall Street Journal* revealed that African American males in their forties and fifties are more than twice as likely as their white counterparts to leave the workforce because of ill health, especially heart disease and hypertension.[12] Such interruptions cannot come without some loss of earnings and increase in the overall black unemployment rate.

Last but not least, many feel that some consideration ought to be given to ethnicity *within* racial groups. All of the above discussion has been based on the assumption that blacks and whites are ancestrally monolithic within their own separate backgrounds, but clearly that is not the case. Middle aged whites do not see themselves in particular European terms to nearly the same extent as their parents and grandparents did, but cultural characteristics do linger, and some contend that these are still sufficiently strong to count as a factor in what sometimes are quite big gaps in income and earnings. And such disparities unquestionably exist within the general white population. The 1990 census found that Greek Americans, for instance, had family incomes half again as big as those of Cajuns, the descendants of French Canadians who live in southern Louisiana. Italian Americans fared almost as well as Americans of Scottish descent, even though the latter were on the whole considerably better educated. (The reason for this apparent anomaly, it seems, is that Scottish Americans often use their extra learning to enter into either teaching or the ministry, neither of which is the most highly paid of vocations.) Jewish per capita incomes are nearly double those of non-Jews; indeed, there is a greater per capita disparity between Jews and Christians in the United States than there is between whites and blacks.[13]

Similar gaps exist within the Hispanic and Asian American communities, and although black Americans are a fairly homogeneous group, there is a view amongst many that the point is basically valid about them too. Already we have seen that there is a comparative earnings difference between African American females and males. It would appear that the same is at least as true of foreign and native born blacks. As long ago as the 1960s newcomers from the West Indies were making on average half as much again as African Americans. Since then, second generation Caribbean immigrants have come to earn fifteen per cent. more than the average American, white or black, despite looking no different from U.S. born and raised blacks.[14]

Response of the Authorities

Whatever the explanation for such inequalities, the nature of the response of federal, state and city governments has changed over the past decade. In the early part of the 1990s Washington, D.C., seemed willing to give consideration to minority arguments. Apparently concerned at accusations that blacks, women and others were not getting their fair share of promotions at the workplace, President Bush agreed to the establishment of a Federal Glass Ceiling Commission in 1991. Although devoid of formal powers, it issued a report four years later that confirmed many people's worst fears and whose findings were embarrassing enough to get at least a few big businesses to mend their ways. As one of its first acts when it came into being in 1993, the Clinton administration raised the national minimum wage, a step generally acknowledged to be aimed at helping blacks and Hispanics, both of whom are disproportionately represented in the ranks of the lowest paid.

　　As the 1990s have worn on, however, the authorities have generally been tackling the problem of inequalities from quite a different angle. The national minimum wage was raised again in two stages in 1996-7, but instead of seeing the gaps in terms of possible discrimination or racism, those in power more and more have been viewing them as the inevitable result of misguided entitlements. In particular, white America has been coming to the conclusion that state handouts were a major culprit, as was explained in Chapter 3. Partly in response to such beliefs and out of anxiety to reduce the then huge federal budget deficit, both President Clinton and the Republican controlled Congress agreed to the passage of the landmark Welfare Act of 1996. This transferred much of the running of such programmes from Washington, D.C., to each of the fifty states, and replaced welfare with 'workfare'. In like manner, the state of California sought to deny welfare benefits to illegal immigrants in the mid-1990s (see Chapter 10). The success of these latest efforts is debateable, but there can be little doubt that the response has changed.

Conclusion

Social theorists who attempt to draw conclusions about unemployment and income disparities between blacks and whites can be divided into two fairly distinct camps: those who believe racism is the root cause and those who do not. The Left stresses the consistency of the statistics. That official data show continuing higher joblessness and lower income levels among blacks as against whites by virtually unchanging ratios over the decades is to them solid evidence that racism is pervasive, if perhaps more subtle than before. For its part, the Right emphasises the need to compare like with like and contends that when this is not done, the results can suggest evil when there may be none. When this is done, studies demonstrate that African Americans earn as much as comparably qualified Caucasians, sometimes more.[15]

Both approaches have their drawbacks. There is much to commend in the insistence of conservatives that social scientists take the time to examine by race people in highly comparable situations. The trouble is, however, that the black population is by no means identical to the white one. The former is even now on the whole less well educated and less experienced than the latter, differences that continue to owe at least something to past racism. The opportunity to make true contrasts is therefore rather limited, and the studies done have of necessity been so few and far between as to be statistically dubious. Meanwhile, simply looking at jobless and income figures by race, as the Left would have us do, will not suffice. Apart from the likelihood that official data are compiled in an unsatisfactory way, such figures can at best only show the effects of racism, not the original intent. Can something as personal and subjective as this ever be detected? Some have tried to find out by sending applicants of both races with very similar qualifications to interview for the same job. Two surveys conducted in the early 1990s showed a slight preference for Caucasian candidates, but by such a small margin as not to be highly meaningful.[16] Questions have also been raised about the applicants in these exercises, with sceptics wondering whether the black ones were pretending as earnestly as the whites to want to fill the vacancies concerned. It is known, many conservatives argue, that testers of both races were aware of the surveys' purpose and so might have behaved in such a way during interviews as to create a self-fulfilling prophecy.

Thus we are in a sense little further forward. Even the most determined attempts to establish evidence of racial hiring discrimination by secretly testing employers have been of no real avail because one does not know for certain what was going on in the minds of the examiners and the manner of their demeanour during interviews. Indeed, no real proof of bias of any sort can be made without being privy to the innermost thoughts of all concerned, and that clearly is an impossibility. But while one can never establish for sure the extent of prejudice, one can safely conclude that it still exists and is one of a host of factors behind the rather poor performance of African Americans in the labour market.

Notes

1   J.M. Berry, 'Jobless Rates for Blacks, Hispanics Fall', *Washington Post*, 6 February 1999, p. A1.
2   R. Ho, 'Small Firms Are Half As Likely to Hire Blacks As Large Firms, Study Says', *Wall Street Journal*, 28 August 1997, p. B2.
3   W.G. Bowen and D. Bok, *The Shape of the River* (Princeton, N.J.: Princeton University Press, 1998), pp.119-120.
4   B. Staples, 'When a Law Firm Is Like a Baseball Team', *New York Times*, 27 November 1998, p. A42.
5   N. Munk, 'Hello Corporate America', *Fortune*, 6 July 1998, p. 138. However, an accompanying survey found that four-fifths of corporate African Americans believed in 1998 that average skilled whites were more likely to end up on higher rungs of a firm's ladder than were 'black superheroes', thereby suggesting that the mid-century baseball analogy might apply more to promotion than to hiring, at least in the world of business as distinct from law firms. See S. Branch, 'What Blacks Think of Corporate America', *ibid.*, p. 142.
6   This, at any rate, is the phrase used to describe Florida A&M, a historic black university that has succeeded in recent years in getting many of its students into corporate jobs upon graduation. See *ibid.*, *loc. cit.*
7   C. Duff, 'Surging Economy Bypasses Black Men', 3 June 1997, p. A2.
8   'Give All Americans a Chance...', *Washington Post*, 20 July 1995, p. A12.
9   *Statistical Abstract of the United States, 1997*, Table 74.
10 J. Taylor, *Paved With Good Intentions* (New York: Carroll & Graf, 1992), pp. 24-5.
11 D. D'Souza, *The End of Racism* (New York: The Free Press, 1995), p. 301.
12 'Work Week', *Wall Street Journal*, 10 December 1996, p. A1.
13 S. and A. Thernstrom, *America in Black and White* (New York: Simon & Schuster, 1997), pp. 541-3.
14 Taylor, p. 25.
15 See D'Souza, p. 302, where a U.S. Government economist is quoted as saying wage differentials between black and white males in their twenties are negligible when controlled for such factors as age, experience, geography, and so on. According to the Thernstroms, p. 446, a 1991 survey showed that black men earned 9% more than their white counterparts 'with the same education – as defined by skill'.
16 Taylor, pp. 29-30 and Thernstrom, pp. 448-9.

6 Crime, Health and the Media

Crime

If the main source of income for black females according to popular perception is the welfare cheque, the main source of income for black males in the minds of many is crime. A national survey in 1990 showed that over half of non-black people questioned thought African Americans were more violent than whites, and that African American men were especially dangerous.[1] The mere prospect of encountering a black male along an urban pavement, particularly if he is not well dressed, is often enough to cause a white woman to cross the street. White motorists who think nothing of driving through Hispanic or Asian American neighbourhoods frequently have second thoughts about doing so through a black enclave, even in daylight.

Statistics seem to bear out these fears. Crime rates are coming down in numerous respects across the United States and among all the racial and ethnic groups. But those for African American males still are inordinately high. Although blacks comprise a little under 13% of the total population, they constituted in 1997 nearly two-fifths of all those arrested for aggravated assault, possession of weapons and rape. More than half of all those arrested for murder and upwards of three-fifths of those detained for armed robbery in that year were black, the great bulk of them African American males. The figures for young black males are even more alarming. Fully one-third of all black men in their twenties are either behind bars, on parole or on probation. More black males are in prison than in college or university. The incarceration rate of African American men is four times that of South Africa during the most repressive days of apartheid.[2]

Less well known is statistical evidence demonstrating that African Americans are also the principal victims of crime. Black men are murdered at more than seven times the rate white men are, and the ratio between black and white women is nearly as high. Department of Justice statistics reveal that in 1996 African Americans were an eighth again as likely to be victims of property crimes and a quarter again as likely to be victims of violent crimes as Caucasians. Public opinion polls repeatedly reveal that blacks fear for their physical safety even more than do whites. The reason for the apparent discrepancy in the statistics is that the bulk of offences involving African Americans is of a black-on-black nature. In 1995, for instance, more than 90% of the blacks who were murdered died at the hands of a fellow African American. By the same token, about 70% of all violent crimes against whites are committed by whites, according to the FBI.[3] Interracial offences are in many ways limited. Yet with the exception of 'hate crimes', which by some measurements more commonly consist of white attacks against blacks rather than the other way round,[4] public perceptions are otherwise. As President Clinton once put it: 'Violence for white people all too often comes with a black face.'

Is the behaviour of African Americans, especially African American youths, really that bad, or is the public at large reacting irrationally on the basis of spurious figures bolstered by media stereotyping? Everyone except the more hardcore racists would agree that crime is a personal shortcoming and that the great majority of blacks, like the great majority of other racial and ethnic groups, are law abiding. What needs to be ascertained is whether African Americans as a group are somewhat more disposed to illegal activity than others, for whatever reason.

We have seen that black arrest rates are extremely high. Civil rights supporters maintain that this is the result of bias on the part of police and their local authority superiors, so many of whom are still white. The Rodney King and O.J. Simpson cases revealed only too well the racist sentiments of certain officers in the Los Angeles Police Department. Allegations of 'racial profiling', the practice of stopping and detaining black motorists in particular for drug checks, has led many to wonder if the same is also true of state troopers. However, African Americans figure prominently in arrests made in Washington, D.C., a city whose police force is majority black. The same is also true of urban centres like Atlanta and Detroit that not only have black mayors but also black controlled councils. Meanwhile, with the possible exception of New York just about all big-city forces have undergone improved training and screening procedures of their staff. And some say that differences in black-white arrest rates are in any case distorted by the fact that the latter group is generally richer and so can better afford private attorneys who can often prevent formal charges being made. In all probability more pertinent evidence comes from ordinary members of the public. The National Crime Victimisation Survey for 1993, for instance, showed that African American victims of violence identified the perpetrators as black in nearly four cases out of five, with even higher black-on-black identification rates for robberies. A little more than half of all white victims of crimes that year established their offenders as black.[5]

Of course, such figures deal largely with crimes against individuals. African Americans and white liberal sympathisers contend that with regard to crimes against property or offences against moral codes the record is by no means so clear. According to them, positions of social class facilitate or, alternatively, hinder an individual's ability to get away with offences. Poor people, a disproportionate number of whom are black, do not necessarily have a more inherent personal proclivity to crime than the better off, but they are more likely to get caught. If they indulge in gambling, prostitution or theft, they do so in the open because they have relatively little access to buildings and closed doors and so are quite likely to get apprehended by the police. Thieves who work in offices have a greater array of less detectable criminal options, ranging from computer fraud to mutual price fixing arrangements in private dining clubs, activities not available to the disadvantaged. So subtle and clever are these crimes that victims may never realise that they have been swindled and so never report the offence at all.

Thus it is quite possible that the gap in overall black and white crime rates is not nearly as wide as superficially appears. If African Americans still seem to be somewhat more disposed towards wrongdoing, it could well be because of faulty information gathering and because of economic factors less applicable to members of other races. Persistently high African American unemployment rates do create a pool of black men who feel they have few opportunities in the legal world of work. On the other hand, as has been pointed out in an earlier chapter on unemployment, conservatives stress the reverse – namely, the various ways in which criminal activity reduces one's chance of securing a job. And there is the question of whether white wariness of African Americans, especially African American males, is more a precaution against or a source of crime. 'As long as the dominant message sent to impressionable black boys is that they are expected to turn into savage criminals,' writes Ellis Cose of *Newsweek*, 'nothing will stop substantial numbers of them doing just that.'[6]

Putting aside these 'chicken and egg' arguments, one finds it difficult to deny a greater disposition on the part of African Americans as a whole to resort to violence than is true of whites, Latinos or Asian Americans. Here, too, socioeconomic circumstances play a big part. Despite the recent collapse in the 'crack' trade, inner city homicides, especially those committed by young black male members of street gangs upon each other, still occur at a higher rate than elsewhere and so continue to skew the statistics. That said, Americans are not altogether incorrect to speak of 'black crime' in everyday conversation in the same way they refer to 'Italian crime' in their discussion of the Mafia and similar organisations.

The connotation that the former phrase carries of a particular kind of wrongdoing involving the threat or actuality of bodily harm, however politically charged and at times exaggerated, is grounded at least partly in fact. Public circumspection of African Americans in certain urban settings, while by no means always to be condoned, is understandable.

The Criminal Justice System

If there is a disparity between arrest rates of blacks and others, especially for non-violent offences, does the same hold true for convictions and punishments? Once again, the official figures are staggering. Though African Americans make up little more than one in eight of the total U.S. population, they account for nearly half of all those behind bars.[7] Half as many again are estimated to be either on probation or parole. There is a strong suspicion in some circles that the system of criminal justice is tainted with racial bias, not least because the great majority of judges and jury members are non-black.

The problem with such figures is that they do not tell how the accused of various races and ethnicities are handled at each consecutive stage of the justice system. Instead, they merely provide isolated snapshots of certain stages, particularly those at the very beginning like arrests or at the end like imprisonment. Table 6.1, however, gives information about intermediate stages in the system as published by the U.S. Department of Justice in 1993. The data here are based on the experiences of over 10,000 adults with cases proceeding through state courts in the nation's 75 largest counties comprising about three-fifths of the total African American population.

Table 6.1   The U.S. Justice System's Treatment of Blacks and Whites, 1990-1991

	Blacks	Whites
Prosecuted after being charged with a felony	66%	69%
Convicted after prosecution	75%	78%
Sentenced after prosecution	51%	38%

Source: P.A. Langan, 'America's Justice System Does Not Discriminate Against Blacks' in P.A. Winters (ed.), *Race Relations: Opposing Viewpoints* (San Diego: Greenhaven Press, 1996), pp. 141-2.

In two of the three stages, prosecutions and convictions, blacks appear to have been treated more leniently than whites. A similar study reveals that in 1992 blacks were more likely than whites to be acquitted or have the charges against them dismissed in twelve of fourteen categories of felonies. Nor is the disparity in the other direction shown in Table 6.1 about sentencing necessarily the result of bias. According to some observers, other legal factors like prior convictions and the severity of the crime – violent offenders are imprisoned at a very high rate – account for the difference here rather than race. Furthermore, the difference in the length of the average sentence to be served by the two groups is so small as to be statistically insignificant – five and a half years for convicted African Americans, five years and five months for whites.[8]

There are two areas of sentencing, however, where accusations of racism do perhaps have to be taken more seriously. One of these is the drug trade, which at one point was growing exponentially in the United States, particularly the trafficking of cocaine. Like theft and fraud, the peddling and use of illegal substances have produced markedly varying arrest and conviction rates at least in part because of differing ways they were being practised in different neighbourhoods.[9] In low income communities inhabited by a lot of blacks they are often done in concentrated open air markets where undercover police agents find apprehending offenders relatively easy. In scattered middle class, largely white districts they are done behind closed doors, often in the comfort of one's own home. Enforcement is therefore more difficult and in any case does not always get the attention it deserves because the police know that addicts there are more likely to end up in treatment.

This aspect of the campaign critics can for the most part tolerate, however grudgingly. Much more objectionable to them are federal sentencing guidelines that have made punishments for the sale or possession of crack cocaine a good deal harsher than those for the powdered variety. The authorities justify this on the grounds that the former is a more raw and pure form of narcotic than the latter and so is more likely to create disorder and mayhem on the streets. But critics say the distinction is artificial as both forms of the drug ultimately lead to dependency. According to them, the real reason for penalising crack more severely is its usage by blacks, whereas powdered cocaine is taken mainly by whites. Whether the Government is deliberately trying to lock up more of what it regards as potentially criminal blacks before they become a serious danger is hard to prove. Unquestionably, however, the mandatory minimum sentences given even to low level drug offenders, a major plank in the War on Drugs campaign, were an important factor in the nearly six-fold increase in the number of African Americans incarcerated between 1986 and 1991.

According to many, still greater evidence for racial bias in the justice system lies in the area of death penalty convictions. Contrary to what might be expected, however, the argument is not that the bias is based on the race of the defendant but on the race of the victim. Convicted murderers of whites are more likely to be executed than convicted murderers of blacks. Given that the majority of people who murder whites are white and that the preponderance of those who murder blacks are black, as Table 6.2 shows, this means that Caucasians stand a greater chance of being hung, lethally injected or electrocuted than do African Americans.

Table 6.2 U.S. Homicides, 1998

Races Involved	Number
Black murderers, black victims	3,067
White murderers, white victims	3,205
Black murderers, white victims	449
White murderers, black victims	205

Source: FBI, *Uniform Crime Reports for the United States, 1998* (Washington, D.C.: U.S. Department of Justice, 1999), Table 2.8, p. 17.

A study of almost 2500 murder cases in Georgia in the 1970s found the likelihood of white defendants being sentenced to die approaching twice that of black defendants. No comparably detailed survey has been made since then, but more recent official statistics indirectly corroborate this finding. Thus Justice Department figures released in 1994 show that while about 60% of those serving murder sentences are black, nearly five times the portion of African Americans in the total population, only 40% of prisoners on 'Death Row' are black. In other words, African Americans are underrepresented in facing the death penalty compared with other groups for murder.[10]

Why should this state of affairs lead to allegations of racism? The answer, it seems, is that in applying the death penalty, the judicial system in the USA considers black lives less valuable than white ones. Critics contend that there can be no other explanation for the fact that although half of all homicide victims in the United States from 1977 to 1992 were African American, 85% of prisoners executed were convicted of killing whites.[11]

This, they say, simply could not happen if society cared about the death of blacks as much as it does about the death of whites. Others disagree, arguing that murders can be of a different character. Those involving blacks tended to come following a heated dispute or in the midst of a fight, whereas those involving whites often were more calculated and cold blooded and so punished more harshly. The statistics do not take into account variables like the reliability of witnesses, plea bargains and the fact that many states do not have the death penalty. No doubt such points do need to be considered, but for many a more plausible explanation is that white juries are simply more likely to identify with victims of their own race than with those of another. Empathy that reaches across skin colour lines has rarely been all that abundant in America.

Indeed, the belief that race is of importance in jury trials has led to calls for reform of the selection procedures of men and women summoned to give verdicts. Critics contend that as matters stand too many juries are being created consisting of members of just one race who are reluctant to pass judgement against those of their own skin colour in racially contested cases. The 1992 'Rodney King' trial, in which four white Los Angeles police officers were acquitted by a jury containing no blacks of using excessive force against an African American motorist, despite videotaped evidence to the contrary, is a notorious case in point. But the controversy can cut both ways, as the acquittal of black celebrity O.J. Simpson in 1995 by a panel that included no white males illustrated only too well. Reformers want racially balanced juries, which they see as representing a cross section of different groups' differing experiences of the law. They believe that in some instances minority jurors might have a fuller, more realistic picture of the ways in which the criminal justice system operates than does the white mainstream. Even middle class African Americans, let alone poorer ones, are a good deal more inclined than suburban whites to question the notion of complete police integrity. Some argue for a kind of affirmative action programme in jury selection in which blacks, whites and others would be represented roughly in line with their overall numbers in the local population. Yet others insist that the present arrangement of having racially balanced jury pools, if not actual juries, is almost always enough to ensure fairness and maintain public confidence in the system. The process of exclusion by lawyers on one side or another already makes deciding jury composition a difficult enough chore. To insist on a particular racial or gender makeup to boot would render the task impossible.

Health

Statistics about the state of health of African Americans are about as disquieting as those pertaining to crime. There are some illnesses that other minority groups suffer more than African Americans, but as the biggest non-white group and the one with the highest death rates from most diseases blacks arouse the greatest amount of concern. As with crime, the figures show something of an improvement in recent years, but not enough to close the gap with most others. Below are some of the figures that government and independent agencies have produced:

- The life expectancy of African American men in 1997 was 67.3 years. This represents an increase of nearly two and a half years over the corresponding figure for 1990 but remains at about five years less than that for men as a whole in the nation and a rate lower than that in many Third World countries. The life expectancy of African American women is somewhat higher but also lags that of the rest of the female population by several years.
- The infant mortality rate of blacks is twice that of whites.
- National Institute of Health officials estimate that blacks are six times as likely as whites and more than twice as likely as Hispanics to develop AIDS. The disease remains the leading killer of African Americans aged 25 to 44, though there has been a decline in the death rate of blacks from it recently.
- Blacks have significantly higher death rates from cardiovascular diseases, pneumonia, diabetes and cancer than do members of other groups. Their death rate from strokes is twice as high as that of white people. In the case of asthma and some infectious diseases the gap between African Americans and other groups is widening.[12]

It is important to appreciate that the above are figures for blacks in the U.S. in general. Certain specific black communities have much worse health records. Thus in Washington, D.C., a city that is about three-fifths African American, the life expectancy of black males is 57.9 years, the second shortest in the country. Only Oglala Sioux men of the Pine Ridge Red Indian Reservation in South Dakota, who live an average 56.5 years, are likely to die younger, and they are a much smaller group of people.[13] A study in a prestigious medical journal revealed that two-thirds of boys in Harlem could expect to die before they reach the age of 65. Indeed, the study showed that they have less chance of surviving even to 45 than their white counterparts nationwide have of reaching 65.[14]

A number of explanations have been advanced for this alarming state of affairs. Some of the more popularly held ones centre on depravity. Statistics showing homicide to be a leading cause of death in African American males between the ages of 15 and 34 and the continuing high incidence of new HIV cases in the black community serve to reinforce lurid preconceived notions. Yet to put matters into perspective AIDS, firearms and the like account for but a small fraction of all black mortalities in any given year.[15] And medical researchers involved in the above study of Harlem say that the low life expectancy of males there is much more likely to be the result of high rates of heart disease and cancer than violence or transmission of fatal illnesses through sex and drugs.[16]

The conventional view among the more sober minded has been that economic factors are largely to blame. African Americans with their greater joblessness and generally lower incomes are almost twice as likely as Caucasians to have no health insurance.[17] Lacking money, they tend to visit GPs less often than whites and consequently get hospitalised relatively more frequently because they do not seek care until their condition has become advanced. To many, however, this cannot be the whole or even the main part of the story. In the economy of the 1990s, black poverty has shrunk and income differentials with whites have in many instances narrowed. Sociological barriers to economic progress like teenage pregnancy have gone down. Meanwhile Latinos, who are also comparatively poor and who are, if anything, even less likely than African Americans to have medical insurance, tend to stay healthy longer than both whites and blacks.[18]

The sheer intractability of the black-white health gap is prompting searches for new or additional explanations. Investigations have shown a genetic predisposition on the part of African Americans to certain life threatening problems, but it is only slight and is essentially restricted to a handful of disorders like prostate cancer, sickle cell anaemia and underweight births.[19] Increasingly experts are stressing the non-physiological aspects of race as a factor. In particular, they are attaching much significance to studies showing the desirability of a patient's having access to a physician of his or her own skin colour. Yet the fact that only 4% of all U.S. doctors are black greatly reduces the chances of this happening for African American patients,[20] and the fear is that the odds are about to become slimmer still. Already fewer blacks are being accepted into medical schools in California and Washington State in the wake of successful anti-affirmative action ballot initiatives there. More declines are expected as the campaign spreads to other parts of the country, with dire consequences anticipated especially for the inner cities, where African American physicians are much more likely than Caucasian ones to set up practice and where they are badly needed.

No less unsettling is evidence of disparate handling of black and white patients. Research published in 1994 revealed that seriously ill elderly African Americans get worse care than other equally sick Medicare beneficiaries at every type of hospital, though the double standards were far less glaring at big-city teaching institutions, where the majority of senior citizen blacks get treatment.[21] Another study discovered that doctors were much less likely to recommend cardiac catheterisation tests for blacks and women as for white men with identical complaints of chest pain.[22] Even preventative services like flu shots and mammograms were made available a quarter to a third less often to blacks than to whites of comparable incomes and insurance coverage.[23]

Contrary to what might be expected, findings such as these have not given rise to much black-white acrimony. The consensus opinion seems to be that if racism is involved, it is more because of subtle differences in the ways doctors view their African American and Caucasian patients rather than something more overt and sinister. Doubtless, too, an awareness that education, culture and behavioural patterns also play a part has helped to temper feelings. However, the same cannot be said of all medical controversies linked to pigmentation. For some time left-wing observers have been contending that the disproportionate dumping of toxic hazards and waste near minority communities and all that that implies for the health of poor blacks and others constitutes a type of environmental racism.[24] But other voices in the 1990s have taken the allegations to an entirely new level. Thus as regards homicides, Louis Farrakhan has asserted that white hatred is responsible for so many blacks killing each other. Law enforcement groups have the wherewithal to halt black-on-black violence but do not and, indeed, willingly turn a blind eye because Caucasians need the organ donations. 'You've become good for parts', he told an audience in Ohio in 1994.[25]

Such utterances might be dismissed as the feverish conjectures of political extremists like the leader of the Nation of Islam movement. However, they are not always limited to fringe elements. Another early 1990s survey revealed that two-thirds of African Americans thought that the Government allowed illicit drugs to be made readily available in ghettos in order to harm black people. A later poll showed that two-fifths of them entertained at least halfway seriously rumours that AIDS had been created in a medical laboratory to eliminate blacks.[26] A recent revelation that researchers working for the Federal Government monitored but did not treat hundreds of syphilitic black men in Tuskegee, Alabama, between 1932 and 1972 despite the availability of penicillin from the 1940s onwards has fuelled black mistrust of the U.S. medical establishment.[27] Meanwhile, on a less conspiratorial note, some experts argue that racial difficulties in general contribute to African American health problems, notably the much higher incidence of hypertension resulting from supposed hostility when dealing with white prejudice.

For the purpose of a study like this, racial statistics pertaining to crime and health are not of such concern in themselves as of the impact they have on race relations. Indeed, the raw figures are, if anything, almost a source of comfort these days inasmuch as they seem to indicate that U.S. blacks have turned a corner of sorts. Since 1990, African American life expectancy has gone up, while the number of most types of felonies and misdemeanours committed by blacks has gone down. Both trends are thus far rather slight and not of long duration, but they are there all the same and so are encouraging.

These improvements notwithstanding, the continuing racial gap in the crime and health statistics has a bearing on a number of seemingly unrelated public issues. Shorter black life expectancy is one reason for African American activists being especially opposed to proposals to raise the age of eligibility for federal old age pensions and health benefits (Social Security and Medicare, respectively). Proportionally fewer blacks than whites are around to collect each time the age threshold is lifted, and some minority politicians suspect that race rather than fiscal savings is the primary motivation behind such moves. The frequent shifting of convicted blacks to rural white areas, where as inmates they are tallied as part of the local population, adds to census controversies inasmuch as in the view of some it causes some government aid based on numbers to go to the wrong communities. The policy of a good many states to deny the vote not only to those in prison, on probation or on parole, but also to those with past convictions, however distant, is said to show how not just the criminal justice system but also the political process is biased against blacks. At present, an estimated one African American male in seven cannot cast a ballot for this reason.[28] Indeed, belief that the criminal justice system as a whole is inherently unfair was one motive for the African American community rallying behind President Clinton to a greater degree than did a good many whites during the 1998 Monica Lewinsky crisis.

It is, however, primarily in the ordinary everyday interactions between blacks and whites that the figures have the most consequence. The statistics reinforce the worst stereotypes. Noting the relative number of black HIV infections and AIDS cases, some Caucasians are inclined to conclude that perhaps many African Americans are, after all, hypersexual drug addicts. The figures increase the overall sense of distrust in the country. Whites look at the statistics on crime and conclude that every African American they encounter is a potential thief, mugger or worse. Blacks look at these and corresponding figures dealing with health and conclude that the criminal justice system and the medical establishment are both somehow plotting against them. Such figures also help cause discrimination and in such a way as to widen the conceptual divide between blacks and whites about racism. White cab drivers who refuse to pick up black male passengers, however well dressed, for fear of being robbed, are accused by African Americans of harbouring ignorant prejudices. Caucasians, on the other hand, see such behaviour as little other than an exercise in prudent judgement based on past experience. To them, this is rational discrimination and is quite different from the irrational sort of those panicky suburbanites who used to sell their homes at the first rumour of blacks moving into their neighbourhood. But to black males, who only know that the end result is the same and that they are being excluded in some way, such niceties are ridiculous, even offensive. Not only do they disagree with whites in their definition of racism, as we saw in the Introduction to this book, but they are also at odds with them as to whether racism is the sole cause of discrimination.

All things considered, the ramifications of whites and blacks viewing topics like crime and health through differing lenses are considerable. At the individual level, they can arouse strong emotions like fear and indignation. At the national one, they create and add to disagreement. With the possible exception of welfare, no areas of public interest have done more to poison relations between America's two largest racial groups than these. This is because they all – crime, health and welfare alike – to a very large extent touch upon the deep sensitivities of personal morality and behaviour and are linked to long held stereotypes. Combatting such stereotypes is therefore perhaps one way of alleviating the problem. It is a task that the media, with their access to huge audiences, are on the face of it well placed to accomplish. Some, however, think they have failed and have possibly made matters worse.

The Mass Media

There are those who think the news and entertainment industries occupy a special place in the dehumanisation and demonisation of blacks. Taken together, the press, the motion picture industry, radio and television, especially the latter, are thought in certain quarters to be the main purveyors of negative images and subliminal messages that reinforce existing notions of black social deviance of the sort discussed earlier in this Chapter. Elsewhere, others take the opposite view and claim that the media bend over backwards to depict African Americans in the most glowing light possible, even to the point of going to absurd extremes. Both sides allege that the newspapers and mainstream networks, not to mention the minor ones, have a hidden agenda in their portrayals, though they disagree strongly as to just what that agenda is. And both claim that all this occurs in current events as well as fictional viewing entertainment.

Sitcoms and Dramas

To take the latter first, civil rights activists and their supporters accuse the visual media of not doing justice to the variety of black life in contemporary America. Black actors and actresses are said to be used only comparatively rarely and placed more often than not in farcical roles. The casting might not be as bad as it was in the 1940s and 1950s when African Americans were generally only accorded parts that made them subservient to others – notably, as butlers, maids, chauffeurs, and so on. And the buffoonery is never as great as that in *Amos 'N Andy*, a popular mid-century comedy series about two ill-educated rural blacks making a new life in a northern city. But the insult has been thought to have been there all the same, as can be seen in the television airing of numerous short-lived sitcoms rather than serious all-black shows in the early to mid-1990s. The purpose of such programmes, claim the activists, has been little more than to fulfil white expectations of being able to laugh at blacks and so reinforce age old notions of Caucasian intellectual superiority.

More or less the reverse is said to be true of 'serious' shows. Here audiences are not so much spoilt for choice as denied any real viewing at all. According to one critic writing in 1995, there have been fewer than ten black dramatic series in the half century or so of American commercial television, and the reason is discomfort. Drama, unlike comedy, revolves around power, something that makes Caucasians feel uneasy when African Americans exercise it. To spare awkwardness and tension amongst the general public, such scripts are almost never screened, and when they are the black characters are placed in circumstances where their authority is either shared or diluted in some way. The two police commanders in the 1990s television series *Homicide* and *NYPD Blue* were argued to have been illustrations of this.[29] Even when content dictates that African Americans should feature strongly, white characters are allowed to take precedence. Motion picture films of a fairly recent vintage such as *Mississippi Burning*, *Glory* and, some say, *Amistad* all provide examples.[30]

To other commentators, however, blacks have been given too prominent a role in films and fictionalised television. They do not worry about the silliness of black sitcoms as such; after all, they reason, whites too have taken part in many ludicrous series. Rather, it is the proliferation of such scripts in the Nineties as a whole that upsets them. The sheer number of black programmes appearing on the 'small screen' at the start of the new autumn schedules in certain years has, they allege, been out of proportion to the number of blacks in the country at large. The amount has been such as to increase the cultural separation of the two races, with African Americans at one stage watching so many different programmes from whites as to take the country a step further down the road of social fragmentation. Elsewhere, the desire of producers and directors to include blacks in the casting is said to have been carried to such lengths as to give rise to anomalies like having film versions of best-selling novels star African Americans in roles in which the original characters were Caucasian. The brilliant sonar operator who saves the day for the U.S. Navy against the Soviets in *Hunt for Red October* is one example, as is that of a highly sympathetic character in another popular film of the late 1980s, *Bonfire of the Vanities*. Both of these changes reflect an additional complaint of some: the alleged choosing of whites rather than blacks for villainous roles and the supposed inability or unwillingness of the mass media to show African Americans in a negative light in fictionalised programming. The bad guys, they complain, are almost always white, and as often as not 'WASPs' at that.[31]

As might be surmised, the truth lay somewhere between these two extremes. There have been years in the recent past when African Americans have been given a big portion of television roles. In 1993-94, for instance, blacks played 18% of all characters portrayed in total programming, about half again as many as their numbers in the overall population would merit. But equally, there have been times when African Americans have been underrepresented, and in the second half of the Nineties their appearances have been gradually diminishing to the point where at one stage all of the 'Big Four' networks (ABC, NBC, CBS and Fox) were planning to have only Caucasians star in their new shows for the 1999-2000 season.[32] Meanwhile, the fact that there have been spells when blacks figured prominently in sitcoms but not dramas and occasions when the reverse was true has for some heightened the sense of racial unevenness.

A similar conclusion may be reached concerning the other allegations. If Hollywood has been guilty of placing blacks in roles in which they do not belong, television can be accused of omitting them where they might be more often expected. *Seinfeld* and *Friends*, two enormously popular sitcoms of the 1990s, had for all intents and purposes no African Americans in them at all; this despite their Manhattan settings. Comedy has provided the milieu for many of the all-black shows, and the humour in some of them has been clownish and demeaning and so unthreatening to whites. But at the same time, a number of the later black sitcoms like *Living Single* and *Martin* put a reverse construction on the old foolishness. Rather than playing up to whites, many of the characters slyly ridiculed them and poked fun at mainstream lifestyles.

As regards differing viewing tastes, surveys have revealed that the ten most popular television programmes regularly watched by blacks are rarely those followed by whites and vice-versa, a situation made possible by the generally greater airing of African American programmes in the 1990s compared with previous decades.[33] However, the polarisation is not total, and there is evidence to suggest that some 'crossover' viewing is being done by younger audiences, especially white teenagers anxious to watch what they regard as culturally up-to-date black performances. There is evidence, too, that sitcoms with an anti-Establishment flavour to them but featuring few blacks like *The Simpsons* and *Roseanne* have at times enjoyed a certain African American following.[34] Thus the polarisation is not complete on the black side of the colour line either, and if a viewing cleavage does exist it might well be more by class and age group than by skin pigmentation. In the meantime, it is possible to argue that the growth of black shows, such as it has been occurring, is just another example of how viewing has become more specialised in the U.S. with the onset of multichannel cable and satellite television rather than representing a form of catering to minority demands.[35]

News and Current Events Programmes

And what of non-fiction television that must rely on external developments for scripts? Here much depends on the type of event being covered. There is relatively little controversy in connection with sport, at least in terms of media presentation. African American athletes are featured every bit as prominently as Caucasian ones, and many have become heroes to whites as well as to blacks. Rather, the difficulty lies in news stories, in particular those pertaining to crime, health and poverty. If fictionalised television programmes like *The Cosby Show* have glossed over black socioeconomic problems, the news media have been accused of drawing too much attention to them. Minority leaders resent what they see as the overrepresentation on TV screens and in newspaper columns of the black male as the embodiment of drugs, disease and lawlessness and of the black female as being welfare dependent. Right-wingers, meanwhile, attack the press, radio and television for supposedly defining black America in terms of inner city problems. The two sets of criticism seem to be one and the same but in reality are quite different and are aimed at differing parts of the mass media. The former is social in origin and expresses a worry about slights and humiliations in the lives of ordinary African Americans resulting from the perpetuation of unflattering stereotypes. It is directed primarily at the local news stations that feature such everyday stories. The latter has political roots and reflects a concern that black poverty is being exaggerated to promote affirmative action and other left-wing policies. It is aimed largely at the national networks and organs of opinion, which the Right feels are dominated by liberals and are in league with the various civil rights organisations.

Of the two, it is the civil rights groups that have made most of the running in recent years. The NAACP has accused news stations of sensationalising those crime stories that have black perpetrators and white victims. Ishmael Reed, an African American novelist, once compared the coverage of blacks in some news stories with that of the Jews in the Nazi press in pre-holocaust Germany.[36] So concerned was the Reverend Jesse Jackson about the portrayals that in 1994 he announced a Commission on Fairness in the Media. In response, the media claim that their stories are not an invention and that if African Americans figure well in crime related news items it is because a preponderance of wrongdoing is being committed by blacks. They contend that viewers can also see on the nightly news African Americans who are police officers, judges and citizen heroes similar to those on the sitcoms and crime shows. Meanwhile, the news staff have long been of more than one race, and their greater involvement in editorial comment has reduced the incidence of glaring bias in latter years. But many blacks remain unconvinced.

Some African Americans suspect the mass media of scripting race relations with an entirely different purpose in mind, to render the issue of race a thing of the past. Allegedly guilty here is almost the whole of contemporary television – talk shows, drama series, sitcoms and commercials alike – that subtly preaches the message of race sameness by pairing black and white actors and actresses and having them get along. Newscasters of both races at local as well as the national level play their part by making casual remarks between items suggesting familiarity and genuine friendship with each other, and Hollywood is said to be not immune by having race deleting themes in films as diverse as *Forrest Gump*, *Lethal Weapon* and *Driving Miss Daisy*.[37] In all of these formats racial problems are played down to the point of being almost non-existent, and on the rare occasion when they do occur, they are presented in an individual rather than a group context. To critics, such a portrayal might be a step forward from the old days when African Americans got at best patronising treatment, but to them it is insidious. It ignores the reality that the majority of African Americans are still not middle class. It is an attempt at opinion engineering inasmuch as it implies that the road to better relations is through personal contact and not formal structural procedures like affirmative action. Last but not least, it deludes the white public into thinking that basically all is well between the races when it is not. Hence, they say, the amazement of most Caucasians in 1995 not only when a largely non-white jury acquitted O.J. Simpson of murder charges but also when blacks across the country cheered the verdict. Until then, whites, conditioned by seeing so much apparent racial harmony on TV, evidently thought that they and African Americans saw eye-to-eye on the trial.[38]

Not that whites necessarily should have been surprised at this reaction. Earlier televised real life encounters between blacks and the Los Angeles Police Department such as the 1991 Rodney King affair and the 'South Central' riots a year later ought to have long dispelled any notions of goodwill fostered by fictitious TV shows about minorities and the LAPD. Of more concern to us, however, is how well the networks fared in their coverage of these infamous developments. The answer, it seems, is mixed. On the one hand, the continuing violence in 1992 was in the main treated with restraint. In contrast to their handling of the race riots of the 1960s, the media this time were less sensational in publicising looting and arson while they were happening and less inclined to spread rumours, with the result that there was less incitement of others to take part. On the other hand, newsroom editorial decisions came in for plenty of criticism. Whites alleged that only those parts of the much watched videotape putting police and not Rodney King in a bad light were aired in 1991. Blacks insisted that too much was made of minority attacks on a white lorry driver innocently caught up in the riots a year later and not enough of his rescue by a black man.[39]

Thus it would seem that the mainstream media have been unable to win. Faulted by the Right for presenting the standing of blacks in too bleak terms for supposedly furthering the civil rights agenda, they have been criticised by the Left for painting too rosy a picture in an attempt to undermine the need for preferential policies. Denounced by whites for sanitising race in matters of crime, the newspapers, radio and television have all been attacked by black spokespersons for emphasising skin colour too much in this area. Likewise, their editorial decisions have been seen as racially biased in two opposite directions in times of crisis. Of course, the reason they have been caught in this crossfire is that at bottom most mainstream organs of opinion, especially the major television networks, have adopted a centrist approach towards race, as with so many other issues. In their endeavours to please everyone there have been times when they appear to have satisfied almost no one. Not surprisingly, for this and other reasons their audience share underwent decline when still other news sources and formats became available.

Alternative Media

The alternative media vehicle that most reflects dissatisfaction with the mainstream networks is talk-show programming. A form of this has existed on the traditional airwaves for years. But the more popular examples like *The Oprah Winfrey Show* are generally non-political and are taped before they are broadcast and so lack a certain spontaneity. They also do not adhere to a particular line on those occasions when contentious public policy matters do arise. Much more common is talk-show radio, which began to proliferate in the late 1980s and early 1990s thanks to the development of satellite technology, enabling syndicated talk-show programmes to be distributed nationally in an economic way. Add to this the improved voice quality made on incoming telephone calls and the art of entertainment that many talk-show hosts assiduously cultivated, and it is easy to understand why the phenomenon grew exponentially in the Nineties. The most famous of the radio talk-show hosts, Rush Limbaugh, had at one point a weekly audience of twenty million people listening on more than 600 stations across the country.[40]

Talk-show radio unquestionably has its good points. It is a powerful tool for bringing people closer to government. It arguably provides a good snapshot of public opinion on key issues of the day. Yet some people are worried by it. They contend that talk-show hosts are more inclined to amuse than inform. They accuse such hosts, who are almost always strongly conservative in their views, of demonising their opponents, beginning with President Clinton, and of polarising issues to such an extent as to threaten the political system. In the case of race relations, which studies show consistently appears in the top ten of the most discussed topics on radio talk-shows, humour is said to be used as a device for transmitting prejudice.

For his part, Rush Limbaugh says that as regards African Americans his biting comments are reserved for civil rights leaders and their policies, not blacks themselves. Right-wing bias, if it exists, serves to offset what he and other conservatives perceive to be the overly leftward leanings of the more mainstream media. As an example, such people point to *Eyes on the Prize*, a lengthy PBS television documentary aired a few years ago about the early modern civil rights movement. It was said to have described racial discrimination as a chronic condition of American society fifty times without a single contrary opinion. Limbaugh says that his 'Excellence in Broadcasting' network is an antidote to such onesidedness. Besides, he and others like him contend that there is an element of unpredictability in interactive programming. Talk-show hosts can serve as a megaphone on the issues of the day, but the very nature of live calls from listeners means that they cannot set the agenda for what is going to be discussed or censor the views of dissenting listeners. Indeed, Limbaugh claims to welcome telephone calls from liberals so as to sharpen the debate and make the programme more interesting.

Others, however, maintain that some genuine hatemongers have made it onto the airwaves in recent years and that their virulent language is damaging racial harmony. Included in this group are said to be certain black talk-show hosts who have been known to disparage Jews and occasionally other minorities like Hispanics. Those worried by such developments are inclined to favour some kind of legal curtailment through tighter control over licensing or tougher punitive measures for inflammatory remarks. In making these proposals, reformers have encountered the opposition of free speech libertarians, conservatives who say that honest airings help defuse rather than exacerbate racial tensions, and some more detached observers who see talk radio as little more than a harmless exercise in preaching to the converted, given that hosts and listeners tend to be already of like mind.[41] It is a debate as yet unresolved and one that at times has seemed almost as big as the race relations issue itself in America.

A similar discussion has taken place in connection with the Internet. The source of concern here is the springing up of well over a hundred 'hate sites' by 1998. Critics, worried about the potential impact on black-white relations, would dearly love to see some kind of regulation but are at a loss to see how it can be accomplished in view of the anonymity of cyberspace messaging and of the fact that banning altogether Internet use is now clearly out of the question. Others, noting that the number of hate sites is easily more than matched by the thousands of 'bulletin boards' and 'chat rooms' devoted in a less controversial way to race every week, are less anxious. The conversations posted in these places for millions to see are often frank and sometimes bitter but rarely invidious. Their honesty, like that of the radio talk-show participants, is prompted by the facelessness of the whole procedure and in the opinion of many can help to clear some of the air between the races in a way that the public dialogues in President Clinton's recent 'Initiative on Race', for instance, could not possibly have hoped to do. Of course, not everyone is agreed that the anonymity of the Internet makes it the best place for such conversations; total honesty would require them to be done face-to-face. But even these critics for the most part acknowledge the value of the Internet in helping to overcome inhibitions, something that is essential if the nation's racial and ethnic problems are ever to be solved.

Meanwhile, this same anonymity is helping some African Americans overcome racial obstacles. Hundreds of black and other minority entrepreneurs are setting up shop in cyberspace, many with good results in the late 1990s because certain race conscious white consumers are prompted to buy on the basis of what the product looks like rather than who is selling them. In commerce, the 'Net allows minority business owners to avoid real life tensions by hiding their racial identity. No less important, Web based businesses usually require far less capital than comparable physical operations, thereby removing another hurdle for minority entrepreneurs. This aspect of the Internet, unlike perhaps the billboards and chatrooms used by ordinary members of the public, does not provide a possible answer to racism as such. But in a business sense it can help equalise matters.

Other Minorities

There is another type of alternative media that in its own way has come to challenge the dominance of mainstream journalism and programming. This is the rise of the Spanish language media, which has developed by leaps and bounds in step with the growth of the Latino population in the U.S. Whereas in the 1960s, virtually everything was broadcast in English, today there are about fifty television and hundreds of radio stations whose programming is completely in Spanish. Hispanics also have their own cable TV networks. One of them, Univision, claims over four hundred affiliated stations. Spanish language radio and television do not challenge the 'Anglo' media along overtly political lines, but by emphasising different aspects of an event they do help make the United States appear a less self-absorbed country. Thus when in the mid-1990s the mainline English language networks were covering in almost microscopic detail the goings on in connection with the O.J. Simpson murder case, Univision and its cable rival Telemundo were featuring less sensational but more significant items about Latin America to their viewers. Even when they cover the same stories as ABC, NBC and CBS, they do so in a different manner. Accounts tend to be longer, with more depth than is usually seen on the English language networks. In part, this is a matter of economics. The Spanish language media have less money than the established national networks. As there are fewer reporters to fill in the same amount of airtime, each story is of necessity longer. But the greater length is also attributable to the traditions of Latin American journalism, which are more analytical and relay a stronger point of view than does the U.S. variety.

In some respects, Asian Americans and Hispanics are now at the same stage of network media representation as blacks were in the 1950s and 1960s. They do hold a reasonable share of newscasting and reporting posts, something that did not apply to African Americans a few decades ago. But they continue to be relegated to relatively minor and stereotyped parts in serialised programmes. For example, a 1998 survey revealed that less than 4% of the leading prime time television roles that season involved Latinos, even though they made up 11% of the population.[42] Most Hispanics are portrayed as poor immigrants. Asian American men tend to be cast in an unsexual light and so hardly ever get any lead roles. There has yet to be either a prominently positioned Spanish- or Asian American series on any of the mainstream networks as happened for blacks in the first half of the 1990s. The reason these networks have yet to apply such offerings to America's other minority groups is largely market induced. In the case of Asian Americans, analysts say, it is because their numbers are about only a third that of the black population. In the case of Hispanics, it is because an estimated forty per cent. do not watch English language television.[43] Furthermore, neither Latino nor Asian culture is as familiar to the rest of the country as is black culture. In these circumstances, launching a sitcom or drama series that hardly anyone is going to watch is simply not viable for any of the major networks.

Conclusion

Indeed, commercialism is key to understanding so much of what has been taking place in the mass media as regards race relations over the years. Lack of diversity in the networks' executive offices is undoubtedly a factor in the above problems, but in the final analysis the country's newspapers, radio and television stations and motion picture industry are all businesses, anxious to make a profit. If the leading media corporations now air or screen a disproportionate number of productions featuring whites at the expense of blacks, it is just as likely to be out of financial considerations as any other. It has long been a piece of Hollywood wisdom that whites will not go to see a film that they perceive to be about blacks, and so the decision to give Caucasian actors and actresses a large presence in otherwise black films. Presumably the same is true about the 'small screen'. True, several surveys over the years have shown that blacks as a group tend to watch up to fifty per cent. more television than do whites.[44] On the face of it, this should prompt the likes of ABC, NBC, CBS and Fox to air more all-black programmes, as indeed did happen in the early to mid-1990s. But with complaints about sitcom stereotyping on the rise and with African Americans increasingly indifferent to mixed race drama series, the major networks have come to see this as a not particularly viable course of action.

Of course, the main networks are not altogether oblivious of other considerations. The inclusion of African Americans (or, indeed, members of other minority groups) can make for good art as well as possibly good business. A diverse group of actors lends a degree of authenticity to police or hospital programmes like *E.R.*, while also broadening the shows' attractiveness to black and white audiences, at least in theory. But there can be little doubt that money is the ultimate determinant, as can be seen in the readiness of the networks to drop quickly underperforming programmes, whether black or white.

Much the same can be said for non-fictional media programming. Television stations have been accused of employing newscasters and reporters of various racial and ethnic backgrounds for all sorts of ulterior motives. The Left sees it as an attempt at glossing over tensions by having blacks and whites working together in apparent harmony. The Right suspects a subtle plot to promote affirmative action. Yet just as likely is a simple desire to capture as wide ranging an audience as possible by having people on the air with whom viewers of all groups feel they can identify. Likewise, in all probability the driving force behind journalism's presentation of crime stories is not race, as some allege, but information provision and in some instances sensationalism. Newspapers and local media stations emphasise violent crimes because they are matters of public interest and the publicising of such events sells copies and attracts attention. A disproportionate number of these cases continue to be committed by blacks. As long as crime remains a staple of the press and other news outlets, that unfortunate reality will keep being reiterated for the sake of profit and ratings. The actions of the mainstream mass media may have social and political consequences, but the motivation behind them is often monetary.

Notes

1   S. and A. Thernstrom, *America in Black and White* (New York: Simon & Schuster, 1997), p. 259.
2   FBI, *Uniform Crime Reports for the United States, 1997* (Washington, D.C.: U.S. Department of Justice, 1998), Table 43, p. 240; also J. Coleman, *Long Way To Go* (New York: Atlantic Monthly Press, 1997), p. 400; and The Milton S. Eisenhower Foundation and the Corporation for What Works, *The Millennium Breach* (Washington, D.C.: First Edition and Printing, 1998), p. 32.
3   R.T. Schaefer, *Racial and Ethnic Groups* (New York: Addison Wesley Longman, 1998), p. 233; Thernstrom, p. 263.
4   Five-eighths of the 8500 known such offenders in 1997 were white; one-fifth were black. See FBI, *op. cit.*, Table 2.39, p. 62.
5   Thernstrom, pp. 271-2.
6   E. Cose, *Rage of the Privileged Class* (New York: Harper Collins, 1993), p. 110.
7   African Americans constituted 46% of all state prisoners in 1996, according to Schaefer, *loc. cit.*
8   P.A. Langan, 'America's Justice System Does Not Discriminate Against Blacks' in P. Winters (ed.), *Race Relations: Opposing Viewpoints* (San Diego: Greenhaven Press, 1996), p. 143; also Thernstrom, pp. 273-4. These sentencing figures pertain to grown ups. In the case of juveniles, the racial gaps are proportionally greater. Thus one Justice Department sponsored study has found that judges on average jail Caucasian youths charged with violent offences 193 days, a few months less than their black and Latino counterparts tried on similar charges in corresponding circumstances. The report, 'And Justice for Some', does not tackle the question of why minority youths get relatively severer treatment, but some social scientists speculate that the reason lay not so much in overt discrimination as in stereotypes, with judges influenced, for instance, by the defendant's adult-defiant dress or single-parent background, factors that by definition are not applicable to older offenders. See F. Butterfield, 'Racial Disparities Seen As Pervasive in Juvenile Justice', *New York Times*, 26 April 2000, p. A1.
9   African Americans comprise 15% of the nation's drug users but 33% of those arrested and 57% of those convicted on drug charges. See M.A. Fletcher, ' "Crisis" of Black Males Gets High-Profile Look', *Washington Post*, 17 April 1999, p. A2.
10   Thernstrom, pp. 274-5.
11   Schaefer, p. 234.

12   D. Brown, 'AIDS Death Rate in '97 Down 47%, *Washington Post*, 8 October 1998, p.
     A1; A. Bettelheim, 'AIDS Update: Are Researchers Closer to a Cure?', *CQ Researcher*,
     4 December 1998, p. 1064; P.T. Kilborn, 'Health Gap Grows, With Black Americans
     Trailing', *New York Times*, 26 January 1998, p. A16. Although there has been a decline
     in the rate of African American mortalities from AIDS in recent years, it has not been as
     dramatic as that for members of other racial and ethnic groups, with the result that
     blacks accounted for nearly half of all AIDS cases and deaths in the U.S. in 1998. See
     L.K. Altman, 'Focusing on Prevention in Fight Against AIDS', *ibid.*, 31 August 1999,
     p. D5.

13   D. Brown, 'Death Knocks Sooner for D.C.'s Black Men', *Washington Post*, 4
     December 1997, p. A1.

14   Schaefer, *loc. cit.*

15   Out of a total 282,000 African American deaths in 1994, a year in which both AIDS
     related mortalities and the murder rate were near their peak in the nation, the syndrome
     and firearms together accounted for less than a tenth – 16,000 and 11,000 respectively.
     See *Statistical Abstract of the United States, 1997*, Tables 129, 133 and 141.

16   Schaefer, *loc. cit.*

17   According to Census Bureau data, two out of every nine blacks but only a little more
     than one ninth of whites are without such coverage. See R. Pear, 'More Americans
     Were Uninsured in 1998, U.S. Says', *New York Times*, 4 October 1999, p. A1.

18   35.3% of Latinos were without health insurance in 1998. *Ibid, loc. cit.* Kilborn, in
     another article in the *New York Times* ('Denver's Hispanic Residents Point to the Ills of
     the Uninsured', 9 April 1999, p. A1), puts the figures for Latinos down to their having
     the most menial of jobs; to recent laws requiring immigrants having five years'
     residency before they can qualify for Medicaid, the government sponsored scheme for
     the poor; and to language barriers. Presumably much of this would also apply to Asian
     Americans, about a fifth of whom are uninsured, according to Pear.

19   Kilborn, 'Health Gap Grows…', *loc. cit.*

20   P.T. Kilborn, 'Filling the Needs of Minority Patients', *ibid.*, 14 February 1999, I, p. 16.
     According to H.B. Noble, 'Health Care Systems in U.S. Called Separate and Unequal',
     ibid., 27 April 1999, p. F12, 90% of whites have a white doctor, but only 40% of blacks
     have an African American one.

21   S. Blakeslee, 'Poor and Black Patients Slighted, Study Says', *ibid.*, 20 April 1994, p.
     B9.

22   African Americans as a whole were referred 60% as often as Caucasian males, and
     black women only 40% as often. See A. Goldstein, 'Georgetown University Study
     Finds Disparity in Heart Care', *Washington Post*, 25 February 1999, p. A1.

23   W.L. Leary, 'Health Care Lagging Among Blacks and Poor', *New York Times*, 12
     September 1996, p. A18.

24   Schaefer, p. 236.

25   Quoted in D. D'Souza, *The End of Racism* (New York: The Free Press, 1995), p. 488.

26   Thernstrom, p. 515.

27   L. Richardson, 'Experiment Leaves Legacy of Distrust of New AIDS Drugs', *New York
     Times*, 21 April 1997, p. A1.

28   P. Thomas, 'Study Suggests Black Male Prison Rate Impinges on Politics', *Washington
     Post*, 30 January 1997, p. A3.

29   P. Farhi, 'Amos 'N' Andy Standby', *ibid.*, 8 January 1995, p. C1.

30   D. Britt, '*Amistad* Slips Past the Wall', *ibid.*, 19 December 1997, p. C1; also D.
     Nicholson, 'What Price *Glory*?', *ibid.*, 21 January 1990 p. G1. As regards the all-black
     films that Hollywood has turned out in recent years, the African American director

Spike Lee cites ignorance on the part of executives more than racial power psychology as the main reason for their being weak and restricted to overdone urban based themes. He also chastises 'the fickle black audience' for not viewing when an independent African American director does try 'to correct the record with a serious film'. See his article 'Black Films: The Studios Have Got It All Wrong', *New York Times*, 2 May 1999, IIA, p. 23.

31   J. Taylor, *Paved With Good Intentions* (New York: Carroll & Graf, 1992), pp. 230-33.

32   P. Farhi, 'In Networks' New Programmes, A Startling Lack of Diversity', *Washington Post*, 13 July 1999, p. A1. However, within a month of their original decision executives of the leading networks reversed course and added at least 17 minority characters to new and returning shows for the 1999-2000 season, possibly as a result of threatened NAACP boycotts. See L.E. Wynter, 'Networks Need to Find a Better Balance with Minority Roles', *Wall Street Journal*, 8 September 1999, p. B1. It is important to stress that the foregoing applies to the main networks, as emerging ones like UPN and WB are following in the footsteps of Fox in its early days by airing a great many minority shows.

33   See, for instance, the leader article 'Watching TV Viewers', *New York Times*, 19 May 1992, p. A22; also L. De Morales, 'TV Networks Adding Some Colour for Fall', *Washington Post*, 21 May 2000, p. A1. African Americans underview even mixed race drama series. NBC's late *Homicide*, to which whites widely tuned in and which earned much critical acclaim, 'never cracked the black top 20' of favourite TV programmes. *Law and Order*, *E.R.*, and *NYPD Blue* have also performed indifferently in the African American ratings. See Wynter, *loc. cit.*

34   P. Farhi, 'Amos 'N' Andy Standby', *loc. cit.*

35   Two cable networks, HBO and Showtime, while white owned and operated, devote considerable airtime to African American oriented programming, much of it socially aware and of good quality. The result is quite strong minority loyalty. The subscriber base of HBO, for instance, is 22% black, or upwards of double the percentage of African Americans in the total population. See H. Goldblatt, 'In the Black', *Fortune*, 11 October 1999, p. 60.

36   D'Souza, p. 262.

37   In a rather similar vein, some regard the 1997 film *Amistad* as at least in part a piece of social propaganda. By deliberately leaving the audience with a positive ending emphasising the way in which some twenty years before the Civil War the Supreme Court allowed black mutineers aboard a Spanish slave ship to return as free men to Africa, director Steven Spielberg was said to be offering the country an exit 'from what ails us now – a form of escapism akin to the months long debate over a slavery apology' out of the affirmative action issue. See F. Rich, 'Slavery Is Bad', *New York Times*, 6 December 1997, p. A19.

38   B. DeMott, 'We're All Just One Big Happy Family', *ibid.*, 7 January 1996, II, p. 1.

39   L. Williams, 'Minority Journalists Question Reporting on Riots', *ibid.*, 28 June 1992, I, p. 19.

40   K. Jost, 'Talk-Show Democracy: Are Call-In Programmes Good for the Political System?', *CQ Researcher*, 29 April 1994, p. 372.

41   *Ibid.*, *loc. cit.*

42   P. Farhi, 'In Networks' New Programmes...', *loc. cit.*

43   P. Farhi, 'A Television Trend: Audiences in Black and White', *Washington Post*, 29 November 1994, p. A1.

44   *Ibid.*

7 Politics

Black Officeholding

In political representation as well as in other areas, blacks have long lagged whites. During the first quarter of the twentieth century not a single African American was elected to Congress. Even today, more than seventy years and several civil rights acts later, blacks account for only 7% of the total number of men and women in the U.S. national legislature while comprising about 12% of the voting age population. Across the country, a mere 1.5% of the 8000 or so elected offices have been filled at any given time by African Americans in the 1990s.[1]

These figures are, however, possibly misleading. While African Americans undoubtedly hold a disproportionately small share of the political pie, the rate at which they have been making advances is impressive. Since 1970, the number of black elected officials has sextupled, and their congressional representation since 1965 has increased eightfold. During the past thirty years African Americans have been elected mayor of upwards of a hundred cities with a population of 50,000 or more, including the two largest, New York and Los Angeles. In the historically hostile South, 290 towns and cities of all sizes had black mayors in 1996, up from three in 1968. Similar progress has been made in the state legislatures, where it is not now altogether unheard of for African Americans to hold a higher proportion of seats than their voting age numbers would suggest.[2]

For some, statistical increases tell only part of the story. When one considers voting patterns the picture is perhaps not as bleak as it seems to be at first glance. Unlike whites, whose political allegiance is more or less evenly divided between the two major parties in the U.S., black loyalties in modern times have been almost exclusively to the Democrats. Whether as a cause or as a result of this, Republicans rarely bother to field black candidates. In the opinion of some, a good case can therefore be made for simply looking at the racial and ethnic profiles of elected Democrats to determine more accurately whether African Americans are getting their share of offices. Table 7.1 suggests that nationally they are, with about a seventh of Democrats in the 106th Congress elected in 1998, the same fraction of those who voted in the 1992 Democratic primaries, being black,[3] and African Americans faring none too badly in other recent Congresses.

Table 7.1 Number of African American Democrats in 1990s' U.S. Congresses

Congress	Date Elected	Black Democrats	Total Democrats	% Black Democrats to Total Democrats
102nd	1990	25	323	7.7
103rd	1992	38	315	12.1
104th	1994	39	251	15.5
105th	1996	40	252	15.9
106th	1998	38	256	14.8

Sources: Facts on File, 1990-1996; also T.M. Neal, 'In 106th Congress, New Faces But Little Change in Diversity', *Washington Post*, 8 November 1998, p. A12.

Residential patterns also provide some evidence that African American political representation might not be quite as poor as initially seems. A little more than half of all blacks in the United States live in the South. Traditionally, this area of the country has had fewer elected offices at the local and even the statewide level than other regions of the country. One part of North Carolina, for instance, has a school district that is more than 500 square miles in area. In the North, a territory that size would be broken up into a multitude of school districts, each with its own elected governing body. About two-fifths of all African Americans live in the country's biggest cities, where for historical reasons there are proportionately fewer elected offices than in the smaller towns and cities inhabited largely by whites. The greatest difference in the number of black and white elected officials occurs by far and away most often at the local level of politics where the decision making process is least significant and voter turnout is usually the lowest.[4]

Demographic trends and earlier civil rights successes are also part of the story. Relative to that of whites, the African American electorate is both growing and generally becoming more politically mobilised. True, the disparate treatment on the part of the authorities of certain types of drug offences has resulted in proportionately greater black disenfranchisement, as was explained in Chapter 6. But by and large African Americans are increasingly able and willing to take part in the political process. Whereas in the 1960s blacks made up one tenth of all potential voters, today they constitute an eighth. Thanks to the 1965 Voting Rights Act, which banned literacy tests and other procedures that certain states employed to try to deny non-whites the right to ballot, the number of blacks registering to vote has risen dramatically, from six million in the 1960s to more than 13 million now. While both that figure and the percentage of African Americans who actually show up on election days represent a lower rate of electoral participation than is the case for whites, the averages conceal many variations. African American political involvement is capable of rising to quite high levels in response to individual candidates. Thus when a white supremacist ran for governor of Louisiana in 1991, an estimated 80% of all registered blacks in the state turned out to vote against him.[5] There was a high rate of participation when the black leader the Rev. Jesse Jackson ran in a number of primaries to try to win the Democratic Party's nomination for president in the 1980s. As African American voters overwhelmingly support African American candidates whenever possible, this increased taking part in the political process has inevitably led to more black officeholders.

Up to a point, electoral arrangements have also been instrumental in promoting this result. Chief among these is 'racial redistricting', or the erstwhile practice of redrawing constituency boundaries along skin colour lines so as to capture as many minority voters as possible in certain areas. It is a step that has proved so controversial as to merit a separate section of its own towards the end of this Chapter. Suffice it to say here that, as with school busing and affirmative action programmes, proportional representation of sorts was to be the model. Once created, race based electoral districts would prompt the political parties to nominate black- or Hispanic only candidates and so create a foregone electoral conclusion in terms of race or ethnicity and get minorities elected to office in closer proximity to their ratio in the overall population.

Racial redistricting started in the 1980s, but particularly large numbers of majority black and majority Latino districts were created following the 1990 census, and the big jump in the number of African American congressmen in 1992 as shown in Table 7.1 is to a great extent a reflection of this. In time, the Supreme Court would declare many such districts with their highly artificial boundaries (see, for example, Figure 7.1, p. 121) to be a kind of gerrymandering and so unconstitutional. Yet even though several of them had disappeared by the time of the 1998 mid-term elections, the number of African Americans in Congress has not dropped much, causing some, though as is explained below by no means everyone, to think that the process has left a durable legacy of minority officeholding.

Yet perhaps the most significant reason of all for the increase in the number of black officeholders in the U.S. is changing racial attitudes. There is today a growing willingness on the part of whites to vote for black candidates. It is a trend that is true in many parts of the country. Thus in Virginia, once a slave state, Douglas Wilder, the black Democrat candidate, defeated his white Republican opponent in the race for governor in 1989. Large urban centres in the West like Los Angeles, Denver and Seattle, where African Americans are in a distinct minority, have elected black mayors. In certain instances it can in fact be an asset to be black. In 1989, whites in Manhattan cast their ballots for David Dinkins to become mayor of New York City partly out of a belief that as an African American he would be able to say and do things about black crime that a white city leader would be too inhibited to attempt.[6] In 1998, several black politicians won office in statewide elections in such scattered places as Colorado, Georgia, New York and Ohio.

Nor is it just at the state and local levels that this change in white attitudes has been occurring. Time and again many white Americans have expressed a political liking for General Colin Powell, the black Chairman of the Joint Chiefs of Staff during the 1991 Gulf War. Exit polls conducted on Election Day in November 1996 indicated that had he chosen to run he easily would have defeated Bill Clinton for the presidency. When Jesse Jackson stood in early rounds for president in 1988 he got his greatest percentage of votes in states with a relatively small black population.[7] Of course, some white voters will cast their ballot according to skin colour if there is little else to distinguish a Caucasian candidate from a black opponent. Others will never vote for an African American. The same Douglas Wilder who won in Virginia in the late 1980s lost his party's New Hampshire presidential primary a few years later because the voters 'viewed him through the prism of race'.[8] All in all, however, there has been a growing receptivity among whites to the idea of backing African American candidates in racially divided contests, and this has been a very important explanation for the greater number of African American officeholders in recent years.

The Power of the Black Vote

U.S. political observers debate not only the outlook for blacks as regards representation but also in terms of influence. The traditional view is that socioeconomic and demographic conditions mean that blacks cannot hold much weight. They have less money than whites; they are thought to be more caught up in personal difficulties and so allegedly have less time for politics than the latter; and their concentrated numbers in parts of the country mean that there are whole states where their voice has little impact on senatorial and gubernatorial campaigns. In 1990, for instance, African Americans made up less than 5% of the electorate in no fewer than twenty one states.[9]

The counterview is that segregation is breaking down and that the increasing dispersal of African Americans from urban to suburban areas gives blacks the opportunity to exercise the swing vote in more and more marginal seats. According to this view, it is concentration of another sort, that of black voters in the Democratic Party's ranks of supporters, that affords them a certain amount of leverage. In the opinion of social scientists Stephan and Abigail Thernstrom, the Democrats would have lost every presidential election of the past quarter century but for the African American vote. The fact that five out of six of those blacks who did turn up at the polls in 1976, 1992 and 1996 cast their ballots for Jimmy Carter and Bill Clinton more than offset the plurality of votes their Republican opponents received from the Caucasian electorate in those three presidential campaigns.[10] If so – the analysis appears to make no allowance for the entry of Reform Party candidate Ross Perot in the two latter contests – then one can say that the tendency of African Americans to vote as a bloc not only has an impact on black but also white officeholding.

There are two schools of thought about the desirability of this state of affairs for African Americans. On the one hand are those political scientists who see it as beneficial, permitting blacks to gain influence in the Democratic Party and extract concessions from its leadership from time to time. In this view, Democrat support for civil rights legislation in the 1960s and affirmative action in the 1970s and 1980s was borne out of such considerations as much as through genuine conviction. On the other are those who see repeated support for the Left as detrimental to black political interests inasmuch as it encourages Democrats to take blacks for granted and Republicans to write them off as a permanent lost cause. In this view, African Americans are only really courted during mid-term elections when the turnout is low and the parties make special efforts to bring out their most consistent supporters – blacks and trades unionists in the case of Democrats, Christian coalition groups in the case of Republicans – in order to win. But once the contest becomes nationwide, as during presidential campaigns when appeals need to be made to a broader electorate, African Americans tend to be forgotten.

Events of the past decade for the most part seem to have verified this latter thesis. In 1998, Democrats, worried about possible impeachment proceedings against their President, made a particularly noteworthy effort to drum up the African American vote during the mid-term campaign that year. But in the 1992 and 1996 contests for the White House, the Democrats, fretful in the wake of three successive presidential defeats in the 1980s that they were becoming too closely associated with black people, thus driving away white voters, played down their African American links. Bill Clinton did, of course, want their votes but went out of his way not to be seen as pandering to blacks to get them. In 1992, he even engaged in some public rebukes of a few of the more controversial African American public personalities, much to the annoyance of Jesse Jackson.

Some expect this pattern to continue indefinitely. Yet others contend that America's party of the Left owes blacks a big debt for the way in which they rallied to its defence at a crucial moment in 1998. Furthermore, they say, the apparent patching up of quarrels has not taken place in isolation. With crime and illegitimate birth rates dropping and with welfare caseloads declining, many of the issues that, rightly or wrongly, have been associated with African Americans in the public mind have lost their potency. The perception that minorities are no longer getting something for nothing, at least not to the same extent as before now that workfare has largely replaced welfare, should mean that race will no longer work against the Democrats as it has done in the past. The party need not fear that being beholden to a special interest group like African Americans will necessarily repel other voters.[11] If true, then blacks could find themselves being wooed in future presidential elections about as much as in certain past mid-term ones and so constitute more of a proper power bloc in the Democrat Party, whether the by then ex-President Clinton exerts much of an influence or not.

The Clinton Factor and Black Philosophy

Indeed, relations between African Americans and Bill Clinton have been the subject of much comment. Nominally a left-wing politician, Clinton has helped undo some of the social safety net built for the poor over the decades. Food stamps are now harder to get, and welfare benefits are today more restricted and limited than before. Both of these developments affect African Americans quite deeply, since a disproportionate number of them continue to figure prominently in the ranks of the poor. Yet despite this the President continues to generate a lot of enthusiastic support from black people as a whole. In 1996 he attracted a bigger percentage of the African American vote than did most of his fellow party members running for

Congress.[12] When legal and political pressures seriously began to mount on the President during his second term of office, African Americans were the least inclined of all racial and ethnic groups to want to see him resign. As a demonstration of their fidelity, 88% of those African Americans who turned out to vote in the 1998 mid-term elections cast their ballots for Democrats.[13]

To some extent, all this is the result of perceived shared circumstances. The President was raised among poor blacks in rural Arkansas and knows African American culture, from soul music to Baptist church services. His personal trials and tribulations in the late 1990s were, African Americans argue, the result of a warped criminal justice system biased against him as they believe it has been against them. But personalities and policies also play a part. Mr Clinton is a fundamentally outgoing man. Blacks sense that he is more at ease with them than virtually all other white political leaders are and feel that he is not only aware of discrimination but also has given great thought as to what causes it. Once secure in office, he devotes considerable energy to race relations, appointing significant numbers of African Americans to his administration, visiting black communities, defending affirmative action programmes in the face of at times considerable congressional pressure and launching initiatives like his recent national dialogue on race to bring together various groups. In the midst of the 1998 crisis resulting from his private life, he made a State trip to several countries in Africa, the longest such visit ever made by a president and one in which he expressed regret at America's past role in slavery. The simple fact that the President, unlike all his predecessors of the past thirty years, is willing to address the highly thorny issue of race wins him many points with U.S. blacks.

Evolving attitudes on the part of African Americans also form a part of this at times apparent contradiction. There are signs that in recent years some blacks have tentatively begun to rethink the social arrangement that government has had with them ever since the 'New Deal' of the 1930s. They have not turned against the notion of state intervention nearly to the same degree as those whites won over by the Reaganomics of the 1980s and the 'Contract with America' advocated by Newt Gingrich and the Republican Right of the 1990s, but at least a few are coming round to the view that some change of approach is perhaps advisable. Chief among them are members of the expanding African American middle class who are not dependent on social programmes and a few of whom are starting to show the same class attitudes as their white equivalents, as we saw in Chapter 4 on housing.[14] Yet also said to be included are some low income blacks who have grown disenchanted over the years with programmes that have failed either to better their lives or improve crime- and drug ridden inner city communities.

Of course, a lot of African Americans retain the broad view that society is best served by having large, protective government. Even many of those who are well off see their newly acquired status as fragile and their individual destinies still highly intertwined with those of black people as a whole. Certainly, activist civil rights leaders have not amended their big government outlook. Nevertheless, a debate of sorts has started to occur among African Americans, thereby making it possible for President Clinton to enact with his Republican opposites welfare reform and budget cuts without alienating too much this section of his party's electoral base. His good fortune in presiding over the country at a time of great economic health and so progressively fewer welfare claims has not hurt matters.

Indications that African Americans are becoming a bit more open to the idea of making do with less state assistance can perhaps be seen in their reaction to the Nation of Islam movement. For years, a tiny minority of blacks has admired the movement's leader, Louis Farrakhan, for articulating their frustration with American society's failure to change as fast as they would have liked. Most, however, long regarded his anti-white, anti-Semitic remarks as extreme, if not inflammatory, and kept their distance. But when in the mid-1990s Farrakhan began to attack blacks themselves for at least some of the shortcomings in the African American community, more began to listen. Farrakhan was at this time particularly critical of African American males for their tendency to get involved in crime and drugs at the expense of their families. When he proposed a 'Million Man March' in Washington in 1995 as a preliminary step towards personal renewal, hundreds of thousands answered the call by flocking to the capital, where they pledged to take more responsibility for their lives in all sorts of ways, including becoming more civic minded. Whether the Black Muslims can claim the bulk of the credit for 1.7 million more African American men voting in November 1996 than did in 1992 is difficult to say. Some believe other factors to be behind this,[15] though Farrakhan definitely did make a contribution. Meanwhile, attendance at Farrakhan led rallies has fallen off again as the militant leader has reverted to his earlier racist message. But when his talk was more mainstream and included exhortations to self-help, Farrakhan was being heeded. With blacks, it would seem that appeals to rebuild from within do not necessarily fall on deaf ears, even when coming from a controversial source.

In point of fact, there has always been a certain strain of social conservatism among America's blacks. Surveys reveal time and again that they favour by quite a large margin such right-wing proposals as the reintroduction of school prayers, automatic life sentencing for third time convicted offenders of serious crimes, and the sale of public (council) housing to sitting tenants. A smaller percentage, but still a majority, back proposals to cut benefits to single mothers on welfare who continue to have children.[16] The question is why this social conservatism does not get translated into political conservatism and more blacks do not follow the examples of Clarence Thomas, the Supreme Court Justice, or Ward Connerly, the anti-affirmative action businessman in California, and think more fully along Republican Party lines. A variety of explanations has been put forward: memories of the 1960s when Republicans opposed the civil rights movement; the willingness of Presidents Reagan and Bush to play the race card in emotive party political broadcasts during electoral campaigns in the 1980s; and attempts by right-wing politicians of the 1990s to 'downsize' government, which has given many African Americans jobs over the years.

There are, of course, signs of possible change. As we have seen, a black middle class is growing. Black immigrants are entering the country in ever larger numbers and bringing with them little or no bitterness. At the same time, certain Republican leaders are reconsidering their position. Former party head Newt Gingrich began speaking of the need to win minority votes after some setbacks in the 1996 elections. If subsequent actions seemed to indicate that the then Speaker of the House of Representatives was more interested in attracting the Asian and Latino rather than African American vote, others have reached out differently. Jeb Bush, the second son of the former president, has said that his victory in winning the governorship of Florida in 1998 stemmed from his ability to appeal to all races and ethnicities, blacks included. 'Compassionate conservatism', a major theme of older brother George W. Bush during the 2000 presidential campaign, has drawn a big endorsement from General Colin Powell. By and large, however, U.S. blacks remain a group with essentially a single political outlook. Old habits die hard, and in contrast to their liberal counterparts the new black conservatives, such as they exist, are as yet too inhibited to stand for office.[17]

Black Pressure Groups

To a certain extent, the existence of separate black political organisations and pressure groups is another reason for the tendency of many African Americans to think one way but vote the other. Founded for the most part several decades ago to secure equal opportunity for blacks in somewhat different areas and through varying methods - the NAACP using the courts to secure integration; the National Urban League concentrating on improved social services - some such organisations like the Southern Christian Leadership Conference have connections with the black Baptist Church and so are imbued with a certain moral conservatism. Officially apolitical, they nevertheless have had an affinity for the Democratic Party arising out of civil rights legislation of the 1960s. Some in recent years have become more actively involved in partisan politics, invitations to Republican Party presidential candidates to appear at NAACP conventions notwithstanding. Starting in the late 1980s, umbrella organisations like the National Black Leadership Forum were created to forge a coalition of black institutions, including the churches, in part to get African Americans to register and vote. As we have seen, the more strident Nation of Islam movement separately lent its weight to achieving this goal. More recently, the NAACP has begun working with feminist and trades union groups to try to halt the passage of anti-affirmative action measures.

Operating parallel to the above are the 'caucuses' that have sprung up as subgroups in virtually every organisation in the U.S. The Congressional Black Caucus is the best known of these. Formed in the late 1960s with only a handful of members, it subsequently grew to nearly forty congressmen and women, making it one of the more prominent pressure groups inside the national legislative branch. At one point it had $2 million in funds to fight campaigns for black political candidates.[18] State assemblies also have black caucuses, and each of the main departments of the U.S. Government has its own African American subgrouping, as do professional and advocacy associations like those for lawyers, university lecturers and even the elderly.

The impact of these numerous bodies in recent years has been rather mixed. There was a time when the biggest ones almost invariably got national attention and were courted by leading politicians, including presidents. But this is no longer always the case, partly for political reasons. The influence that the Congressional Black Caucus once exerted on 'Capitol Hill' enabling it to secure sanctions against South African apartheid in the Eighties, for instance, has largely melted away now that the Republicans have control of Congress. The leading civil rights groups have been wracked by internal problems. Finance scandals, accusations of sexual misconduct on the part of some leaders and a growing feeling of being out of tune have shaken the NAACP for much of the 1990s.[19] For a while, the organisation was having to devote so much of its energies to debt repayment that its legal advisory role was going neglected. The National

Urban League, having only fairly recently changed leadership and lacking a grassroots base, is still not all that well known in the African American community. It too was having money problems. Given that there are not all that many black corporate executives in the country and that African American trades union leaders, while competent, somehow lack charisma and so a 'cutting edge', it is little wonder that in the opinion of some there has been a void in black leadership for much of the past decade.[20]

Of course, none of this is to say that the efforts of black pressure groups have been altogether without results in recent years. The NAACP's united front with others might not have been enough to prevent the passage of an anti-affirmative action ballot initiative in Washington State in 1998, but it did suffice to help the Democrats regain some congressional seats from Republicans in the mid-term elections of that year. More likely than not, the organisation's boycott threats were the main reason for the decision of the major TV networks to abandon their initial all-white casting plans for new serialised programmes in 1999. And NAACP attempts to ostracise South Carolina as a tourist venue for its continued flying of the Confederate flag above the state capitol building in Columbia is showing signs of bearing similar fruit. Furthermore, there is the view that an argument can be made for drawing a distinction between the civil rights group's leadership and its more ordinary members during the bad spell of the mid-1990s.[21] In the main, however, the impression is one of questionable impact in recent years. For all the new initiatives and broadened range of work, the NAACP has still to address core economic, educational and related problems facing much of the African American population.

Race Based Congressional Districting

The debate about the effectiveness of African American political bodies is next to nothing in comparison to that which has raged for much of the 1990s about race based congressional districts. As we have seen, these are in essence constituencies designed to promote black officeholding, and they arose out of perceived shortcomings of civil rights legislation of an earlier generation. The 1965 Voting Rights Act guaranteed blacks the right to vote. If need be, the new law empowered both the courts and the Federal Government to intrude in local electoral procedures in all sorts of unprecedented ways to make sure that African Americans were able both to register and cast their ballots unimpeded. Basically the legislation worked. Straight away blacks went to polling stations in increasing numbers and exercised this most basic right of citizenship without fear or harm, a situation that continues to exist today.

Yet while the 1965 Act guaranteed equality of opportunity in the American electoral system, it did not guarantee equality of outcome. The difficulty was that as a minority group in a 'winner takes all' system of voting, African Americans could find themselves winding up with no elected officials of their own, even if a very big number of them did duly take part in the electoral process. The greatest risk of this occurring was in the South where public officials had a long history of rigging the voting system and where it was feared that single member voting districts in which blacks were likely to be elected would be replaced by larger citywide and countywide constituencies where whites outnumbered blacks and so would win. In response to pressure from civil rights organisations, Congress amended the Voting Rights Act in both 1970 and 1975 to end 'at large' voting designed to disenfranchise blacks. In 1982 it went a step further and allowed the creation of race based electoral districts to ensure that African Americans and other minorities got at least a certain number of seats.

In order to create race based electoral districts, state authorities under the watchful eye of the Federal Government were obliged to redraw constituency boundaries. However, because African Americans still tended to have a lower voter participation rate than whites, the redrafting was often done in such a way as to include within a boundary not just a plurality but a definite majority of African American inhabitants to guarantee the desired result. Creating a constituency that had more blacks than members of other groups in it was deemed to be not enough to ensure success. It was thought that African Americans should make up at least 50% of the population, preferably a good deal more.

The upshot was the creation of snakelike or Z-shaped constituencies that had little in the way of geographic compactness or shared community interest to them other than linking together as many African American neighbourhoods as possible. Figure 7.1, on the next page, shows what critics see as one of the most notorious examples of racial gerrymandering. The 12th congressional district created in North Carolina in 1992 wound its way for upwards of two hundred miles through a variety of tobacco fields, financial centres and manufacturing towns. It was an exceedingly slender district whose boundaries in places were scarcely any wider than the main north-south interstate highway it often tracked until they were altered at Supreme Court order later in the decade.

Altogether more than fifty such fancifully designed congressional districts with majority black or majority Hispanic populations had been created by the early 1990s, a great many of them in the wake of the 1990 census revealing the latest residential patterns of minority voters. Up to this point most of the discussion about the pros and cons of race based districting had been confined to political backrooms and offices of federal examiners in Washington, D.C. But now it erupted more fully into the public domain. Thousands of whites who found themselves in new majority black districts complained that their votes suddenly had no chance of influencing the outcome. Fears were expressed about a race driven electoral spoils system worsening relations between blacks and whites. Lawsuits began to be filed for a reinstatement of former constituency boundaries. For their part, civil rights lawyers contended that majority black and majority Hispanic districts were needed as a remedy against past voting discrimination and as a sure way for minorities to get more equal representation.

Figure 7.1 The 12th Congressional District in North Carolina, 1992-97

A further complication for Democrats was that while race based redistricting increased the number of liberal African Americans in Congress, it also worked to the benefit of Republicans. This was because of the 'wasted votes' syndrome that racial redistricting tended to foster. Because most African Americans vote Democrat and because they were being bunched in extra numbers in certain constituencies, the Democratic Party's black candidates were winning unnecessarily large majorities, even allowing for lower turnouts. Fewer black Democrats were being left in neighbouring, often marginal constituencies where they might have acted as decisive 'swing' voters in close campaigns. The possibilities arising from this were not lost on Republican Party strategists who convinced both Presidents Reagan and Bush to let racial redistricting proceed apace in the 1980s and early 1990s so as to dissipate Democratic Party strength. In exchange for helping to elect a few more black representatives, Republican Party advisors were hoping to decrease even more the delegations of white Democrats. This opportunism was effective. In the 1992 elections, African American Democrats gained thirteen seats in the House of Representatives this way while non-black ones lost twenty one (see Table 7.1, p. 110). The Republican Party reaped even more handsome dividends in 1994 when it won enough borderline seats so as to gain control of Congress itself for the first time in forty years, partly as a result of the creation of so many majority black and Hispanic seats. The Clinton administration, worried by the opposition's gains yet anxious not to upset the Democratic Party's African American constituents, maintained a studious silence on the subject.

In disputes such as these, it is the judiciary that is the final arbiter. But the Supreme Court, while having reached several important decisions in the mid- and late 1990s, has yet to be entirely conclusive on the matter. Thus about half way through the decade it ruled that the shape of the 12th congressional district in North Carolina amounted to racial gerrymandering and so was unconstitutional. A similar case concerning the 11th congressional district in Georgia reached the Court early enough for new boundaries to be drawn up in time for the 1996 elections. In Texas and Louisiana, too, the Court found constituencies where race was thought to be too much of a factor in determining district lines, and so these were declared invalid. But such decisions were all based on instances of more obvious geographic distortions. Elsewhere in the South, as in the West where many Hispanics live, there are specially created 'majority minority' constituencies that are perhaps irregular in shape but relatively compact and that encompass actual communities. Thus far the Court has not invalidated these and is reviewing them as and when they appear before it on a case by case basis rather than in a single sweeping judgement. Despite several redistricting appeals in recent years, the highest judicial body in the land has yet to settle clearly on a single standard for evaluating the use of race for drawing up constituency boundaries. Decisions have been close, with the nine justices usually split 5-4. It has to be said, however, that as time has worn on the majority on the bench has hardened in its view that just about anything involving skin colour in connection with redistricting is constitutionally suspect.

Some Wider Considerations

While the justices deliberate, academics and others have weighed in with a spate of theoretical points. Heated arguments have taken place about whether only black politicians can effectively represent black voters and whether African Americans and other minorities are better off politically concentrated in the race- and ethnic based districts that remain or with their influence more disseminated. Some have been exploring the possibility of there being means other than redistricting to ensure black and Hispanic representation. A few scholars have called for the overhaul of the electoral system to achieve this end, thereby prompting widespread discussion in learned circles on the merits and defects of full-fledged proportional representation schemes.

But the basic question being asked while there is still something left of race- and ethnic based districting is whether black candidates can appeal to whites. Some question the evidence provided earlier that they can. According to them, focusing on the success of people like ex-Governor Wilder of Virginia is wishful thinking. There have been times past when African American candidates seemed to be getting more white votes, only for this trend to fall away again. Nor do the doubters draw much comfort from the fact that every African American congressman or woman whose district the Supreme Court switched from majority black to majority white and who nonetheless chose to stand was voted back into office in both the 1996 and 1998 elections. In American politics, incumbents usually win. The real test, they maintain, will come once these politicians eventually step down and whether Caucasians in these areas decide to nominate, let alone vote for, another black. The fact is that a number of African American politicians who have built strong biracial constituencies have been able to do so only after gaining the advantage of incumbency by winning first in black majority districts. As Cynthia McKinney, one such black beneficiary from Georgia, put it in an interview: 'Had the [race based]district not been drawn, there is no way you would have me in Congress, no way.'[22]

A related issue is how much African American politicians will have to bend in order to secure the white vote. Despite being quite conservative on a number of moral issues, most blacks have, as we have seen, liberal political beliefs. The question therefore arises whether these candidates will sometimes have to betray the wishes of their black constituents or their own convictions on such matters as government intervention, taxation and social spending in order to appease more right-wing Caucasian electors. They concede that the dispersal of black voters from one to several constituencies that would accompany the end of race based districting might force some movement towards the Centre by white conservative politicians as well, but they counter most of the burden would be placed on blacks.

Yet opponents of race based congressional districting beg to differ. They maintain that white attitudes to black politicians are changing, and they contend that having influence in politics through swing voting in marginal constituencies is in the long run more important for African Americans than having a guaranteed but limited number of black faces in Congress. Leverage in a greater number of districts will ensure that there is effectively more, not less, black legislative representation. Nor, they claim, is this all. The creation of less overwhelmingly minority constituencies would also make African Americans' own representatives feel less secure and complacent. These men and women, too, would have to become more attentive and vigilant, and therefore their constituents would benefit as well. Indeed, the whole country stands to gain as the racially polarising tactics of those candidates of either colour who currently are voted in by virtually all-black or all-white constituencies would have to stop. Black-white relations would improve as politicians were forced into making more and more of a biracial appeal.[23]

Black Militancy, Black Moderacy

Many would say that the target of these last implied criticisms on the African American side of the colour line is the Congressional Black Caucus, more than four-fifths of whose members in the early to mid-1990s were voted in by an almost overwhelmingly minority electorate. The power base of these congressmen and women was so typically black that, according to some, it could almost entirely disregard white sensitivities. Thus about a decade ago much of the Caucus was demanding that the U.S. Government pay reparations to the descendants of slaves. A few were supporting those who sought to exempt themselves from paying income tax for this reason. Some tried to forge links with the black nationalist movement, and in 1991 the Caucus came out against the Persian Gulf War on the grounds that it was likely to lead to a disproportionate number of black deaths given the racial complexion of the U.S. Army. Of course, the Caucus has endorsed more mainstream positions, and its membership is by no means monolithic. But its leftist views have in the past often been regarded as being out on a limb, and because of this Republicans were keen to ignore it once they gained control of the House of Representatives in 1994, especially as many Caucus members were alleged to have excluded or cold shouldered Gary Franks, the sole black Republican Congressman at the time.[24]

For some, the contrast between the Congressional Black Caucus and many African American city mayors cannot be emphasised too much. The former in its political heyday of the late 1980s/early 1990s was full of racial rhetoric and stressed the need for black empowerment. The latter have generally been much more bipartisan and pragmatic in their approach. In part, this is owing to differing functions of the two types of elected posts. Local government is concerned with daily needs like street cleansing and road repairs and so is by nature more practically minded. Congressional politicians deal with national and international affairs that are by definition more theoretical and ideological. Age is another distinguishing feature. African American municipal leaders are by and large younger than their congressional counterparts. They belong to a generation that grew up after the civil rights struggles of the 1960s and so tend to have fewer feelings of bitterness than the generally older black politicians found in Washington. For many, however, the main explanation of the comparative moderacy of the one and the militancy of the other is the racial makeup of the home constituency.[25] Most whites earnestly hope that the end of race based districting will lead to more temperate black politicians, just as the dispersal of an increasing number of African American voters into the suburbs and beyond should lead to more moderate white ones.

Conclusion

African Americans have undeniably made strides in securing greater political representation as time has passed, but their future in this area is at least as uncertain as that in any other. Thus whereas there can be little doubt about increasing residential integration, however slow, as the twenty first century unfolds, legitimate concerns have been expressed as to how much of a voice blacks will have in the U.S. political process in the coming years. Many of the fears have to do with racial redistricting. The recent decisions of the courts to do away with some of the more egregious examples of 'majority minority' constituency boundaries have raised real questions about future numbers of African Americans in public office. Even if existing black congressmen and women representing these former safe seats continue to get reelected by white voters through the advantage of being already in office, no knows how their racial kin will fare in the next generation.

Some say that it is not black faces that matter so much as black interests. According to this view, the dispersal of African American voters from one to several constituencies that would accompany the end of race based districting will force some move towards the Centre by white conservative politicians anxious to capture the African American 'swing' vote in marginal seats. There is room for this view, but just as plausible is that the same will be forced upon black liberal candidates, and the whole process begs the question of whether white politicians can truly represent black interests. Then there is the matter of whether blacks would ever be inclined to constitute a proper swing vote, even if they do get the numbers in certain places. The overwhelming majority of African Americans support the Democrat Party and have done so for years. There are definite reasons for this, and these seem to be growing in number with each passing year.[26] There are also certain advantages that accrue from it. But equally, there are disadvantages, and some wonder whether their inability or refusal to play off one political party against another at the polls is doing more harm than good to African Americans. Two groups who seem to have fewer qualms about such ploys are the Hispanic- and Asian American communities. Their circumstances and attitudes form the basis of the next chapter.

Notes

1   S. and A. Thernstrom, *America in Black and White* (New York: Simon & Schuster, 1997), p. 288; R.T. Schaefer, *Racial and Ethnic Groups* (New York: Addison Wesley Longman, 1998), p. 237.
2   E. Cose, 'The Good News About Black America', *Newsweek*, 7 June 1999, p. 30; also Thernstrom, pp. 286-7.
3   *Ibid.*, p. 290.
4   *Ibid., loc. cit.*
5   L. Duke, 'Blacks Mobilised Against Duke', *Washington Post*, 17 November 1991, p. A12.

6   Thernstrom, p. 296.
7   J. Taylor, *Paved With Good Intentions* (New York: Carroll & Graf, 1992), p. 232.
8   C. Page, *Showing My Colour* (New York: Harper Collins, 1996), p. 241.
9   A. Hacker, *Two Nations* (New York: Chas. Scribner's Sons, 1992), p. 200.
10 Thernstrom, p. 291.
11 S.A. Holmes, 'Why Both Parties Wooed Black Voters This Year', *New York Times*, 8 November 1998, IV, p. 4.
12 Clinton captured 84% of the black vote in the 1996 presidential election, whereas 82% of African American voters supported Democratic Congressional candidates as a whole that year. See 'Portrait of the Electorate', *ibid.,* 10 November 1996, p. A28 and T.M. Neal, 'Democrats Fear Loss of Black Loyalty', *Washington Post*, 3 August 1998, p. A1.
13 '1998 Voter Profile', *Facts on File, 1998*, p. 782. The profile was based on exit polls on 3 November that year.
14 M.K. Frisby, 'Clinton Stays Popular with Blacks In Spite of Fraying of Safety Net', *Wall Street Journal*, 13 June 1997, p. A1.
15 The decision of the Democratic National Committee to change its focus from simply registering black voters to getting them actually to appear at polling stations is particularly cited. See M.K. Frisby, 'Both Parties Take Stock of Jump in Black Turnout', *ibid.,* 13 February 1997, p. A20.
16 Thernstrom, pp. 303-4.
17 'Black, Yes; Democrats, Maybe', *Economist*, 18 August 1998, p. 25.
18 Taylor, p. 235.
19 Younger blacks in particular are apt to regard integration as no longer being the panacea for problems. Many see litigation, the NAACP's traditional way of defending or advancing black claims as counterproductive or even futile in these days of more conservative minded judges and justices. See M.A. Fletcher, 'Mfume Takes NAACP Helm Today', *Washington Post*, 15 February 1996, p. A3; also D. Masci, 'The Black Middle Class: Is Its Cup Half-Full or Half-Empty?', *CQ Researcher*, 23 January 1998, p. 66.
20 G. Jones, 'The Wellspring of Black Leadership', *Wall Street Journal*, 17 October 1996, p. A22.
21 According to the black journalist and author Clarence Page, for example, while those at the head of the NAACP lurched from crisis to crisis in the mid-1990s, those in its more than two thousand chapters stayed 'as dynamic as ever, tackling all manner of local racial eruptions and local issues...'. See *Showing My Colour* (1996), p. 211.
22 Quoted in E.J. Dionne, Jnr, 'The Minorities' Vote', *Washington Post*, 1 December 1998, p. A25.
23 C.M. Swain, *Black Faces, Black Interests* (Cambridge, Mass.: Harvard University Press, 1993), p. 203.
24 Thernstrom, p. 301; also D. D'Souza, *The End of Racism* (New York: The Free Press, 1995), p. 479.
25 Thernstrom, pp. 298-300.
26 In addition to the 'Clinton Factor' and the impact of the 1998 impeachment hearings, it would appear that a new race card might have emerged in U.S. politics recently. Whereas before it was Republicans, beginning with Richard Nixon, who made skin colour an issue in the hope of driving whites into their fold, now it is said to be Democrats who 'polarise around race', only this time 'to scare up the black vote' so as to recapture lost regions like the South. In Georgia, Maryland and North Carolina, Democrat charges of racism against Republican opponents got African American voters to turn out in much greater numbers in the 1998 mid-term elections than in those of four

years earlier. According to some, the President's similarly dubious portrayal in 1999 of right-wing congressional opposition to two black nominees, one for the judiciary and one for an ambassadorship, was done with an eye to gaining even more of the African American vote in the 2000 elections. See P.A. Gigot, 'What Nixon Taught Dems About Race', *Wall Street Journal*, 29 October 1999, p. A18.

8 Middleman, Model and Silent Minorities?

The Kerner Commission, set up by President Lyndon Johnson more than thirty years ago to investigate the causes of the many urban riots of the 1960s, painted a bleak portrait of racial affairs. America, it warned in its 1968 report, was becoming 'two nations, one black, one white, separate and unequal'. Relations between African Americans and Caucasians were deteriorating rather than improving, and unless drastic reforms were undertaken immediately, the 'continuing polarisation of the American community' would ultimately lead to an explosion big enough possibly to destroy the country.

Needless to say, no such thing has happened. There have been tensions and confrontations between blacks and whites in the past few decades but hardly any disturbances on a large scale. Residential segregation, which the Commission saw as being at the root of much of the problem, is no longer a very great issue. Other difficulties like discrimination in employment and education were already starting to break down even before the panel of experts was completing its findings. Yet if the Commission was unduly pessimistic about the state and future of black-white relations, it was in the opinion of many overly optimistic that racial affairs need be viewed only through a simple two-dimensional lens. For the fact is that in a great many urban neighbourhoods, the USA has in the intervening decades in effect become several nations: one black, one white and a host of others from virtually every quarter of the globe.

These other groups have sometimes been known as 'middleman minorities' because of their propensity to bring together producers and consumers in commercial transactions and because in aggregate they have averaged somewhere between blacks and whites in most of the traditional socioeconomic standings. Yet the expression is rather misleading. By no means are all people of yellow and brown skin in the United States entrepreneurs, and while Asians, Hispanics and others might taken together rank somewhere in the middle of America's two largest groups in terms of health, education and income, taken separately they clearly do not. Even within the Asian and Latino communities, such wide variations exist as to make generalisations difficult, at times almost meaningless.

129

Hispanics

Socioeconomic Standing

In the past, Hispanics experienced many of the same difficulties as African Americans, albeit usually in a somewhat milder form. In the southwestern states, Mexican American migrant farm labourers endured exploitation almost on a par with that of the southern black cotton and tobacco worker. They were confronted with school and housing segregation, though mainly out of local practice rather than state law. Puerto Ricans in New York and New Jersey may have lived in ghettos like 'Spanish Harlem' and shared a common deprivation with blacks, but Cubans were for the most part able to carve out comfortable enough lifestyles for themselves in Miami and other parts of southern Florida. All in all, the generally less pronounced forms of prejudice that collectively faced Latinos enabled them to fare somewhat better than African Americans by most economic and social yardsticks. The one exception was higher education, where proportionately fewer Hispanics got university degrees than did blacks, but this was largely ascribed to language difficulties that, it was assumed, would disappear as assimilation took hold.

For much of the past ten years, however, a new pattern has been in place. Hispanics still face many of the same problems as other minorities, but they appear as a group to have coped rather less well. Census Bureau statistics reveal that while real median household income rose for most of America's racial and ethnic groups between the late Eighties and mid-Nineties, for Latinos it fell. By 1995, the poverty rate among Spanish speaking people in the United States had surpassed that of blacks. In that year, Hispanics accounted for 24% of the country's poor, up from 16% a decade earlier, and amounting to a portion more than double that of their numbers in the country. Three out of every ten Hispanic families were officially classified as poor in 1995, and they were also overly represented in the ranks of the nation's most poor.[1] Admittedly, real median household incomes for Latinos have risen a bit since the mid-1990s while their poverty rate has fallen somewhat. But the same is broadly speaking true of the other main groups in the U.S. during this time span, as everyone has benefited from the rising tide of several years of economic expansion that has lifted all boats, including even those of the most lowly paid workers. Unlike the others, however, it took Hispanics nearly a decade to get back to the real levels they had reached in 1989.[2]

Such countertrends baffle many experts who are aware that it all cannot be put down to something as simple as laziness. The work ethic of Latinos is well known and recorded. Their 5.8% unemployment rate in the spring of 1999, for instance, was almost exactly midway between that of whites at 3.6% and blacks at 8.1%.[3] Even during the worst periods of the early and mid-1990s, when anti-Latino feeling in California and elsewhere was high, their national jobless rates still did not quite match those of African Americans. Indeed, the participation rate of Hispanics in the country's labour force as a whole is higher than that of both the other groups. A seemingly obvious explanation for the disappointing performance is immigration. The sheer flood of Latino newcomers, many of whom have been arriving easily and illegally across the long Mexican border over the years, is pulling down national Hispanic averages in the ethnic 'league tables' in a way that does not apply to others. Unlike many Asians, for instance, Latinos tend to come with few qualifications and so usually land only routine jobs like fruit picking, gardening and housework that others, including blacks, disdain because of the low pay and lack of promotion prospects. Their illegal status heightens their chances of staying poor inasmuch as they cannot become unionised or make formal complaints without alerting the authorities. Knowing this, unprincipled employers have paid them at or sometimes even below the most basic levels. This is particularly true during those periods when xenophobic sentiments are strong, making even the documented ones reluctant to stand up for their rights.

To all outward appearances, there seems much to be said for this view. The trouble with the immigration argument, however, is that it fails to take into account the fact that native born Hispanics are also suffering sluggish income growth compared with others. There are, of course, exceptions. A number of Spanish speakers in the U.S. are upwardly mobile. In Los Angeles alone there are now about half a million middle class Latino households, three times as many as in 1980. Nationally, more than half of all native born Hispanic Americans possess or are buying their own home. By 1998, there were more than a million Latino owned businesses in the country, double the number in 1993.[4] Cuban Americans, many of whom are older, well-educated middle class exiles from the Castro regime, or descendants of such, have done well in economic terms. However, government statistics show that even among Latinos born in the U.S. real average earnings have not been rising particularly fast and that poverty levels have not fallen as markedly as those of other groups.[5]

Lack of education is a likely culprit. Less than 60% of Hispanic high school students completed their secondary education in 1995, compared with nearly 87% of blacks and more than 90% of whites.[6] The language barrier is a commonly cited reason for this poor performance. But Hispanic spokespersons claim that their young are often made to do with underfunded, substandard schools, while others point to the economic necessity of Spanish speaking adolescents having to go into the world of work to help support large families. Whatever the reasons, Latinos are the least likely of the major racial and ethnic groups to go on to higher learning, and the gap between them and African Americans in this respect is made wider by the fact that there is no Hispanic equivalent to the one hundred or so historic black colleges in the U.S. The failure of the authorities to keep them in school has resulted in millions of Spanish speaking U.S. citizens entering the labour force with marketable skills scarcely any better than those of illiterate immigrants. In the past, Hispanic school dropouts got reasonably well paid blue-collar jobs, but owing to structural changes in the economy this type of work has become rarer and a good deal less financially rewarding. In California, for example, a number of Americans of Mexican background are still concentrated in the textile industry, but not as many as before, and their real earnings have declined several thousand dollars annually since the late 1960s because of competition from cheap foreign labour.[7]

Yet a strange amalgam of cultural factors would also appear to be at play in the worsening economic fortunes of Latinos vis-à-vis other groups. Second- and third generation Hispanics in many respects seem to have become accustomed to some of the worst aspects of modern day urban life in the U.S. without abandoning altogether the very values and customs of their parents and grandparents that have traditionally held them back in a material sense. Teenage pregnancy, itself an explanation for both poverty and an incomplete education, is now a relatively more common occurrence among Latinos than either whites or blacks. In 1995, 11% of all Hispanic girls between the ages of 15 and 19 gave birth compared with 10% of African Americans and 4% of Caucasians in this category. Admittedly, Hispanic teenage mothers are more likely subsequently to get married than are their counterparts in some of the other racial and ethnic groups. The pressure to retain the family structure is rather strong in Latino culture. But by the same token, this means that they are also less apt to seek gainful employment, bowing to the demands of their husbands to stay at home with the children. Thus increasingly and at an earlier age Hispanic nuclear families are confining themselves to one income rather than two until the children become a good deal older.[8]

There is also the matter of religion. Generally Roman Catholic in upbringing and often coming from Third World societies where birth control is unknown or avoided, they tend to have large families, making it harder for many to stay above the poverty line.[9] Bigger family size not only increases the need for income but also makes it more difficult for those Hispanic women willing and able to go out into the world of work to find childcare. At the same time, the higher birth rate also keeps the Latino population younger than other groups. The median Hispanic age is twenty six, several years less than the corresponding figure for the rest of the country.[10] As most people's earnings increase as they get older in their working years, this aspect of demography should not be overlooked when considering the reasons for lower median and average Latino incomes.

Puerto Ricans

One subset of the Hispanic community, however, does not seem to be underpinned by especially strong family structures. This is Puerto Ricans, after Mexicans the second largest and arguably the most enigmatic of the many Spanish speaking groups in the USA. Census Bureau indicators reveal that nearly half of all Puerto Rican families are headed by a single parent and that at almost any given time they are twice as likely as African Americans and more than three times as likely as other Latinos to be on welfare. Precisely why this is the case is something of a mystery. Some believe their ranking as the economically worst off ethnic group in the country to be the result of their special status. Coming from a Caribbean island that is U.S. territory, they automatically have full access to voting rights and various assistance schemes. Classified as Americans, they take the easy course and live off welfare benefits unavailable to other newcomers. Others say it is the reverse side of the citizenship coin that is the cause of their problems. Being able to come and go as they please between the mainland and their home island, they do not settle and so do not progress in the same manner as Cuban Americans, another Caribbean émigré group with full citizenship rights but who do not remotely contemplate returning to their place of birth until the end of the Castro regime (and now possibly not even then). Still others cite the concentration of Puerto Ricans in the northeastern part of the USA, especially in New York City and northern New Jersey, whose local economies at times have not been as dynamic as those elsewhere, as the main explanation for their poor performance. Whatever the reason, the impoverishment of much of what constitutes a fairly significant portion of Spanish speaking individuals in the U.S. is an additional explanation for lagging Latino figures as a whole.[11]

At the same time, the Puerto Rican experience is in many ways atypical. Immigrants from the Dominican Republic, who also recently have settled in large numbers in the northeastern part of the U.S., share some of the same problems. But most Latinos do not, and it is important to recognise that comparatively few Hispanics are on welfare. The bulk of Latino poverty is one of low wage work and overcrowded households and has little to do with unemployment or the deliberate seeking of benefits. Most disadvantaged Hispanics belong to the working rather than the non-working poor and normally seek little official help. Indeed, many cannot now do so because of recent legislative changes requiring at least five years' residency before one can claim benefits. The distinction is important, for it means that Latinos tend to see poverty in a rather different light from disadvantaged blacks and whites. The former are more apt to construe it as a workplace problem with raising the national minimum wage, exposing unscrupulous bosses and passing legislation against occupational hazards as the main priorities. Spokesmen for the latter are inclined to regard poverty more from an entitlement perspective with restoration of recently cut benefits being the main goal.

Hispanics and Politics

For quite a while, Latinos were facing political difficulties commensurate with their social and economic problems. At both the state and national levels, they were very much on the defensive, fighting rearguard actions on several fronts simultaneously to keep what they felt was their due. Nowhere was this truer than in California, where in 1994 Republican Governor Pete Wilson drove through Proposition 187, a statewide referendum that sought to end a variety of welfare and social benefits to illegal immigrants perceived to be living off the public coffers. But it also applied to Hispanics residing in other southwestern states like Arizona and New Mexico where the white led 'English Only' movement aimed at the removal of Spanish from all official documents, and, indeed, to Spanish speaking people in those many parts of the U.S. where anti-minority feeling in general was on the rise because of non-assimilation fears.

Today, however, it would seem that political fortunes have improved for Latinos. The watershed came just as conditions were looking their bleakest in 1996. In the prelude to the presidential and congressional elections of that year, the Republicans announced that they intended to do nationally what they had already done statewide in California: deny food stamps and medical benefits to undocumented newcomers. Meanwhile, Governor Wilson was lending his support to Proposition 209 outlawing affirmative action programmes in his state. Alarmed at these developments and worried that other states would follow suit if whites in California got their way over preferences, large numbers of Latinos across the country were galvanised into taking up citizenship and becoming registered voters. More than 400 000 new Hispanics turned out to register and vote in Texas alone that year.[12] Although those in California failed to defeat Proposition 209, Latinos in general did manage to get the political parties, especially the Republicans, to sit up and take more notice. In 1997, the Republican controlled Congress backpedalled somewhat on the immigration act of the year before and made it easier for thousands of refugees and asylum seekers from earlier civil wars in Central America to remain in the U.S. Like the Democrats, the Republicans have now taken to having their leaders deliver speeches to Hispanic organisations and printing bilingual party documents.

Of course, such appeals would never be made if party leaderships on both sides of the divide did not believe that there was at least some opportunity of getting political reward. Yet both do. Democrats are convinced that they have a good chance of securing the bulk of the ever larger Latino vote because of the immigrant bashing image of the Republicans and because they are convinced that their party's message and agenda about maintaining social services and improving minimum wage levels are in tune with the needs and aspirations of poorer Hispanics. Republicans admit that they have an uphill struggle as regards image, especially in California where former Governor Wilson's actions have not been forgotten, but they contend that they have culture and economics on their side. Often coming from rural Third World societies, Latinos tend to be natural supporters of the Republican Party's 'family values' agenda. The liberal line that the Democrats take on abortion and gay rights offends not just the traditionally Roman Catholic Hispanics but also those who are joining the highly conservative Pentecostalist churches in great numbers. The entrepreneurship of many Latinos puts a number of them economically speaking to the Right of much of the Democratic Party, and Republican enactment of a $400 per child tax cut in a recent budget has gone down well among those numerous Hispanic households that contain large families.

Thus the Hispanic vote could go either way in future elections. Much will depend not just on the message of the two parties but also on how it is delivered. Already there are signs that Republicans are exercising extreme care in their attempt to overcome past mistakes, tailoring their message to different sections of the Latino population as they campaign. With the most recently naturalised Hispanic immigrants they emphasise social conservatism. For those who are longer established, they stress economic conservatism. The Democrats in their own way are being equally selective.

In this connection, one cannot help but conclude that the political position of Latinos today is better than it was just a few years ago and probably superior, too, to that of blacks. There are fewer Hispanic than African American members of Congress – only 20 in 1999 - and not nearly so many of national renown. But Hispanic voters by their rapidly growing numbers show signs of cornering important statewide and local offices. In California, the speakership of the state assembly at Sacramento changed hands from one Latino politician to another in 1998. In Arizona and New Mexico, there are entire counties where just about all elected posts are in Hispanic hands, a number of them for some time. The total number of elected Spanish-American officials in the country now exceeds 5000.[13] Furthermore, Latinos, by virtue of their demographic concentration - more than three-quarters of them live in five of the six most populous states in the nation[14] - and their discernment once inside polling stations, voting usually on issues rather than along strict party lines, cannot so easily be taken for granted by one political grouping and written off by another. The fact that both main parties are assiduously courting them is bound to reap them handsome rewards. Whether these rewards can eventually spill over to economic success for Hispanics as a whole remains to be seen.

Hispanics and African Americans

Generally speaking, relations between African Americans and Latinos have often been more complex than the circumstances would seem to warrant. For a start, there is a basic difference in the way each group sees the other. Blacks are apt to regard Hispanics as racially closer to whites and therefore better able to assimilate and avoid discrimination. Most Hispanics have at least some European blood, and a number could outwardly be mistaken for Italian- or Greek Americans, against whom today there is no real discrimination. African Americans believe it is for this reason that there are fewer social constraints to Hispanic-white marriages than black-white ones and that property values do not necessarily get marked down as sharply in some suburban neighbourhoods for Latino entrance as when blacks move in. On the other hand, a good many Hispanics see African Americans as part of the majority culture from which they themselves are excluded. Blacks as native speakers of English are steeped in U.S. traditions and do not have to worry about deportation. The fact that most African American politicians have Anglo-Saxon sounding names gives them something of an advantage over Hispanic candidates with xenophobic white voters.

This gulf extends to deeper political perceptions as well. A number of African Americans comment bitterly on what they regard as the scant participation in the struggle against discrimination by Latinos, who all the same are said to be only too willing to reap the benefits of whatever victories have been won. In the autumn of 1996 the Hispanic activist group La Raza did stage a large march on Washington, D.C. But in the opinion of at least one writer this was little more than another attempt on the part of that organisation to push Latino politicians 'to compete with African Americans for the status of most-discriminated-against minority'.[15] For their part, Latinos say that they have never fit neatly into a civil rights mould. Being a diverse group, they do not have much of a shared history or common experience to draw upon and so unlike U.S. blacks are not entirely clear about what they dislike. Among some Latinos there is the largely unspoken feeling that while they perhaps have gained from the civil rights movement in general, they have profited less from the advance of African Americans into office in particular. Like most whites, a majority of blacks have not bothered to learn Spanish or share power in certain cities like Houston and Los Angeles where there are large numbers of Hispanic voters. Conversely, African Americans have complained at times about favouritism in the opposite direction – notably, the awarding of most business contracts to Latino entrepreneurs in Denver in the early 1990s when that city had an Hispanic mayor.[16]

Yet it is demographic change that is most at the root of the uneasiness between the two minority communities today. Simply put, Hispanics will soon outnumber African Americans. The latter, long accustomed to being the senior partner in whatever coalitions that have existed between the two groups in the past, are afraid of being relegated to subordinate status. Exacerbating the tension is a belief on each side that it is at times involved in a 'zero sum game', that any gains of the one can only come at the expense of the other. Undoubtedly this is what has been happening in political contests in many of the bigger cities where fleeing whites have abandoned power to blacks presiding over ever more numerous Spanish speaking inhabitants. Moreover, competition for the same type of jobs, housing and neighbourhood control is bound to be keen if Hispanics continue to increase greatly in number while the socioeconomic profiles of the two groups go on resembling each other so strongly. Some think the contest more or less already lost. Writing about newcomers to the U.S., a substantial percentage of whom come from Mexico and Central America, one black writer has observed:

> The ever-accelerating flow of immigrants has vastly complicated relations...rank-and-file blacks are increasingly resentful of immigrants; in this era of dwindling distinctions between citizens and non-citizens, African Americans find themselves competing for jobs, social programmes and affirmative action advantages with the new arrivals, and often end up as the losers in the competition.[17]

Meanwhile, among African Americans, whites are seen as preferring Latino immigrant workers to native black ones. It is also sometimes asserted that Caucasians, in an attempt to preserve their majority status, will ensure that some groups of new immigrants like middle class Hispanics will be considered 'white' even if they do not intermarry. Some believe high earning and well-educated Asians already to have achieved this status.

Asian Americans

More typical than Hispanics - indeed, the epitome - of what some sociologists in the U.S. call 'middleman minorities' are Asian Americans. They do well running small businesses in both the central cities and the outlying suburbs of many metropolitan areas. Different sub-groups tend to be represented in different entrepreneurial fields. Thus self-employed Japanese American businessmen are often concentrated in horticultural services. Asian Indians and Philipinos tend to be found in the health service industries. Chinese Americans own a disproportionate number of restaurants, while Koreans are strongly represented in family run grocery and fruit and vegetable stores. Similarly, in corporate America Asians are well established in middle management ranks and also do well in the professions, although they rarely reach the uppermost levels.

Indeed, in a number of respects Asian Americans constitute a top rather than a middle ranking group. At three per cent., they have the lowest divorce rate of any racial group in the United States. They also have the lowest unemployment, mortality and teenage pregnancy rates. In the world of education, they are overachievers. By the mid-1990s, just about half of all Asian Americans in the 25-year old to 44-year old age group were university graduates, and on college entrance exams they perform significantly better than whites, despite the fact that many are first- and second generation immigrants having to overcome language hurdles. Perhaps the best known statistics about Asian Americans pertain to earnings. In terms of both median and average household income, their levels are higher than those of any other racial and ethnic group, including whites.[18]

Asian Americans in general have been so successful that the epithet 'model minority' rather than 'middleman minority' is now often more commonly applied to them. Caucasians in particular hold this image of them and seem to be doubly willing to praise Asian Americans because they have achieved so much without recourse to protests or demands. Although Chinese- and Japanese Americans in particular have experienced prejudice and discrimination in the past, with the latter group having been interned in camps in the U.S. during World War Two, they appear to have overcome virtually all obstacles without resorting to political or violent confrontations with the established order. To whites, Asian American success is proof that anyone can get ahead in the United States with the right attitudes and qualities. Yet to many it is a bit of sweeping judgement, for despite the undeniable virtues like thrift, frugality and hard work of a lot of Asian immigrants and their descendants, many do have certain advantages over Hispanics and other newcomers. They often reach America with greater resources than arrivals from elsewhere. It is by no means unusual for Korean fresh produce grocers, for instance, to have college degrees and arrive by dint of having family already in the U.S. They tend to turn to the likes of the produce business as a career because of language and other barriers to the originally chosen fields. Other attributes that have helped them to succeed are strong organisational skills and clannishness. East Asian immigrants in particular have their own credit pools that enable them to bypass banks and get loans at low rates of interest from each other. They tend to give jobs only to members of their own family whom they put to work for long hours and at low pay.

For these reasons and others Asian Americans are usually reluctant to apply the 'model minority' phrase to themselves. Many of them think that their successful image is more perceived than real. Their income might seem high, but this overlooks the fact that in their extended family households there are often more than two breadwinners. Given that they tend to live in states like California, New York and Hawaii, where the cost of living is dear, the real purchasing power of their earnings is not as great as at first seems. Furthermore, statistics show that at specific education levels whites usually earn more than their Asian American counterparts of the same age, even though the educational attainment of the latter group is often at least as good. They do get promotions, sometimes to quite senior levels, but as has been pointed out before they almost never reach the very top. Meanwhile, a number of highly trained Vietnamese, Hong Kong and mainland Chinese who emigrated to the United States to escape war or for political reasons often spend years working at jobs below the level and status they left at home.

In fact, to a number of Asian Americans images of success are not just a distortion of reality but an outright disservice. An estimated 30% of Southeast Asians ranging from Philipino farm labourers to illiterate refugee Hmong tribesmen from Laos and Cambodia are in need of welfare assistance. Behind the glittering façade of exotic Chinatowns in cities like San Francisco and New York, a quarter of families live below poverty levels. As is the case with Latin American, African and Caribbean immigrants, first generation Asian arrivals have disproportionate numbers in the low paying service occupations. Wide discrepancies exist in income. For every Asian American family earning $75,000 a year or more, there is another making $10,000 p.a. or less.[19] Yet because the perception is that Asians have succeeded, these less well off groups often get overlooked and denied help for social service programmes to learn English or find jobs. Meanwhile, in schools those Asian American pupils who do only modestly well sometimes face criticism from teachers who expect them to fulfil the academically bright image. Many Asian Americans contend that the 'model minority' label is just another example of ethnic stereotyping, the result of white America lumping together all those from the other side of the Pacific Rim simply because so many vaguely share the same physical characteristics.

But it is the impact on other groups of the success label that most worries Asian Americans. The implications of the argument of those whites who hold them up as a shining example is that others must somehow be responsible for their own low status. Such reasoning has been known to induce individual poor whites to commit arson, beatings and other forms of 'hate crime' against Asians in years past. Collective resentment is stronger, however, among non-Caucasian inner city residents who see 'middleman minorities' as an alien, exploitative group using their profits to overtake poor blacks born and raised in the USA on the socioeconomic ladder. Tension has at times been particularly acute with Korean American shopkeepers, whose cultural reserve and wary treatment of some patrons has not gone down well with those African Americans living in the ghettos. The fact that the dominant white culture tolerates if not applauds such quiet, apparently mercenary behaviour and by extension blames the poor for their inability or unwillingness to copy it only adds to the pain. Some militant black activists have gone so far as to suspect collusion between the U.S. Government and Asian immigrants in the form of tax breaks and special grants to prevent African American economic development.[20] Conspiracy theories and paranoia have not of themselves led directly to confrontations between the inner city poor and Asian shopkeepers, but they do not help matters and some say would probably not exist if white America were not so forthright in its praise. Once again, the 'model minority' image is not necessarily doing Asian Americans any favours.

Asian Americans and the Ballot Box

In the realm of politics, Asian Americans tend to have a muted voice. They are big players in Hawaii where the Governor and both Senators are of Pacific Islander descent. The Governor of Washington State is a Chinese American. Elsewhere on the mainland, however, they possess relatively little influence, despite having the potential for carrying the 'swing' vote in parts of important populous states like California and New York. In the early 1990s, when race based congressional redistricting was very much in vogue, Asian Americans, unlike blacks and Hispanics, were unable to get constituencies of their own created. Even in San Francisco and Los Angeles, two cities where great numbers of them live, Asian American voters remained largely split up into different legislative districts. As a result, they tend to be under-represented in Congress, and with the exception of an appointment at the Commerce Department late in President Clinton's second term of office no Asian American has reached the Cabinet.

Numerous explanations have been put forward for this comparative lack of influence. Although their numbers are growing rapidly, they still account for only four per cent. of the total population. More than half of all Asian Americans are foreign born, and while naturalisation rates did increase in 1996 as they did with Hispanics in response to anti-immigrant legislation, many remain non-citizens. Recent Asian immigrants often have little experience of democracy and arrive with a general mistrust of government. Developing political cohesion for them is especially difficult in that they come from many diverse countries and unlike most Latinos do not even have a common mother tongue to bind them together. Cultural factors have often been cited for their reluctance to seek public office (and, for that matter, their failure to climb to the very top of the corporate ladder). To become a political candidate in Western societies requires assertiveness and a willingness to extol one's own virtues and therefore to invite criticism, traits that are said to be alien to the Asian mind. Meanwhile, particular episodes like the 1996 campaign finance controversies in which amongst other things several high profile Asian American businessmen gave large sums of money to the parties, especially the Democrats, have from time to time caused this community as a whole to feel unfairly smeared and so shy away from politics.

In contrast to blacks and to a lesser extent to Latinos, those Asian Americans who do take part in the political process do not necessarily vote Democrat. In the 1996 presidential election, for instance, more cast their ballot for the Republican candidate Bob Dole than for Bill Clinton. Some dismiss this as another attempt at conformity with white middle class USA on the part of Asian Americans, but they and Caucasians do find themselves similarly placed on a number of issues. If anything, proportionately more Asian American students than whites have been denied the higher education of their choice because of affirmative action programmes. As high income earners they have, like affluent whites, been hit hard by past 'tax and spend' policies of the Democratic Party. Tough Republican talk on crime appeals to inner city Asian businessmen. In the meantime, like anti-Castro Cuban Americans, a number of Asian Americans have a special reason of their own for being attracted to the Republican Party. Of the two main political groupings in America, the Republicans are the ones who have the reputation for being traditionally harder on communism, a stance that resonates well with Vietnamese-, Korean- and Taiwanese Americans, all of whom still tend to have a Cold War mentality. On the other hand, many Asians are drawn to the Democrats' liberal position on immigration, and many more voted for Clinton in 1996 than did in 1992 for this reason.[21] As with most Hispanics, neither of the major political parties can automatically make assumptions about the Asian American vote.

Native Americans

If the label 'model minority' as applied to Asian Americans is somewhat inaccurate and misleading, the term 'silent minority', which has sometimes been used in connection with Native Americans, is increasingly regarded as patently false. As long ago as the 1960s an activist organisation known as AIM confronted the Establishment on several occasions with protests and demonstrations about past mistreatment and state interference with Red Indian practices. In 1992, Native Americans in general expressed outrage over 500th anniversary celebrations of the first voyage to the New World by Christopher Columbus, a man who to them was a racist exploiter. Since then, they have become vocal about what they construe as ethnic stereotyping and assaults on their culture. Hollywood may have progressed from portraying American Indians as sullen savages in westerns. But the same is not true of professional sporting teams like football's Washington Redskins and baseball's Atlanta Braves, whose names and logos are regarded as demeaning and whose crowd and mascot practices allegedly cheapen tribal culture. As regards the land, long a sore issue because of broken treaty rights by government, corporations and private individuals alike and more recently because of mismanagement of trust funds by the Interior Department, Native Americans have become more outspoken about what they construe as the vandalising of sacred sites. At South Dakota's Mount Rushmore National Monument, for instance, Indians say that the four enormous busts of U.S. presidents carved into the Black Hills defile a spiritual landmark. Yet for all this, some maintain that the continuing political impotence of Red Indians renders the traditional label still valid. 'They don't form large voting blocs and most cannot afford the kind of access other Americans have', argued Cheyenne U.S. Senator Ben Nighthorse Campbell when opposing a 1997 congressional bill aimed at tightening federal control over the tribes. 'They are truly the "silent minority".'[22]

Any concrete results of increased Indian outspokenness have been relatively few and far between. In terms of cultural slights, they have managed to get more than six hundred sporting teams to change their insignias and mascots to something less offensive.[23] But to date all the substitutions have been at the college and high school levels, not with the professional organisations. Similarly, white America has agreed to change the names of certain battle sites and establish a new national museum honouring Native American history and culture in Washington, D.C., but no move other than a few cash offerings has been made to compensate them for lost lands. Since the early 1970s, the tribes have been granted increased autonomy in everyday matters like housing, education and law enforcement, but final control still rests in the hands of civil servants.

Oddly enough, one area of defeat has turned out to be a boon to at least some of the American Indian tribes. This is funding, which has been cut for the better part of twenty years now, despite the growth in the Native American population and the initial objections of most of the tribesmen. In the early 1980s, the Reagan administration began reducing government assistance to Native Americans as part of its laissez-faire approach to the economy. It was felt that the various aid programmes were creating on the reservations a culture of welfare dependency, robbing the Indians of any kind of initiative needed to improve their lot. The cuts continued for a decade and received new impetus in the mid-1990s when the Republicans gained control of Congress and curtailed public spending further as part of the overall effort to balance the federal budget.

To fill the shortfall created by these cuts, the Indians wholeheartedly began building bingo halls and casinos so that today there are gambling sites on reservations in more than half of the fifty states. Yet whether the idea will prove to be a panacea for the problems of Native Americans is a matter of opinion. Certainly it has turned out to be a good source of income and employment, with a few tribes like the Pequod in Connecticut getting staggering windfalls. The more typical picture, however, is of modestly successful operations, and for some of the Plains Indians who live on the more remote and agriculturally less productive reservations in the western half of the country there has been no benefit at all. The Oglala Sioux, whose Pine Ridge Reservation in South Dakota has seen 90% unemployment and alcoholism and suicide rates running five times the national average, did not have the money to complete the building of a permanent casino and are now in debt to contractors.[24] Elsewhere the question is whether gambling might not create more difficulties than it solves. Already there have been unseemly arguments over tribal membership and the right to share in the profits. Alarm is also being voiced at the appearance of compulsive betting on the part of individual Indians. Others fear the involvement of organised crime.

It is, however, the legal aspects of the gambling issue that have thus far created the greatest furore. Some of the casinos have been built in states where gambling is illegal or highly restricted. That the Indians have been able to get away with this is because of the special status the Supreme Court bestowed on them in the 1830s as sovereign nations exempt from local and state laws. Their immunity has long rankled with some other residents who resent the ability of the tribes (though not individual Indians) to avoid having to pay taxes or being sued in the courts. Now the tribes can engage in what some see as a morally dubious practice not permitted others in places and reap big profits. Worse, their new economic strength resulting primarily from the booming casinos appears to have given some Indians the confidence to dismiss other state laws. Stories abound about many of them doing as they please with regard to hunting and fishing. In those areas propaganda can aid the cause of white supremacists. At the very least, it has served to increase calls for change, if not an end to affirmative action.

An Update – Affirmative Action in Retreat?

Partly out of a belief that the policy was not working and partly because of the then fragile state of the economy, public opinion began to turn more and more against affirmative action in the early 1990s. Popular clamour saw to it that some of the more egregious aspects of the policy were immediately done away with once they came to light. Thus as far back as 1991 'race norming', or the practice of segregating results for civil service entrance exams so that blacks competed only against other blacks and whites versus whites in order to guarantee a certain number of posts for African Americans, came to a sudden end this way. Petitions were gathered, especially among 'angry white males', to start referenda against affirmative action in general. The most famous were in California where they culminated in the passage in 1996 of Proposition 209 ending race- and gender based preferences in all state run hiring, contracting and higher education admissions decisions. Two years later Washington State followed suit, and today an organisation called the American Civil Rights Initiative is hoping to sponsor several anti-affirmative action plebiscites across the country. Meanwhile, ever since 1994 the anti-preferences Republican Party has been in control of Congress. But it arguably was in their willingness to go to court that whites made the most headway in scaling back affirmative action programmes during these years.

In the 1950s and 1960s it was liberal activists who turned to the judiciary for help in racial matters. In more recent times, however, it increasingly has been conservatives who have tended to do this, partly in the genuine belief that the civil rights movement has gone too far and partly because they know they are apt to get a more sympathetic hearing nowadays. Throughout the 1980s and early 1990s Presidents Reagan and Bush systematically appointed right-wing justices to the Supreme Court whenever vacancies arose, and although President Clinton has subsequently redressed the situation somewhat, conservatives continue to outnumber liberals on the bench of the highest judicial body in the land. The shifting balance of power in the Court can be seen in the stance it has taken on this issue in the past decade or so: a decision in the late 1980s that workplace affirmative action could not be introduced at the expense of existing jobs; a series of rulings in the early 1990s making it harder for women and where the growing suburbanisation of America has led to Indians and members of other groups living cheek by jowl, some of the tribes are alleged to have blithely violated zoning laws. In Washington State, for instance, one tribe built a rock concert stadium with its gambling takings adjacent to quiet residential areas.

Such assertiveness is beginning to produce a reaction. In 1997 a bill was introduced to the Senate that sought to require the tribes to waive their immunity from lawsuits before they could receive federal funds. A similar bill in 1998 aimed simply at stripping Native Americans of their sovereign status. Neither became law because of residual congressional sympathy over past injustices and the continuing financial hardships of many tribesmen and women. But some observers believe a turning of the broader tide is discernable. According to the *Economist*, more and more ordinary Americans sense chaos arising out of an aged Supreme Court decision allowing five hundred tribes in many instances to act as laws unto themselves. The 'groundswell of support for the [1998] bill', asserts this periodical, 'suggests that change is in the offing'.[25]

In the Introduction (Chapter 1) to this work questions were asked about the relationship of America's non-black minorities to the colour line. On the face of it, none of them seem to apply to Native Americans. Few in number and living on remote reservations, they cannot exert much influence on black-white relations, even if they so wished. Generally impoverished, they are most unlikely to create a colour line of their own. Members of sovereign nations but still under some bureaucratic control as regards everyday matters like housing, education and law enforcement, they have a uniquely anomalous relationship with the Federal Government, which to them even more than to others is tantamount to white rule. However, despite all this, they are in some ways in the same predicament as America's other non-black minorities. Like Latinos and Asian Americans, they face the choice between assimilation and maintaining their own identity. Like those two, they are intermarrying more than ever before, with implications for their affirmative action entitlements. How American Indians respond to these challenges as well as to disputes over land use, taxation and gambling will determine whether they keep or jeopardise the moral capital that the tribes had so carefully built up with public opinion over the years.

Notes

1   C. Goldberg, 'Hispanic Households Struggle Amid Broad Decline in Income', *New York Times*, 30 January 1997, p. A1.
2   Not until 1998 did the poverty rate for Hispanic families at 22.7% fall below its 23.4% level set in 1989. By contrast, the 1989 black family poverty rate of 27.8% was breached as far back as 1994 and has stayed lower ever since. See C. Babington, 'Household Incomes Are at a High', *Washington Post*, 1 October 1999, p. A3; also *Statistical Abstract of the United States, 1997*, Table 744.
3   J.M. Berry, 'U.S. Jobless Rate Lowest in 29 Years', *Washington Post*, 3 April 1999, p. D11.
4   'A Minority Worth Cultivating', *Economist*, 25 April 1998, pp. 25-7.
5   Goldberg, *loc. cit.*
6   D. Masci, 'Hispanic-Americans' New Clout: Will Hispanics Desert the Democratic Party?', *CQ Researcher*, 18 September 1998, p. 823.
7   Goldberg, *loc. cit.*
8   B. Vobejda, 'Hispanic Teens Rank First in Birthrate', *Washington Post*, 13 February 1998, p. A10. According to some, the importance that Hispanic women attach to motherhood means that males do not have to exert much domestic pressure. Lack of medical insurance and a certain fatalism, 'a feeling that their lives might be cut short by inner-city violence, so going to college and postponing a family is a waste of time', amongst younger Latinas (Hispanic females) are also reasons for their higher teen birth rates. See J. Blair, 'Why Latinas Are More Likely To Be Moms', *Christian Science Monitor*, 28 October 1999, p. 3.
9   In the opinion of the *Economist*, *op. cit.*, p. 26, religion affects Hispanic poverty in another, more abstract way. 'Their Catholicism', it avers, '…gives them a sense of belonging to a larger world, and a certain resistance (at least for now) to American materialism.'
10   R.D. Hershey, Jnr, 'Bias Hits Hispanic Workers', *New York Times*, 27 April 1995, p. D1.
11   R.D. Griffin, 'Hispanic Americans: Can They Find Prosperity and Political Power?', *CQ Researcher*, 30 October 1992, p. 944. Puerto Ricans comprise about 11% of all Latinos in the U.S. While this puts them well behind Mexicans, who make up 63% of people in this category, it still leaves them ahead of Cubans, who at 4% are the third largest such group. See D. Masci, p. 814.
12   *Economist*, *op. cit.*, p. 27.
13   Masci, p. 811; *Economist*, *loc. cit.*
14   The states in question are California, Texas, New York, Florida and Illinois, which together have 166 of the 270 votes needed in the 538 member Electoral College to determine the next president. At present, however, only a little under half of all Latinos are able to cast a ballot, thereby reducing somewhat their ability to constitute the swing vote in the above pivotal states. See M.A. Fletcher and C. Connolly, 'Gore Chases Hispanic Vote on Bush Turf', *Washington Post*, 29 July 1999, p. A1.
15   G. Rodriguez, 'From Minority to Mainstream, Latinos Find Their Voice', *ibid.*, 24 January 1999, p. B1.
16   See R. Gurwitt, 'Blacks and Latinos Are Competing for Political Power', in P. Winters (ed.), *Race Relations: Opposing Viewpoints* (San Diego: Greenhaven Press, 1996), p. 57.
17   See J. Miles, 'Immigrants Take Jobs from Blacks', in *ibid.*, p. 118, where the black writer G. Bikales is quoted.

18 In 1995, for instance, median Asian household income came to $46,356, whereas for whites it was $42,646, $25,970 for blacks and $24,570 for Hispanics. *Statistical Abstract of the United States, 1997*, Table 724. For the other socioeconomic statistics, see R.T. Schaefer, *Racial and Ethnic Groups* (New York: Longman, 1998), pp. 312, 314.

19 *Ibid.*, p. 314.

20 C. Page, *Showing My Colour* (New York: Harper Collins, 1996), pp. 176, 189.

21 D. Carney, 'Republicans Feeling the Heat As Policy Becomes Reality', *Congressional Quarterly Weekly Report*, 17 May 1997, p. 1133.

22 Senators B.N. Campbell and J. McCain, 'Keeping Our Word to the Indians', *Washington Post*, 10 September 1997, p. A21.

23 M.A. Fletcher, 'Crazy Horse Again Sounds Battle Cry', *ibid.*, 18 February 1997, p. A3. (The article's title refers to the bottling of a new brand of malt liquor bearing the name of the 19th century Sioux chief and the indignation this has caused among Native American activists.)

24 P.T. Kilborn, 'For Poorest Indians, Casinos Aren't Enough', *New York Times*, 11 June 1997, p. A1. The destitution at Pine Ridge is such as to have prompted President Clinton to make it one of his first ports of call during his poverty tour of America in the summer of 1999. However, Native Americans in general fare none too well. According to this same article, of the 1.3 million American Indians who live on reservations, half were below the poverty line and 49%, ten times the national rate, were unemployed in 1997.

25 'Indians and the Law', 18 April 1998, p. 29.

9 Affirmative Action

Affirmative action ranks among the most controversial issues in the United States today. To liberals it is the one programme for subordinate groups that really works, the only true guarantee against a resurgence of racism and sexism. To conservatives it is monstrously unfair and epitomises the heavy hand of intrusive government on everyday life. Both sides are adamant that they are after the same goal: a just and equitable society. Yet they are diametrically opposed in how to get there. For politicians, the entire matter is a hot potato. In 1996, President Clinton avoided the topic altogether in his quest to seek reelection, while congressional Republicans quietly dropped a bill that would have put an end to affirmative action for fear of appearing anti-minority. In view of the fact that the policy has become the 'litmus test' in most debates over race, this Chapter is devoted exclusively to the issue and attempts to cover its most basic aspects.

Background

In its simplest form, affirmative action is the conscious effort to recruit people from previously disadvantaged groups for job and educational opportunities. Unlike the 1964 Civil Rights Act, which basically only outlawed discrimination, affirmative action went a step further by encouraging and then all but requiring the hiring and admission of people from targeted subordinate groups. Whereas the former step sought equality of opportunity, the latter aimed more at equality of results. Some liken it all to the beginning of a track race. The 1964 Act did bring blacks up to the starting line alongside whites, so to speak, by banning favouritism based on skin colour. But pre-existing barriers meant that they still could not compete properly. How could a black secure a decent job if because of his race he had been forced to attend an inferior college or university? And how could blacks gain entrance to elite competitive universities when they had been made to go to less good high schools? The answer lay in giving them a bit of a head start. The rules would be changed somewhat so that employers and admissions officers would be made to take them aboard while African

Americans caught up. If blacks were to be represented on campuses and at worksites at anything even remotely approaching their numbers in the overall population, standards would have to be lowered to admit them. However, this was a step that could be justified by past racism, and it was seen mainly as temporary medicine, a small extra push until they came up to scratch with others.

In the mid- and late 1960s the policy essentially meant aggressive recruitment, making an additional effort, or 'acting affirmatively', to find black talent that had been overlooked or ignored and give it the opportunity to develop. Yet it turned out that the pool of such talent was rather shallow, and so before too much longer more specific measures were introduced to achieve this. Strict racial quotas may have been banned by the Supreme Court in 1978, but during the Nixon administration of the early 1970s, a panoply of goals and timetables was brought in to make sure that African Americans got their share of employment and higher education positions. The government agency that supervised such matters, the Equal Employment Opportunity Commission, was given latitude to make decisions detailing how, when and where affirmative action was to take effect for all but the smallest companies and places of learning, and its directives largely remain in force today. Failure to comply invites fines and loss of government business contracts. Meanwhile, just about all the various federal, state and local government departments and agencies have implemented affirmative action hiring and promotion programmes of their own and seek to help minority owned firms by reserving a certain portion of public sector contracts to be done through them. These special allocations, known as 'set-asides', had long come to amount to at least 10% of all federal government business deals by the early 1990s.[1]

Affirmative action underwent change in other ways as well. Initially designed for blacks, it also came to include Asians, Hispanics and American Indians on the grounds that they too have suffered injustice in some form of another. The feminist movement of the 1970s saw to it that women got included as compensation for their generally inferior status in society. In the opinion of many, the scope of the programmes has also been altered so as to go beyond mere employment and university admissions arrangements. The busing of public school children, the redistricting of some congressional constituencies in the 1980s and early 1990s, and more recent efforts to strike a racial balance in juries and grant blacks and Latinos a certain percentage of mortgages, are all now said by many to be a form of affirmative action insofar as they constitute attempts at a rough kind of proportional representation based on ethnicity and skin pigmentation. Even

President-elect Clinton's pledge in 1992 to form a cabinet that 'looks like America' was in the opinion of a number of people another example.

Arguments about the Policy

For most Americans, the affirmative action debate centres on two distinct areas: the impact it has on everyday matters such as employment and higher education, and whether or not the policy can perform broader social good. As regards the former, many whites, especially white males, strongly resent being made to suffer what they see as loss of jobs and college placements to immigrants, a group that by definition never had to put up with historic injustices at all at the hands of the U.S. Government. Special treatment of this sort might not be so bad if it were accorded to all legal newcomers, but such is the nature of the 'racial spoils system' that only the non-white ones can benefit. Recently arrived immigrants from, for example, Russia and Eastern Europe are not permitted to take part, even if they happen to be as poor as arrivals from Colombia or Cambodia. Compounding the dissatisfaction is the belief that affirmative action hinders assimilation. By offering non-white newcomers a set of rewards simply because they are not Caucasian, the policy is said to be encouraging those from Third World countries to see themselves as oppressed minorities rather than as Americans and so remain separate and distinct from the bulk of the population.

A more fundamental criticism and one that opponents voiced well before immigration became a factor is that affirmative action causes reverse discrimination. Instead of blacks, it is now whites who are being targeted for unfair treatment inasmuch as the former are receiving continuing favouritism at the expense of the latter, who in many instances are thought to be the better qualified or more experienced candidates. African American high school graduates are admitted to many colleges and universities with lower entrance exam results than are whites. Caucasian applicants have been known to be barred from taking tests for local authority jobs to meet deadlined hiring goals. If some see this as a fair way of making up to African Americans for past harm, then others counter that by the 1990s those being favoured are not the same as those who suffered earlier legal discrimination. Conversely, the victims nowadays are those whites so young as not to have even been born when the sins of certain previous generations were taking place and yet who are being made to pay the price, even if they are poor.

Critics wonder just how long a policy that was originally conceived as being short term is going to be made to last. But it is the inherently divisive nature of affirmative action that opponents claim upsets them the most. By constantly making distinctions between people on the basis of pigmentation, the policy is keeping race to the fore in the national mind. In so doing, it is not only stoking tensions but is acting in flat contradiction to the pleas of the late Dr Martin Luther King, Jnr, that Americans should judge each other 'not by the colour of their skin, but by the content of their character'. Somehow, critics contend, the goals and aspirations of the early civil rights movement have become perverted.

For their part, proponents of affirmative action counter that such arguments are either misplaced or deliberate diversions. They insist that racism persists, albeit in a more subtle form today than before, and that while some progress has been made in 'levelling the playing field' over the years, preferential policies are still needed to give certain groups a more equal footing with others. They point to continuing disparities between blacks and whites in income and employment rates, to the findings of the Federal Government's 'Glass Ceiling Commission' on job promotions and to well documented slurs and epithets of the sort made by senior executives of the Texaco Oil Company in late 1996, as proof that highly placed whites are not all that favourably disposed towards blacks or other minorities. Remove affirmative action, they argue, and the moderate gains of the past few decades will stop. Indeed, matters will go into reverse. White employers and admissions officers will go back to taking on board solely their own kind. The condition of blacks will then relapse to where it had been prior to the 1970s, with African Americans lagging Caucasians even more than they do at present.

In contrast to critics, supporters maintain that affirmative action has the capacity to be socially beneficial. They say that it is essentially about inclusion, not exclusion. Properly implemented, it widens, not narrows, the pool of candidates to be considered, a process that can help whites, even white males, who might otherwise be bypassed or overlooked because of nepotism or the 'old boys network' way of doing things. Supporters concede that in the short term affirmative action often pits whites against others, but offsetting this is the bigger number of blacks gaining acceptance and being able to act as role models for younger members of their own race. At the same time, the existence of affirmative action reduces the chances of minorities thinking, reasonably or not, that they are victims of job discrimination when events do not go their way. All in all, backers of the policy claim that terms like 'reverse discrimination', 'quotas' and 'societal damage' are little more than red herrings concocted by white men fearful of losing their long held privileges.

As for the historical argument, many supporters see no reason for at least some of the beneficiaries being able to come from later generations. In their opinion, an entire race can be entitled to restitution for past wrongs in rather the same way as Jews who are descendants of those whose lands and bank accounts were seized in Europe during World War Two are now claiming restoration. Some maintain that even if affirmative action has taken on a life of its own and survived well beyond that which was at first intended, blacks are still entitled to continued special treatment, as three decades of preferences cannot possibly make up for three centuries of slavery and Jim Crow laws. Whatever the merit of such arguments, there can be little doubt that they and others like them concerning the impact of affirmative action on businesses, social class and black psychology have increasingly occupied many peoples' minds as the years have gone by.[2]

Results of the Policy

Perhaps a good deal of the debate about preferential policies might die down if it could be demonstrated that they work. Unfortunately, this is not easy. Studies showing the direct impact of the policy on subordinate groups have been rare and not particularly up-to-date. The fact that affirmative action policies have been adopted nationwide also hampers the investigation. Had New York, for instance, shunned racial preference schemes while California went ahead with them, then analysts might over time have been able to draw valid conclusions about the effectiveness of the policy by looking at racial data for the two states. But since the whole of the country embarked on affirmative action more or less together, such contrasts cannot be made. All this notwithstanding, an attempt is made below to measure the effectiveness of affirmative action, precisely because it is so central to the larger issue about whether the policy should be maintained.

Jobs and Education

There can be little doubt today that women and members of racial and ethnic minority groups – especially blacks, Latinos and Asian Americans – play a larger, more visible role in the world of work in the United States. Whereas non-Hispanic whites made up four-fifths of the total workforce in

1982, today they constitute only about three-quarters, and the portion is expected to continue to decline steadily into the 21st century.[3] Inevitably the figures are linked to immigration inflows, especially of Asians and Hispanics, and the categories of work to which they pertain include a host of menial, unskilled jobs. But there is solid evidence of increased minority representation in more desirable forms of employment. According to the Census Bureau, between 1967 and 1991 the portion of African American households earning $50,000 or more (in 1991 dollars) more than doubled from 5.2 to 12.1%.[4] And as we saw in Chapter 3, two out of five blacks now do white-collar work.

The key question is whether affirmative action can be credited with these types of improvements. In the mid-1990s one university professor, a former Equal Employment Opportunity Commissioner, calculated that no fewer than 5.5 million African Americans and Hispanics had been given jobs over the years that otherwise would not have been available to them.[5] Yet others point to minority progress in both jobs and schooling before preferences came into being, with the portion of blacks holding white-collar jobs increasing more than four fold between 1940 and 1970 and the percentage of 25- to 29-year old African Americans who completed high school going up even faster during the same time span. 'There is no reason to believe', maintains Abigail Thernstrom, fellow at the Manhattan Institute, 'that progress in these and other areas would have come to a halt without preferential policies'.[6]

Demographic change and a more tolerant climate of white opinion were said to be two factors already giving momentum to advances towards equality. Another was education, which anti-affirmative action groups say was doing an improved job in the 1960s of giving blacks the necessary skills to enter somewhat higher positions in the labour market. Since then, the quality of much minority schooling has declined. According to critics, the preferential policies of the 1970s onwards might have enabled African Americans to get into top ranking universities in far greater numbers than ever before, but proportionately fewer of them are completing their courses there, which many would say is the real aim. Supporters of the policy put forward a variety of explanations ranging from money to campus climate problems. So convinced is Microsoft chairman Bill Gates of the financial difficulties that he has pledged to spend $1 billion of his vast personal fortune in scholarships over the next 20 years to get more minorities not only to attend but to stay in higher education in general. However, critics say that affirmative action itself is to blame by allowing many African Americans into certain colleges under different and lower standards and then expecting them to compete with generally better prepared students from other groups.

That said, it would perhaps be wrong to conclude altogether that affirmative action has produced no good in this area. Some of the most recent research has found that while African Americans on the whole do receive lower grades and graduate at a lower rate than their white counterparts, those at the more elite places of learning often achieve notable success after they get their first degree. African Americans who complete their courses at the likes of Princeton and Dartmouth earn postgraduate degrees at rates identical to those of their white classmates and, if anything, are even more likely than the latter to obtain second degrees in the more prestigious subjects such as engineering. Indeed, the authors of one large survey discovered that among blacks with similar college entrance exam results, the more selective the college they attended, the more likely they were to graduate, get advanced degrees and earn high salaries in their careers.[7] Sceptics either express little surprise, given that workplaces and postgraduate schools also have preferential admissions, or wonder if this merely goes to show that it is attending a top institution rather than affirmative action that works. In the words of one observer: 'once you have been admitted to the rarefied community of a Harvard or Yale..., you are almost not allowed to fail'.[8] But the authors of the above report, two former 'Ivy League' presidents, contend first and foremost that it is the policy that counts and that allowing admission to people with lesser qualifications from generally disadvantaged groups can produce results over time.

The debate about results centres not only on whether preferences have altered the size but also the character of the African American middle class. Prior to the civil rights revolution, the black bourgeoisie was not only smaller than today but basically confined to the few niches of the economy not exposed to white competition. That, say supporters, has now changed:

> ...rather than simply ratifying the advantages of already affluent blacks, who traditionally advanced by servicing the segregated black community, affirmative action has helped to create a *new* black middle class, resting on professional and managerial positions within white society.[9]

Yet critics of the policy, while not disputing that the black middle class is now more integrated into the mainstream workforce than ever before, nonetheless claim that this group is by and large continuing to lead a sheltered existence. Most African American professionals are employed in the public sector, where federal, state and local governments assiduously practise preferential hiring and promotion and where job security is greater than elsewhere. Those who opt for the private sector tend to shun entrepreneurship; this despite the various set-aside aspects of affirmative action. All told, African Americans in the early to mid-1990s were running barely 3% of the nation's businesses and taking in less than 1% of the total gross receipts in the country.[10] Three-fifths of this miniscule figure came from government contracting preferences, a state of affairs suggesting to some that without official help these firms would fail. Minority businessmen with set-aside arrangements rarely make the transition from the protected government market to the much more competitive private one. Thus for critics, if set-asides have worked it is only in the narrow sense of doling out public money to keep certain businesses alive. Beyond that, they have achieved little, and in the opinion of opponents serious questions need to be asked about how frequently black firms 'leave the comfortable nest that set-asides give them and fly on their own'.[11]

Assessing the Price

Evidence about the results of affirmative action in terms of costs also appears to be mixed. Critics have talked about lower business efficiency resulting from the hiring and promotion of less qualified people. However, studies have shown this not really to be the case. Spending on government- and private sector administration and enforcement of affirmative action has reached an estimated $2 billion, money that presumably could have been spent elsewhere. But one investigation conducted by the University of California at Berkeley found no real loss of productivity. There were cases of less qualified workers being taken on board, but these, it was said, were dwarfed by those where companies genuinely enlisted minorities because of merit rather than skin colour. Another study of thousands of firms in five of the nation's biggest metropolitan areas found that statistical differences in productivity were insignificant between those contractors who complied with federal racial hiring guidelines and those who did not. Apparently most weaknesses in quality of work were soon overcome through in-service training.[12]

On the other hand, assessments about the moral consequences of the policy are a good deal less clear cut. Supporters of affirmative action say that there has been little proof of reverse discrimination. One examination of federal court decisions in job bias cases from 1990 to 1994 found only 21 individual complaints and 22 suits attacking preferential policy plans throughout the whole of the country. More than half the former and almost half the latter were rejected. Even fewer suits have been filed against colleges and universities over supposed double standards in admissions.[13] Yet critics contend that such studies are flawed because whites who encounter reverse discrimination are unlikely to lodge formal complaints. White men at the workplace are said to remain silent out of fear of being labelled as whingers or racists or simply of not being believed. Blue-collar whites, who by some estimates have lost out more than their white-collar counterparts over the years, are said often not to have either the money or the confidence to press their grievances through the legal system. As regards higher education, white and Asian students do not file complaints because in many instances they do not know for sure that they are the victims of discrimination. All they are definitely aware of is that the college or university to which they applied did not admit them. According to critics, a much better indicator than numbers of lawsuits of harm being done is national mood. And this, they say, has at times not been good, with recorded instances of racial tensions at workplaces and on campuses caused by perceived unfairness being too numerous to count. In response, supporters contend that much of the backlash of angry whites, especially during the early 1990s, stemmed from more general economic anxieties brought on at first by recession and then by stagnant incomes and corporate and government 'downsizing' than by preferential policies as such. In their opinion, hostility has abated somewhat now that jobs are more plentiful.

Sometimes supporters and detractors are able to use the same reference point to arrive at quite different conclusions about the impact of affirmative action. A good illustration is the 'parking spaces' analogy. In this, the number of admissions allocated to minorities at elite colleges and universities is likened to that of parking spaces for handicapped drivers outside a shopping mall. Eliminating the reserved space would have only a tiny effect on the parking options for non-disabled drivers but a potentially major one for those with disabilities. All the same, the sight of an open slot will frustrate many passing motorists looking for a space during busy periods. A number will believe that they would have been able to park if the space had not been reserved, even though this is most unlikely since in all probability it long would have been taken by another motorist who had arrived earlier on the scene. Supporters of affirmative action argue that so it is with preferential policies. The number of white students displaced by blacks through race based admissions seems to be large but in reality is quite small. According to one statistical argument, if more than half the blacks at selective colleges had been rejected, the probability of acceptance for another white applicant would rise only slightly, to 26.5% from 25%.[14]

Keeping such policies only marginally hurts members of the majority but significantly benefits the minorities who as a group would not otherwise be able to pursue quality higher education.

Yet opponents, while not necessarily disagreeing with the statistical conclusion, argue that the force of the above analogy is the opposite of what the pro-affirmative action groups assume. Preferential admissions may have affected whites hardly at all, at least as a group, but because so many people, like the drivers in the car park, *think* they have been treated unfairly, a great deal of broader harm has been created. For such opponents, the real results have been worsened race relations, as can be seen in the periodic bouts of tension. The adverse moral consequences of affirmative action may be limited, but the social ones have been larger.

Given the weight of evidence on both sides, such as it exists, a good tentative conclusion might be that affirmative action has not delivered all that its proponents had hoped, but equally, neither has it resulted in everything that its critics originally feared. One could perhaps say that it has not given African Americans real results in education and perhaps not in jobs. At the same time, however, there appear to be relatively few costs in terms of workplace inefficiencies and not all that many whites being cheated by seemingly double standards in college admissions policies.

Yet the impression in recent years has been one of failure. To some, this is the result of timidity on the part of the defenders of the programmes. The onslaught against preferential policies has been such that conservatives have been accorded the luxury of having it both ways in their arguments – namely, that affirmative action should be ended because it has failed (*e.g.*, in educating blacks) and because it has succeeded (*e.g.*, in securing job and college placements for blacks over whites). Others cite the propensity of some pro-affirmative action groups to play into their enemies' hands as a reason for the general negativity. Thus some civil rights activists also minimise progress, afraid that applauding it might suggest that the struggle is finished. The upshot of this double dose of pessimism from the hostile Right and the frightened Left, some say, is a picture of overwhelming gloom and of decades of federal intervention being of little avail. Worse, the refusal of some African Americans to admit improvement feeds on stereotypes. Not only is the public left with the impression that government efforts to aid blacks simply do not work but also that there are factors inherent in the black situation that prevent African Americans from getting ahead. No wonder some liberal writers occasionally feel obliged to round on certain minority organisations. Possibly well intentioned but misplaced

minorities to prove discrimination; and a 1994 declaration that the Civil Rights Act of three years' earlier dealing with workplace bias could not be backdated.

It was, however, in the mid- and late 1990s when the conservative justices truly began to show a mistrust of further government involvement in racial matters. In 1997, they refused to overturn California's Proposition 209, much to the disappointment of President Clinton. Scarcely less momentous was a decision in 1995 on 'set-asides'. The case on which the justices ruled here, *Adarand Constructors v. Pena*, involved a white road contractor who submitted the lowest tender on a guardrail job in Colorado, only to see the Government's contract awarded to a higher bidder who was chosen, at least in part, because he was Hispanic, a member of a minority group. The Court ruled not only that the deal here was unfair on the Caucasian businessman but that favouritism displayed towards minorities in set-asides was generally unconstitutional. The ruling has not put white entrepreneurs completely on a par with their non-white competitors in securing such contracts; for the former still have to prove that they are disadvantaged in some way, whereas the latter do not. Nevertheless, a door has been opened to white run small businesses, especially female owned ones. Then as regards the *Hopwood* case of 1996 the Supreme Court let stand a lower court decision covering Texas, Louisiana and Mississippi that race could not be used in college admissions. Some expect the courts to concur with the latest arguments of the anti-affirmative action camp in California that 'outreach' programmes informing minorities but not Caucasians of college or job opportunities are unconstitutional.

There can be no doubt that all this has had at least some adverse impact on African Americans. Black enrolment at public universities in the above three states plus California is down, but not in uniform fashion.[15] Whether it will stay down is a moot point. Proposition 209 and the *Hopwood* case affected public but not private universities in states such as California and Texas, so famous institutions like Stanford near San Francisco are continuing with preferences. Meanwhile, both these states and Florida have introduced 'percentage plans' as substitutes for affirmative action. In California, those in the top 4% of their public high school graduating classes statewide are guaranteed college admission. In Texas, the threshold applies to the top ten per cent. In neither state do these moves amount to the same concrete guarantee to racial or ethnic minorities as did preferences, but given that certain schools are overwhelmingly black or Hispanic it is hard to see how at least some members of both groups will fail to be admitted.

Equally open to debate is whether the jobs axe has fallen all that hard on African Americans. The two states that thus far have banned preferential hiring in their own public sector positions, California and Washington, do not have particularly large African American populations. Indeed, in each of them both Latinos and Asians are more numerous, and in Washington State, where more than 80% of the population is white, members of even these two groups are not all that common. Rather, the ones who might be most affected in that corner of the country are white women, even though they were not the focus of those opposing affirmative action programmes. As regards federal contracts going to minority owned companies, these have declined in the late 1990s, but not by much. The ingenuity of Clinton administration officials in exploiting the vagueness of Supreme Court guidelines in the *Adarand* case has spared more of these programmes than was originally thought possible.[16]

In other ways, too, the anti-affirmative action campaign has not necessarily turned out as anticipated. To date, the success of the crusade has not been matched at the federal level, where a deadlock between a Democrat controlled White House and a Republican dominated Congress has prevented the passage of any national reformist legislation, let alone an outright ban. Corporate America has got rather used to affirmative action, even if smaller businesses have not, and has made it plain that it will not back conservative moves to take California's Proposition 209 to the country. Already big firms with headquarters in the Pacific Northwest like Boeing, the aircraft manufacturer, and the high-tech company Microsoft have reiterated their intention to continue with preferential hiring even if the state of Washington does not. There are those who would say that it is too early to write off altogether special consideration policies just yet.

Other Groups

Most of the discussion about the racial aspects of affirmative action is conducted in terms of black-white relations. But preferential policies also have a bearing on other minorities. Indeed, their inclusion, particularly that of recently arrived immigrants, in programmes originally intended to be a kind of reparations to African Americans for past injustices has been a source of great annoyance to critics.

Two of the USA's other racial and ethnic groups, Latinos and Asian Americans, have been especially affected. In the case of the former, the impact has been more or less the same as that on blacks. The number of

Latinos admitted to public universities in California and Texas has fallen roughly in line with that of African Americans in the wake of Proposition 209 and lower circuit federal court rulings.[17] As with blacks, the likelihood of future economic success is now cloudier, but for Hispanics there are political implications as well. One possibility is that the brightest Latino students could well be drawn away from studying in California and Texas, the very states where they have the greatest chance to advance in public life because of their concentrated numbers. African Americans, whose population is considerably more evenly distributed across the country, do not face this risk.

With Asian Americans, however, the picture is more complex. Members of this group have been much more of two minds about the supposed attractions of affirmative action than either blacks or Latinos. On the one hand, Asian entrepreneurs have been rather enamoured of it, winning a disproportionate and seemingly ever growing share of federal government set-aside contracts.[18] On the other, younger Asian Americans are apt to feel robbed by it. So many have done so well in secondary school that university entrance requirements have often been raised very high against them to prevent their numerical domination of certain undergraduate student bodies, rather as happened to Jews in America before the Second World War. A further complication is that there are huge educational and economic gaps within the extremely diverse Asian American community, with Chinese- and Japanese Americans because of their almost excessively great pass rates usually losing out more than those of Southeast Asian background in getting to the higher learning establishment of their choice. The impact of all the recent changes is as yet a bit hard to discern, though the indications are that Asian Americans as a whole are coping reasonably well. Their numbers have risen at the University of California's campuses at Berkeley and Los Angeles.[19] Asian owned firms continue to get a good portion of set-aside contracts. Asian American public opinion does not seem too upset at the changes. Some 40% of it backed Proposition 209 in California in 1996, a bigger figure than was the case for either the black or Latino sections of that state's population.[20] It is thought that a similarly high percentage favoured 'Initiative 200', the Washington State equivalent in 1998, even though Democratic Governor Gary Locke, a Chinese American, was against it.

Still another group to consider is those of mixed race. To date, affirmative action has had no separate effect on them because they are not officially recognised as a distinct racial category. The old 'one-drop rule' dictates that those who are part white, part black be regarded as black, and so individuals in this category have been affected by all the recent changes in precisely the same way as other African Americans. Social convention has traditionally permitted those who are of mixed non-black blood more leeway in choosing their racial or ethnic category and so profit according to the circumstances. Presumably many accord themselves a minority status when it is in their interest to do so and they, too, now stand to lose in those parts of the country where preferential policies have been rolled back. But moreso than is the case with those who are pure Asian or pure Hispanic, mixed race individuals in all probability will one day have the capacity to exert influence of their own. As they become more numerous and more organised in their demands to be treated as a separate racial group, people of mixed blood pose a real threat to affirmative action, whose very existence depends on individuals being classified along well delineated racial lines. As the years go by, preferences are less likely to have an impact on them than they are apt to have on the policy. So far, civil rights advocacy groups have staved off a challenge to have the Census Bureau grant mixed racials a separate classification of their own, as we saw in Chapter 2, but many feel it is only a matter of time before change is made and that once this happens the days of affirmative action as America now knows it will be numbered.

Alternatives

As the debate about both merits and results has intensified, more people have proposed compromise solutions. The scope for give-and-take does exist insofar as the general public has consistently shown in surveys over the years that it favours some form of affirmative action, especially outreach programmes to the disadvantaged, although the majority are against anything that smacks of quotas and overt racial favouritism. This is particularly true of white women, whose belief that they have gained from the policy is often offset by its perceived impact on their menfolk.[21] The dichotomy explains the apparent contradiction of certain referenda results across the country in which voters in California and Washington State recently endorsed ballot initiatives but those in the city of Houston, Texas, in 1997 did not. The first two plebiscites explicitly referred to ending discrimination and preferential treatment in their wording, but the latter deleted such terms and, indeed, made it sound as if any form of affirmative action was being jeopardised.

One suggestion widely canvassed for a while was to substitute class for race. Minorities, who figure prominently in the ranks of the poor, would continue to get a lot of preferential treatment, but so too would the worst off Caucasians. The inclusion of the latter would mean that the former could get a helping hand without the dubious air of unfairness and so less public opposition would be generated. Meanwhile, the hitherto largely ignored underclass would finally get assistance that was more meaningful than mere state handouts.

Yet to civil rights groups, the above proposal, while attractive in some respects, has its faults. They argue that class based affirmative action would not create much extra workplace or campus diversity, as more than half of those below the poverty line are white. Colleges and universities would have to provide more money in scholarships than most have available. Furthermore, class oriented affirmative action would not be relevant to all types of preferences. As regards set-asides, for instance, how could one choose a business contractor based on class? Are there many poor ones and, if so, would government departments wish to do business with them? Even if these wrinkles could somehow be ironed out, could a Republican dominated Congress really be trusted to implement broad 'colour blind' programmes to aid the poor while the existing system was being dismantled?

Knowing the singularity of the black experience to past oppression in the U.S., some people favour confining affirmative action to African Americans only. Such a move would revert much of the policy to its original form and do away with a number of the anomalies of certain immigrants being able to claim special treatment but not others. Furthermore, many of the non-black minorities do not need this extra help. Asian Americans are often affluent. Despite some recent socioeconomic reversals, Hispanics of the second- and third generation as a whole seem to be doing roughly as well as some earlier white immigrant groups like Italians at the same stage of residence in the country. The intermarriage rate of both Asians and Latinos with whites is in any case quite high. But here, too, there are problems. The reform would not please special interest groups. Women, Hispanics and Asian Americans would surely protest, as would Native Americans, who if anything are even poorer and arguably have suffered worse historical mistreatment than blacks at the hands of whites. Finally, working class Caucasians, who tend to compete for jobs more often with blacks than with Asians, would have little reason to be enthusiastic about such a change, since they stand to gain nothing. It is thought that some African American leaders, after initially welcoming the suggestion, would express second thoughts out of fear that their people would be isolated against an overwhelmingly opposed public opinion, and so this suggestion, too, has been dropped.

Laissez-faire Republicans generally favour scrapping affirmative action altogether and putting nothing in its place. However, as this is politically unfeasible, a few on the Right moot the idea of having anti-discrimination laws limited to the public sector and leaving the private one to do as it pleases when hiring and promoting employees. Government has an obligation to treat its citizens equally, but businesses do not. Admittedly, some employers are bigoted, but conservatives counter that market forces exert a powerful incentive not to discriminate on racial grounds because if bosses select inferior employees they stand to lose money. Merit, therefore, and not skin pigmentation would be the ultimate determinant in a free enterprise economy, and the 'race neutral' or 'colour blind' aspects of the policy would lower resentment on the part of the aggrieved groups and so be socially beneficial. Yet others wonder if there can ever be such a thing as race neutral hiring and admissions in a society still dominated by whites. With the best will in the world, some Caucasian bosses will gravitate towards employing their own kind either through social connections or what sociologists call the 'affinity impulse'. Other white employers lack this basic good will. Even if the free marketers are right, they continue, and unfettered capitalism somehow did see to it that the most talented were chosen, how long would the process take? It could require years for the vagaries of the marketplace to catch up, and in the meantime minorities would suffer.

Still another possible alternative is to introduce what some people call 'developmental' affirmative action as distinct from the preferential sort that exists today. It is a proposal that like 'blacks only' affirmative action harks back to the earliest days of the policy in the 1960s. Rather than accord certain groups extra consideration like lower entrance requirements when applying for a job or university admission, developmental affirmative action would help bring them up to scratch through special outreach programmes beforehand. As with class based affirmative action, the disadvantaged would be targeted but this time standards would be maintained. Endeavours would be made to reverse whatever it is that has been causing poor performance, an undertaking that the current preferential programmes do not attempt.

A notable provider of 'developmental' or remedial affirmative action is the U.S. Army, which at every level seeks to promote diversity and widen the pool of candidates by offering special training classes to minorities. Able blacks, Hispanics, Native Americans and others who wish to attend the military academy at West Point but who lack entrance qualifications are admitted to a preparatory school for a one-year course at the end of which they must pass rigorous exams. Minorities looking for promotion lower down the ranks are offered similar help. The result is a fully integrated armed service with outwardly, at any rate, comparatively little racial tension because whites know that blacks and others have been made to measure up in advance.[22] Enthusiasts like President Clinton wonder if there are not lessons here for civilians. But critics are sceptical that such a system can be made to operate outside the rigid, hierarchical world of the armed forces. Industries and universities argue that they are not in the business of remedial and mentoring work and cannot bring pressure to bear in the same way as the Army. In the meantime, advocates of colour blind policies say that such programmes are still based too much on race and that the annual 'class composition goals' of West Point and other academies hint too much of quotas.

All of the above alternatives have been well publicised, but there are other, less well known suggestions that have also been put forward. A few black conservatives have advocated making racial, ethnic or gender discrimination a criminal rather than merely a civil offence. If someone can go to jail for stealing a car, the argument goes, he or she ought to be made to spend some time behind bars for damaging another person's livelihood through blatantly racist or sexist behaviour. Racially divisive affirmative action as such could be ended, with minorities relying instead on the old civil rights laws of the 1960s, knowing that they would now be backed by much tougher penalties. Yet critics say that enforcement would be difficult, as discrimination can at times be very hard to prove and a very heavy burden would be put on the shoulders of those making the accusations. Others have suggested means testing to enable disadvantaged people to get jobs or college admissions, but this is seen as being fundamentally the same as class based affirmative action.

In view of these shortcomings, it is small wonder that some see salvation in state sponsored 'percentage plans' of the type mentioned on page 160. Proponents think they offer a real chance of killing two birds with one stone by ending unpopular racial quotas, while establishing a proportionate number of minorities in state college and university systems overall. But if so, then it must be added that gaining admission into higher education establishments is still one thing and staying there quite another. Critics wonder how entrants from the less rigorous high schools will be able to keep pace unless there is a 'dumbing down' of coursework. This is particularly true of Florida, whose 'One Initiative' scheme would grant automatic entry to the highest one-fifth of each secondary school graduating class. Meanwhile others, noting that the new diversity in both California and Texas seems to be taking place only at the second- rather than the top tier state campuses, attack such schemes as a form of latter day 'Jim Crowism'. The upshot, they contend, is that blacks and Latinos are going to largely separate institutions from whites and Asians and so not getting a truly equal education.

Conclusion

Although the foregoing alternatives have their drawbacks and so have largely been unable to get off the ground, it would be wrong to think that some kind of compromise solution will not eventually materialise. Clearly affirmative action cannot go on indefinitely as it is. 'It simply strikes too many people as wrong, and the longer it exists, the more irritated about it many people become', writes one otherwise sympathetic black editor.[23] This is especially true of those who remember that the policy was originally intended to be only temporary.

Yet short of a sweeping decision on the issue by the Supreme Court, something that has not occurred in the past few decades despite numerous cases having been brought forward, outright abolition also seems unlikely. In general, ordinary Americans are opposed to preferences but for social reasons do not wish to end them straight away. Powerful interest groups on both sides of the debate need to be conciliated. And because the issue is thought to be genuinely difficult, a lot of people see compromise as enormously attractive. The question is what kind of middle ground is to be sought, reforming present day affirmative action so that the worst types of abuses are removed but the essential programmes remain intact, or scrapping much of it but removing the sting to minorities by introducing something in its place like school vouchers and tax incentive schemes for the inner cities. Bill Clinton, who promised in 1995 to 'mend it, but not end it', advocates the former course of action; prominent Republicans support the latter. The approach of each of the two sides in Washington, D.C., is quite different, and leaders of both parties will no doubt be tempted to try to define the debate in crude terms by pandering to particular sets of voters from time to time. But at least both in their own way are moving closer towards the political Centre on this issue. Almost surely, the current reevaluation of racial and ethnic preferences is unlikely to produce a complete victory for either side of the debate.

Notes

1   K. Jost, 'Rethinking Affirmative Action: Are Policies Based on Race and Gender Unfair?', *CQ Researcher*, 28 April 1995, p. 376.
2   Whereas opponents see affirmative action dragging companies down by forcing them to hire less qualified employees, proponents see it as a boon that helps such firms keep pace with the consumer profiles of the growing non-white population. While critics say that special preferences chiefly help those minorities who are already in the middle class, supporters contend that they by definition have not been aimed at the hardcore unemployed and poor and so such criticisms are irrelevant. Whereas detractors say that the policy makes blacks uncompetitive and ultimately raises issues of self-doubt in minorities' minds, advocates point out that other preferential schemes like special college admissions for sons of alumni have not in the past had a similar deleterious effect on white male beneficiaries. For a fuller discussion of such arguments, see D. D'Souza, *The End of Racism* (New York: The Free Press, 1995), pp. 332-6; C. Page, *Showing My Colour* (New York: HarperCollins, 1996), pp. 215-38; E. Cose, *Colour-Blind* (New York: HarperCollins, 1997), p 174; and S. Steele, *The Content of Our Character* (New York: St Martin's Press, 1990), pp. 111-25.
3   K. Jost, 'Diversity in the Workplace: Is It Good for Business?', *CQ Researcher*, 10 October 1997, p. 892.
4   E. Cose, *The Rage of a Privileged Class* (New York: Harper Collins, 1993), pp. 36-7.
5   The academic in question is Alfred Blumrosen, professor at Rutgers University law school. See Jost, 'Rethinking Affirmative Action', p. 373.
6   A. Thernstrom, 'Who's Afraid to Debate Affirmative Action?', *New York Times*, 22 November 1997, p. A15.
7   W.G. Bowen and D. Bok, *The Shape of the River* (Princeton, N.J.: Princeton University Press, 1998), pp. 97-8, 116 and 124. The authors do concede, however, that minority students for the most part do not excel academically at these institutions. The average Hispanic admittee in their study graduated at the 36th percentile of the class and the average black at the 23rd percentile.
8   See J. Traub, 'The Class of Prop. 209', *New York Times*, May 1999, VI, p. 44, where it is stated that the 60% black graduation rate at Berkeley so often quoted by certain conservatives in fact rose to 71% for African American students and 78% for Latinos in 1998. 'What is true', this writer goes on to say, *loc. cit.*, 'is that at lower levels of selectivity the gaps can be very large: 72% of white students, but only 39% of black students, typically graduate from Colorado University at Boulder.'
9   See E. Foner, 'Discrimination in Favour of Minorities Is Necessary' in B. Szumski (ed.), *Interracial America: Opposing Viewpoints* (San Diego: Greenhaven Press, 1996), p. 152. The emphasis was in the original quote.
10   D'Souza, p. 280.
11   S. and A. Thernstrom, *America in Black and White* (New York: Simon & Schuster, 1997), pp.450-1.
12   'Does Hiring Minorities Hurt?: Affirmative Action and Productivity', *Business Week*, 14 September 1998, p. 26.

13 Jost, *loc. cit.* One reason could well be that race and ethnicity play little part in admissions outside the more elite colleges and universities. According to one writer, most second- and third tier institutions 'cannot afford to be choosy about academic qualifications if they wish to fill their classes'. See P. Passell, 'Economic Scene: Surprises for Everyone in a New Analysis of Affirmative Action', *New York Times*, 27 February 1997, p. D2. Traub, p. 51, claims only 20% of colleges use preferences in any meaningful way.

14 Bowen and Bok, *op. cit.*, p. 36.

15 In California, there were big declines in the 1997 intake of first-year blacks at the state university system's two best known campuses at Berkeley (especially the law faculty) and at Los Angeles, but not really elsewhere. A similar disparity in new African American admissions occurred in Texas between the state's 'flagship' campus at Austin and the others. See 'Dark Clouds, Silver Linings', *Economist*, 11 April 1998, p. 20; also R.L. Stanfield, 'Affirmative Inaction', *National Journal*, 12 July 1997, p. 1414.

16 D.S. Cloud and K. Ackley, 'As Nomination for Civil Rights Chief Sputters, Lee Quietly Scores Victories on Affirmative Action', *Wall Street Journal*, 31 March 1999, p. A24.

17 *Economist, loc.cit.*; also P. Duggan, 'Texans Push College Diversity', *Washington Post*, 16 October 1998, p. A2.

18 Between 1986 and 1996, Asian American entrepreneurs more than doubled their share, from 10.5% to 23.6% of the Small-Business Administration's '8a' set-aside programme, the largest in the Federal Government. By contrast, the African American share fell from 50.5% to 36.7%, while the Hispanic portion held steady at about thirty per cent. during these years. See R. Sharpe, 'Asian Americans Gain Sharply in Big Programme of Affirmative Action', *Wall Street Journal*, 9 September 1997, p. A1.

19 *Economist, loc. cit.*

20 M.A. Fletcher, 'For Asian Americans, a Barrier or a Boon?', *Washington Post*, 20 June 1998, p. A9.

21 See Jost, *loc. cit.*, p. 374, in which a March 1995 *Los Angeles Times* poll is quoted showing that 54% of white women but only 35% of white men supported affirmative action programmes for minorities. 21% of the former and just 12% of the latter favoured the use of quotas.

22 The image of the U.S. Army having comparatively few skin colour resentments to deal with may be rather idealised. The Pentagon conducted a survey in 1999 that found that two-thirds of all personnel in the armed forces had experienced a racially offensive encounter in the previous twelve months. It was not a question of lack of tensions, but that they only rarely came into the open. See S.A. Holmes, 'Which Man's Army', *New York Times*, 7 June 2000, p. A1.

23 Cose, *Colour-Blind*, p. 173.

10 Immigration

Background

No country on earth has absorbed immigrants in greater numbers or variety or has done more to incorporate them into the national culture than the United States. Since 1820, when records were first kept, America has officially admitted more than sixty million foreigners, and that does not count the large numbers who arrived illegally. According to Census Bureau estimates, there were in March 1998 more than 26 million foreign-born residents in the USA representing almost 10% of the total population.[1] Each year another one million or so newcomers arrive, congregating for the most part in selected areas. Los Angeles, the second largest city in the country, is 40% foreign born.[2] Though there have been times when immigration has been proportionally as great or even greater, the type of people arriving in the past was different. In the late 1800s and early 1900s the newcomers were Europeans; today they are from every corner of the globe. Then they were the 'tired and poor' immortalised in the refrain chiselled into the Statue of Liberty; nowadays significant numbers who come are well educated and even wealthy. Then they were inclined to be diffident and accepting of the cultural and political landscape; today's have been known to be more assertive about seeking change. The sheer scale of the inflow of people who look, sound and sometimes act so differently troubles native born Americans who on occasion are apt to see the USA as a country under siege.

If the characteristics of the typical immigrant into the United States are somewhat different today from what they were a century ago, the factors prompting him or her to go there are more or less the same. They include such time honoured reasons as fleeing religious persecution and political turmoil and reuniting with family members. As always, economic factors are an inducement, and the boom decades of the 1980s and 1990s have reinvigorated the idea of the USA being a land of opportunity. Some, like members of the large retired Canadian community in Florida, come for climatic reasons. Others supposedly arrive to take advantage of what Americans see as their generous welfare system, although the main federal government benefits like Medicare and Social Security are strictly work related and only gradually acquired over the years.

The attractions of the United States to foreigners have generally remained constant over the decades. What has altered, however, are the background circumstances enabling them to come. In part it is a story of transformation and upheaval affecting much of the developed world. In today's era of multinational companies, globalised trade and ever swifter mass communications, it is inevitable that a growing cohort of highly skilled and well trained foreign business and professional people should be living in the USA, as they do in Western Europe and Japan. Cataclysmic events like the fall of the Soviet Union and the consequent civil unrest and disintegration of the former Yugoslavia and other states have set off an unprecedented level of international migration, and America has not been unaffected. Meanwhile, overpopulation and Third world poverty have added to the stream of hopeful entrants into the post-industrialised nations of the world, of which the USA is, of course, one.

Legislation

To a large degree, however, the swelling ranks of immigrants have for a long time been a direct consequence of revised legislation in the United States itself. Particularly instrumental was the 1965 Immigration Act, which shifted the basis of entry from national origin to family reunification. Whereas before basically only Europeans were granted admission, suddenly people from all parts of the world were being invited, especially if they already had relations in the country. According to the 1965 Act, up to 400,000 people were to be permitted entry each year, but close relatives of American citizens were exempted from the quota. Thus, once an immigrant became naturalised, he or she could bring his or her spouse, children, parents and siblings and so reconstitute if need be virtually an entire family in the USA.

The 1965 Act was at first slow to take effect. Europeans, the group originally thought to be the most likely to take advantage of the reform, were by this time beginning to prosper from a protracted period of peace and the advent of what was then called the Common Market. They were less drawn than before. But with the failure to stop communism in Southeast Asia in the 1970s and with worsening economic conditions in Latin America in the 1980s, the system of family preference was starting to result in a dramatic change. Before too long, upwards of a million people were being allowed entry each year, most of them from Third World countries and with at least half of the newcomers arriving on the strength of family ties with those already in the U.S. 'Chain migration' and 'pyramid immigration' began to become commonplace. In one often cited but hardly isolated case, a Philipino nurse who entered the U.S. in the 1970s wound up successfully sponsoring 45 members of her original family within ten years.[3]

Subsequent legislation reinforced this trend. The Immigration Reform and Control Act of 1986 was meant to halt illegal inflows, but it actually encouraged their growth. It created amnesties that allowed nearly three million former undocumented aliens – the great majority of them Latinos – to acquire legal residence and eventually become eligible for citizenship. The hope had been that the pardons, coupled with tough penalties on employers who knowingly hired undocumented workers, would put an end to the anomaly of having irremovable illegal people in the country and allow individuals to start again with a clean slate as regards the law. But within a few years almost the reverse proved to be true. By the late 1980s, a veritable cottage industry for forged documents had sprung up. People were once again entering the country secure in the knowledge that they could acquire good quality counterfeit papers and full of belief that if there had been one official forgiveness leading to permanent residency, it would only be a matter of time before there was another. Then in 1990 Congress passed an additional immigration act switching the basis of entry somewhat more towards jobs. Henceforth, those who were qualified professionals or who had a lot of money to invest in the country were to be given a bit more priority. But the needs of those who had relations abroad were not altogether abandoned, with the result that the overall ceiling on people allowed into the country was raised to 700,000 a year, thus ensuring a protracted influx.

Both the 1986 and 1990 Acts covered regular immigration. A somewhat older piece of legislation dealing with more special types of arrivals also served to increase the inflows. This was the 1980 Refugee Act, which set no upper limit on the number of either displaced persons or asylum seekers allowed into the country. Fifty thousand people was deemed to be the annual 'normal flow' based on an average of the total number of such individuals admitted during the 1970s. But a clause in the Act allowed a U.S. president to raise the number if an unforeseen emergency existed, something that has turned out to be the case in most of the twenty years or so since the passage of the Act. Starting with the crisis of the 'boat people' seeking to escape communism in Southeast Asia in the early 1980s to civil wars in Bosnia, Rwanda and various parts of east Africa in the 1990s, the U.S. Government has found it very difficult to limit the intake to 50,000 people a year. Adding to the problem has been the role of the courts, which whenever confronted with a case of disputed entry, have almost always sided with the would-be immigrant by expanding the categories of permissible asylum seekers to include not only those fleeing political and religious persecution but also people suffering discrimination based on, for example, gender and sexual orientation. Even those Chinese who refused to obey their country's one-child policy were being granted visas.[4]

Backlash

For a long time, Americans barely took notice. Then a reaction came that was ultimately to lead to a virtual national backlash. In the early 1990s, recession struck, and immigrants were increasingly being seen as unwanted people who were taking jobs that rightly belonged to Americans. An extraordinary set of events combined to present immigration as a menacing phenomenon. In 1993, foreigners who had slipped through the immigration net bombed the World Trade Centre in New York City. The media became filled with seemingly endless stories of Chinese smuggling ships, Haitian boat people, Cuban rafters and swarms of Mexican border jumpers, all of which fuelled anxieties about a chaotic world infringing upon the relative peace of the U.S. The inability of Washington, D.C., to halt the inflow of newcomers confirmed the growing doubts of many Americans at the time about the efficacy of big government.

Combined with all this were public expenditure concerns. Unlike the immigrants of the 1950s and 1960s, who in any case were not all that numerous, the foreign born of the 1980s and 1990s were for the most part not especially well educated. A survey completed in 1996 showed that while 12% of immigrants had postgraduate qualifications of some sort compared to 8% of native born Americans, more than a third of all newcomers had not finished high school or the equivalent, more than twice the percentage of the indigenous population.[5] Many came with only pre-industrial skills for a post-industrial society, and although a good number were able to find menial work, others failed to achieve even this, with the result that they were more likely than regular Americans to live in poverty and turn to certain kinds of welfare and other forms of assistance. Indeed, some were popularly assumed to be migrating to the U.S. just to receive these benefits and act as a drain on public resources; this at a time when both the states and the Federal Government were grappling with budget deficits. The perception was widespread in the early 1990s that the needs of immigrants as much as anything else were responsible for the high taxes and punishing interest rates that such deficits entailed.

Not surprisingly, the most pronounced anti-foreign sentiments appeared in California, where the economic downturn of the early 1990s was severest and where immigrants had arrived in the greatest numbers. In 1994, the people of California approved Proposition 187, a referendum that sought to deny basic social services, including education, in the state to illegal aliens. Although soon afterwards largely struck down by the courts as unconstitutional, Proposition 187 signalled to national politicians the depth of grassroots discontent with the Federal Government's immigration policies. Congressional Republicans, hoping to capitalise on anti-newcomer sentiments, made two key policy changes in the immediate background to the 1996 elections. In July of that year, they secured the passage of a landmark Welfare Act, which among other things denied all sorts of benefits like food stamps, Medicaid and housing subsidies to legal immigrants who had not spent at least five years in the country. Two months later the Republicans passed a new immigration act that cracked down on illegal aliens by doubling the number of agents patrolling the Mexican border, fining employers who knowingly hired illegals and even constructing a fence south of the city of San Diego, California, where a good many of the undocumented immigrants had been arriving. Provisions were also made to deport immigrants with criminal records, however minor, and earlier refugees whose homelands had now become politically stable enough for them to return.

Politics and other Difficulties

All the same, sizeable immigration into the U.S. continues more or less unabated. The legal inflow still amounts to about 900,000 people annually, with an estimated another 300,000 coming illegally every year.[6] The much touted legislation of the mid-1990s appears to have come to naught. Why is this the case? Electoral considerations are an important factor. Far from strengthening the Republican grip on power in Washington, the 1996 elections produced another round of gridlock, with President Clinton winning a second term in office in the White House and the Democrats even making a few inroads on the Republican majority in the House of Representatives. Any success that the Right had in attracting the native born white vote was more than matched by the mobilisation of the various immigrant communities, which gave their support to the Left in record numbers. Latinos are usually credited with making this turn of events possible, as it was largely their ballots in 1996 that enabled Clinton to become the first Democrat to win the electoral votes of Arizona and Florida since 1948 and 1976 respectively. However, there was a significant electoral shift with most of the other minority groups as well, to the point where the Asian American vote, which had been almost 2 to 1 in favour of Bush over Clinton in 1992, came close to being equally divided between Dole and Clinton in 1996.[7]

Disturbed by these results and alarmed at continued high ethnic minority turnout in subsequent local and mid-term elections, Republican Party strategists began in the late 1990s to have second thoughts on the matter. They did not altogether abandon plans to curtail immigration; rather, they simply began to think terms of piecemeal legislation. The aim now was only gradually to reduce the numbers and shift the emphasis still more from family ties to job skills as the main criteria for entry. In so doing, the Republicans not only hoped to keep employers reasonably happy at a time of labour shortages but also boost the core constituency for their own party because the new, educated and technically competent entrants would presumably have middle class conservative values. Meanwhile, to appease existing minority voters, the Republicans have dropped some of the more controversial aspects of their recent legislation. In 1997, the Immigration Act of the year before was partially rescinded to allow 150,000 refugees from the civil wars in Central America in the 1980s to stay after all. In 1998, congressional Republicans agreed to President Clinton's request to restore welfare benefits to a quarter million elderly and disabled immigrants. Token cultural gestures were made, of the sort mentioned in Chapter 8. While all this has been taking place, angrier members on the Right have been redirecting their main fire away from immigrants to the U.S. bureaucracy as being most responsible for recent messes. Bills have been introduced to overhaul, even abolish, the unpopular Immigration and Naturalisation Service (INS) for having been inefficient and perhaps even politically motivated when dealing with aliens.

Neither the Republicans nor the Democrats wish to antagonise the feelings of the various ethnic minority groups, especially as they constitute the fastest growing segment of the voting population. This is the primary reason for some of the most recent anti-immigrant legislation being undone. Yet leaders of both parties also failed to achieve meaningful restrictions in earlier years when Latinos were relatively uninvolved in politics and Asian Americans and others were not numerous enough to carry much weight. Clearly there must be other explanations apart from electoral considerations for the longstanding inability of America's lawmakers to tackle the problem effectively.

Many would say that one such explanation is ideological confusion. Whereas other issues are more or less neatly delineated between Left and Right, immigration defies the usual labels and, indeed, often provides some strange political bedfellows. Thus traditionally left-wing environmentalist groups, worried about overpopulation, have been known to join forces with conservatives who advocate preservation of the ethnic and cultural status quo in calling for tighter restrictions. At the same time, traditionally right-wing forces like business interests, free market economists and civil libertarians have teamed up with their frequent adversaries in the immigrant communities to oppose tougher legislation. In Congress, cross-party alliances have been formed, while in various parts of the country civil rights advocates and trades unionists are split about whether the newcomers are likely to be a help or hindrance to their respective causes.

The upshot is near paralysis because coalitions of forces from both inside and outside a government can torpedo legislation. Thus a proposal in the 1980s to issue counterfeit proof national identification cards never got past President Reagan's cabinet because of objections of libertarian conservatives who saw it as the first step down the path towards totalitarianism. A 1990s plan for having a computerised registry of the nation's entire workforce met a similar fate for essentially the same reason. The 1986 Immigration Act of the Reagan administration sought to crackdown on illegal immigration but had to compromise by allowing an amnesty for crop pickers to satisfy otherwise conservative farmers wanting cheap labour. Nearly a decade later a Republican bill in Congress to curb legal immigration came unstuck for a variety of reasons, not least of which was the opposition of employers, this time high-tech firms wanting more foreign workers to compensate for the skills shortage at home. Conversely, the 1990 Immigration Act, in which Democrats increased the number of legal foreign entrants to the country, would have raised the ceiling much further but for the objection of some labour organisations fearing job competition with their own members just as a recession was taking place.

Of course, none of this is to say that there has been no success in curbing inflows in recent years. A longstanding open door policy towards Cuban refugees was ended in the mid-1990s when it became apparent that President Castro was trying to use mass emigration as a safety valve to his country's economic problems and to apply foreign policy pressure on the U.S. The Clinton administration agreed to take in the latest batch of emigres – some 20,000 people on makeshift rafts and boats who had been detained at a nearby naval base – but no more, and so far the new policy has held. However, in related circumstances governments have been less triumphant. Thus the influential Jewish lobby has seen to it in Washington that large numbers of East European migrants of their faith continue to reach the U.S. even though the Cold War has ended. Meanwhile, African Americans, angered at how the mostly white Cuban rafters of the mid-Nineties had eventually been permitted entry for one last time but not the predominantly black Haitian ones suffering similar problems, demanded more evenhanded treatment. In 1997, they got President Clinton to relent and use his executive authority to spare from deportation some of those of the latter nationality who had smuggled themselves into the country. Once again, lobbyists and special interest constituencies were keeping the numbers higher than they otherwise would have been.

Illegals

Coexistent with all this are the unalterable facts of geography. The frontier with Mexico, the country through which the majority of illegal immigrants travel to get to the USA, is two thousand miles long. Throughout the 1990s, border security has been increased with the building of concrete embankments and huge perimeter fences at crossing points near El Paso, Texas, and San Diego, California, where the terrain is relatively flat. Elsewhere the frontier mostly runs across either the Rio Grande or desert canyon or mesa that are too extensive to supervise closely. In any case, the extra border agents hired to patrol these areas have been given such a priority to hunt for illegal drugs, at least 50% of which enter the U.S. via Mexico,[8] that attention has been drawn away from undocumented human traffic. Knowing this, those migrants without proper papers have been circumventing blockaded areas and crossing the desert, enlisting the services of smugglers to avoid the most perilous spots. Most succeed in reaching their destination. A 1997 study concluded that while increased border surveillance has affected migration patterns, it has done little to prevent unauthorised entry. Illegal casual daytripping has been substantially reduced, and undocumented Hispanics already in the U.S. have not been visiting home as often as before. But determined Latinos who want to go north permanently have not really been put off coming.[9]

Yet it has to be said that even if the U.S. authorities could somehow seal off the entire Mexican frontier, the problem of illegal immigration would still not be ended. For all the talk of human smuggling and 'wetback' crossings of the Rio Grande, the fact is that large numbers of undocumented aliens enter the country by other means. The imposition at airports and other places of entry of a substantial fee and a 150-day waiting period for work permits has been of limited value in restricting immigrant practice of applying for asylum on the grounds of supposedly being in danger of persecution at home and then disappearing into the general population. It has been claimed that 'thousands upon thousands' are doing this upon arrival in New York City alone each year.[10]

Many prefer economic diplomacy to detection and enforcement as a solution. If the Latin American economies can somehow be bolstered, or so the argument goes, the pressures south of the border to migrate will be reduced. Expensive surveillance measures could then be cut back, affronted Mexican feelings reduced, and U.S. taxpayers saved a lot of money. Such were some of the hopes of the Bush and Clinton administrations when they respectively negotiated and signed NAFTA with Mexico and Canada in the early 1990s. Neither President saw free trade as a 'quick fix' to the illegal immigration problem. Indeed, both anticipated that the initial impact of NAFTA would be to increase immigration, legal and illegal alike, because the treaty needed free movement of labour to work. But both felt that as time wore on the Hispanic flow northwards would begin to ebb as some firms relocated in Mexico and as the wage gap with the USA gradually narrowed.

To some extent, this has happened. Between 1993 and 1997 Mexican exports to the USA more than doubled, and factories there selling abroad took on nearly an extra 500,000 workers. But many say that the latter figure represents only a modest increase in a nation of more than ninety million people. Most of the benefits have been felt only in the northernmost part of the country along the U.S. border, and it is possible to argue that the limited gains there owe as much to the devaluation of the peso in 1995 as to any treaty. It is still early days, but so far NAFTA has not given the bulk of ordinary Mexicans much incentive to stay put. The predictions of the more cautious analysts that free trade would require up to two generations' time to take proper effect in stemming large scale migration seem all too likely to be realised.[11]

Economic Considerations

Most of the above discussion is based on the assumption that Americans want tighter restrictions. Yet this is not altogether true. For years employers in low skilled U.S. enterprises have sought the services of illegal immigrants as a cheap supply of labour, as have significant numbers of affluent individual Americans for employment in their homes. A scandal of sorts erupted in 1993 when it emerged that one of President Clinton's cabinet appointees had wittingly hired two undocumented Peruvians to work as family nanny and chauffeur. The resultant furore forced the President to withdraw the nomination, even though critics acknowledged that the practice was widespread among wealthier people in the country.

Recently there have been requests on the part of employers for increased legal immigration as well as turning a blind eye to illegal entry. With the economy several years into expansion, labour markets have begun to get tight, and in a number of places an actual dearth of workers has started to appear. So badly needed are computer specialists and software programmers that the number of visas issued under the H-1B programme, which permits highly skilled foreigners temporarily to fill vacancies, was raised from 65,000 in 1998 to 115,000 in 1999, and is possibly set to rise to 200,000 annually.[12] But scarcities also exist at the other end of the labour market, with West Coast fruit growers, for instance, being so concerned about finding pickers that they have backed a pilot guestworker programme bringing 20,000 migrants from south of the border into the country.[13] In many ways, America's large intake of immigrants is not only a question of abundant supply but also large domestic demand.

Coinciding with all this is a tentative shift in public opinion towards greater tolerance of newcomers. A 1997 poll of several thousand ordinary Americans revealed that only 36% of respondents thought immigration should be decreased from current levels, compared with 65% in 1993.[14] A highly publicised referendum held in 1998 by the Sierra Club, one of the oldest and largest environmentalist groups in America, resulted in members refusing to go along with a motion calling upon the Government to reduce immigration as a means of limiting U.S. population growth and preserving natural resources. Whether the people interviewed and balloted had truly come to believe long held pro-immigration arguments that the arrival of low wage, younger newcomers helps both keep down prices and fund Social Security or whether they simply felt less threatened because the economy had improved is a debateable point. The fact is that by the end of the 1990s there was little political capital to be gained from taking a strong anti-immigrant stance. Restrictionist policies were no longer attracting votes among native born citizens, even if they still counted for a great deal among naturalised newcomers. This, too, is another reason for Republicans being more willing to take their time of late in legislating the matter.

Assimilation

Americans seem to have become more willing of late to put up with foreigners permanently coming to their shores. However, it is tolerance of a somewhat different sort that in the opinion of many has a lot to answer for as regards assimilation worries. The United States protects in law more than it ever did differences in language and in culture. Whereas at one time a rigorous 'Americanisation' programme had been in place in which immigrants were strongly encouraged to take up civics courses and learn English in order to live up to the national motto *E Pluribus Unum* ('Out of Many, One'), now a laissez-faire, if not worse, approach exists allowing newcomers to retain or even develop further their roots from their homelands. Previous talk of America being a 'melting pot', or common culture, has in a number of quarters been replaced by new metaphors labelling the country as a 'mosaic' or 'salad bowl', terms that convey a sense of separateness or distinctiveness among different groups.

At the root of the matter, according to critics, are the multiculturalists. These are minority spokespersons, often native born and said to be in many cases self-appointed, who place great emphasis on the need to maintain one's ethnic identity in the belief that all heritages and value systems are in the end of equal worth. None, including the European based ones of white people, is really superior to that of any of the others, and that being the case, there is no particular reason for immigrants to have to abandon their native tongues and traditions for the wholesale adoption of Anglo-Saxon ways. Expecting newcomers to do so is a sign of intolerance on the part of the English-speaking majority. Requiring them to do so is tantamount to a modified form of ethnic cleansing. By spreading such beliefs, multiculturalists are said to be preserving not just foreign traditions in the name of immigrant self-esteem, but they are ultimately threatening the very existence of the country by creating many disconnected and competing ethnic blocs interested mainly in their own rather than the national good.

But critics contend that white policy makers and officialdom have been almost as much to blame. Not only have they allowed themselves to be intimidated by multiculturalist accusations of racism, but they are also said to have permitted immigrants to take advantage of benefits originally intended for others, thereby enabling feelings of separateness to flourish. While earlier waves of newcomers were under the necessity of blending in quickly in the absence of a welfare state, later ones who failed in the workforce were, until the passage of some new laws in the mid-1990s at any rate, spared having to return home by a system of government handouts, whether they were citizens or not. And as critics are quick to point out, even this most recent legislation has been sufficiently undone so as to permit refugees and select groups of new arrivals to continue collecting public assistance. Similarly, the decision of policy makers to extend affirmative action to include others beyond native born blacks has encouraged many immigrants not to think of themselves simply as Americans but more as disadvantaged minorities entitled to special employment and education treatment. Add to this improvements in transportation and communication, making it easy to keep in touch with those in the old country, and it is understandable why a number of observers regard the traditional assimilation 'melting pot' model of the early 1900s to be endangered today. The fact that Mexicans do not have to cross any oceans but can simply arrive on foot into territory that many of them see as historically being theirs only heightens these fears.

Left-wing multiculturalists have had much to say about assimilation. But just as outspoken, if to date less influential, are the right-wing nativists. They also do not place much store in America absorbing aliens, albeit in an entirely different manner. While multiculturalism holds that immigrants should not have to mix in, nativism claims that they *cannot* do so. If most nativists today do not insist that one be born in the United States, as the term implies, they do nonetheless have a very narrow definition of what it means to be an American and argue that the bulk of the most recent wave of newcomers fail to meet it. Unlike those caught up in the great incoming movement of a hundred or so years ago, today's arrivals are overwhelmingly non-European. Between 1990 and 1996 77% of incomers came from Asia and Latin America alone.[15] They are so alien that they have little understanding of basic Western concepts of democracy and civic responsibility, still less of subtler Anglo-Saxon notions of justice and fair play. Any hope of making true Americans out of such individuals is in the opinion of the nativists hopelessly idealistic.

In the view of many nativists, not only can the vast majority of recent immigrants not be assimilated, but many do not wish to be so. As evidence, they draw attention to old-country styles of dress and eating habits among the more senior entrants into the U.S. and the continued widespread use of Spanish rather than English in cities like Miami, even though much of the Cuban population there has been living in Florida for decades. Some nativists suspect immigrants of more overtly sinister intentions. In this connection, all Middle Easterners are seen as potential terrorists in the wake of the bombing of the World Trade Centre building in

New York in 1993, just as Asian businessmen are suspected of being subversive following revelations in 1996 that some had been secretly funding political parties during the election campaign of that year. More generally, nativists worry about the general direction of American foreign policy as the migrants arrive and wonder if the inflow will ultimately work to the benefit of Third- rather than First World interests. For these and other reasons, nativists clamour for such solutions to the immigration 'problem' as reducing, even eliminating, annual inflows; the passage of 'English only' legislation in the U.S.; and the deportation of those who refuse to conform.

Taken together, the multiculturalists and the nativists dominate much of the debate about assimilation in the United States. Yet there are others who also take part in the discussion, and they by and large do not have nearly so many reservations about aliens trying to blend in. Included in the loose ranks of this third group are social scientists and political theorists of both the moderate Left and Right who generally see little danger of the newcomers not fitting in. People in this middle category are inclined to point to surveys such as one published in the *New York Times* in the spring of 1998 showing a preference for English among nearly nine out of ten 18-year old immigrants across the nation as evidence that fears about absorption have been badly overdone.[16] But they cite other forms of everyday practice as well and argue that the devotion of younger immigrants to American tastes in dress, music and consumerism in general, not to mention growing rates of intermarriage, as definite signs that events are for the most part turning out fine.

These more relaxed onlookers concede that sometimes the absorption is only halfway undertaken, but they contend that it is nonetheless proceeding in the right direction. Thus as regards sports, the avid interest that many Latinos of all ages tend to exhibit in baseball to some extent compensates for their general preference for soccer to American football. An exception to this trend can perhaps be found in the area of social morals, where the nightmare of many immigrant parents coming from more inhibited rural developing societies is that their offspring might get caught up in teenage sex and drug activities so prevalent in much of the U.S. Yet many would say that resistance here is a positive rather than a negative step and one aimed more at preventing immigrant children from becoming too American, in a manner of speaking, rather than not American at all. In this context, foreign born mothers and fathers can be said to be doing in the moral sphere what immigrant workers through their energy, ambition, toughness and adaptability are accomplishing in the economic one – helping preserve traditional national ideals better than some of the native born population.

Optimists such as these believe that assimilation is taking place every bit as fast presently as it was during the early years of the 20th century, if not faster. Perceptions are often otherwise because the sheer numbers involved nowadays enable the new arrivals to colonise large chunks of certain cities and so keep the more recent arrivals highly visible and apparently separate. In the case of Latinos there is the further consideration that their immigration pattern has to a large extent been quite different from that of other groups. While most European and Asian newcomers have reached the U.S. in clearly defined waves, the movement of people across the Rio Grande has been an almost continual stream. The steady flow has meant that no matter how quickly Hispanics learn the English language and American ways, their community retains the status of an immigrant, Spanish speaking minority group thanks to the constant turnover. Yet research has shown that considerable numbers of new arrivals regard the *barrios* as little more than starting off places before they move elsewhere and that like blacks, Asians, Hispanics and Arabs are all relocating in the suburbs, sometimes as soon as possible.[17]

Not that there is no cause for concern, even as regards the young. The tendency of certain immigrants to gravitate towards particular types of employment has created job niches by ethnic group of the type described about Asian Americans, for instance, in Chapter 8. And these in turn have reinforced a sense of separation of Mexicans, Philipinos and Koreans from each other, as well as from the native population. The relatively high dropout rate of Hispanics from school to some extent offsets their willingness to learn English. The advent of an 'hourglass' labour market, in which there is an abundance of high and low paying jobs but with the technological revolution and the collapse of unions scarcely any blue-collar transitional ones, has potentially ominous implications. Such developments create occasional talk about 'segmented assimilation', a process in which some incomers follow the classic course of joining the middle class, while others get downwardly absorbed into a hostile underclass, while still others wind up in a kind of nether world of Eurocentrism by day but reverting to immigrant enclaves at night, with children and parents taking different approaches. Meanwhile, sometimes the assimilation cuts both ways. Native-born Americans pick up Spanish words, eat Asian and Mexican foods, and fall under the sway that immigrants of all backgrounds have exerted from time to time in the arts and in the world of entertainment.

But optimists see little reason for undue worry. Employment pigeonholing by ethnic group existed in the past and was eventually overcome. The 'hourglass' economy is serious but dangerous only over the longer term. Two-way assimilation based on food and a handful of words is trivial and possibly a force for good inasmuch as it helps create a progressive American identity that goes beyond the old world of Europe. The main point is that the will to be absorbed in the most important areas – language, suburbanisation, politics – is there. And progress would be greater still were it not for native born segregationist practices like 'white flight' to the outer suburbs and the propaganda of the multiculturalists, which has won over much of the Anglo-Saxon Establishment, though not necessarily the immigrants themselves.

On this last point, recent events would seem to bear out the above analysis. While educators continue to accede to the demands of ethnic activist leaders by promoting multiculturalism in school and college courses, the ethnic rank and file have increasingly become lukewarm, if not indifferent. Thus a suggestion in early 1998 that the San Francisco Board of Education introduce a sizeable quota of minority authors on the city's high school reading lists did not get the universal backing of Asian and Hispanic parents, and after an initial storm the plan was later largely and quietly diluted.[18] To the dismay of La Raza and other minority advocacy groups, about 40% of Latino voters in California later that year supported Proposition 227, which sought to end public bilingual education in the state.[19] Later still in 1998 substantial numbers of Asian Americans in Washington State contradicted the urgings of their spokesmen and voted for Initiative 200, a ballot to end affirmative action there. The swiftness with which these events followed upon each other suggests to some that the average immigrant is becoming disillusioned with notions of special treatment and distinct status. Even some minority politicians at the local level are said to be starting to share the same feelings.[20] However, other observers think differently, and equally recent developments pertaining to immigrants becoming Americans perhaps tell another story.

Naturalisation and Dual Citizenship

During the 1990s, it was not just the number of newcomers to the United States that skyrocketed but also the number of those who went a step further and opted to become U.S. citizens. Whereas about 250,000 foreigners became Americans in 1992, a million did so in 1996.[21] And if anything, the number of applications has grown since, so much so that the government department in charge of such matters, the INS, cannot handle them all. By the end of 1998, the backlog of those applying approached two million people.[22]

Several factors have contributed to this rise, including much of the legislation mentioned earlier in this Chapter. The 1986 Act, which granted a once-and-for-all amnesty to longstanding illegal immigrants, allowed some three million people to become U.S. citizens after several years of permanent residency. Many chose to do this once the option became available in 1993. More applied in the mid-1990s as first California in Proposition 187 and then the country as a whole sought to deny public assistance to certain types of non-citizens. Meanwhile, the cost of renewing visas kept going up while that for becoming naturalised did not, and many saw the latter as ultimately the cheaper alternative. The number of applications spurted to a million in 1996 as elections loomed and ethnic minorities hoped to punish the Republican Party for its stance against newcomers in the Immigration Act of that year. Perceiving most immigrants to be potential Democrats, the Clinton administration is said to have helped by coaxing the INS to launch the 'Citizenship USA' programme to speed up naturalisation procedures in time for the voting. Since then, Mexico has become the latest of several Latin American countries formally to adopt dual nationality. The practical effect of this has been to encourage millions of Mexican emigres to become naturalised U.S. citizens, safe in the knowledge that in doing so they will no longer be losing property ownership and other rights in their homeland.

The rapid growth in the number of immigrants becoming full-fledged Americans has provoked much comment. To all outward appearances, it is yet another sign that assimilation is proceeding apace. Why would so many foreigners be applying, unless they had come to embrace the American way of life? Yet some are not altogether certain. Noting how the surge of applications has coincided with threats to cut off welfare benefits, a number of observers suspect that many immigrants have become citizens for selfish economic reasons rather than out of any sense of acquired civic responsibility. The INS is thought to be guilty of having encouraged them in this behaviour by simplifying tests and watering down citizenship requirements and so devaluing the process to the point where some fear immigrants are taking naturalisation 'about as seriously as joining a health club', in the words of one commentator.[23] Meanwhile, Republicans accuse the Clinton administration of rampant carelessness. According to them, not only did the President indulge in dubious immigration politics in 1996 to boost his chances of getting reelected, but in his haste to simplify procedures he had the INS eliminate many background checks, with the result that thousands of immigrants with criminal records were allowed to become U.S. citizens.

But it is the tendency of the latest set of naturalised citizens to opt for dual nationality that is causing most concern. Whereas earlier waves of immigrants were only too willing to break ties completely with the old country upon becoming Americans, an increasing number of today's newcomers are reluctant to do so. Although the phenomenon of dual citizenship is arguably little more than a reflection of living in an increasingly mobile world where one has a transnational existence with family living in more than one country, many Americans profess not to understand it. They wonder about the loyalty of such people and moot the possibility of wartime defections and the risk of industrial as well as political espionage. Dual citizenship raises awkward questions not just about allegiances and assimilation but also more tangible matters like military service, extradition and taxes.

Once again, particular alarm is voiced in some quarters about Mexico, a country that has century old territorial claims to large tracts of land in the American Southwest. The fear is not just that Mexicans will affect domestic politics by coming in great numbers but still more that they will be tempted to migrate north to try to influence America's policy towards their native country. Others counter that these colonisation theories are irrational and that dual citizenship, far from weakening national identity, will actually strengthen it by encouraging the participation of millions of those who hitherto had felt excluded and alienated from the U.S. political process.

Conclusion

Reflecting on the immigration issue of recent years, one might be forgiven for wondering about the commotion of the early to mid-1990s. The most dire prophecies of pessimists like Reform Party leader Pat Buchanan have not materialised. Newcomers from Asia, Latin America and elsewhere have not necessarily become multiculturalists. Environmental disasters linked to overpopulation are conspicuous by their absence. Economic growth continues apace. Indeed, on this last point some go so far as to say that the prolonged expansion has taken place not so much in spite of but because of immigration. By arriving in large numbers, foreign arrivals managed to fill five million of the more than twelve million jobs that the 'new paradigm'

U.S. economy created between 1990 and 1998. Had it not been for them, America's central bank, the Federal Reserve, would have had to raise interest rates long before it started doing so in mid-1999 to check wage inflation, thereby slowing the industrial, manufacturing and service sectors much earlier than actually happened. Far from causing more unemployment, the newcomers have in fact been playing a big part in keeping it lower than it otherwise would have been.[24] Even the great debate about the case of Elian Gonzalez, the five year old boy rescued on Thanksgiving Day 1999 off a south Florida beach, was arguably more about America's Cuban policy than her handling of asylum seekers and refugees.

Yet it would be wrong to infer that immigration is now for all intents and purposes a dead issue. For one thing, party politics dictate otherwise. The type of incomer who would supplement the core constituency of the Republicans is not one and the same as the sort who would bolster the rank and file support of the Democrats. As long as this remains a fact of American political life, the controversy of who should gain entry will not go away, the silence on the matter of presidential hopefuls George W. Bush and Al Gore during the 2000 election campaign notwithstanding. For another, the ground on which the protagonists contest the issue keeps shifting. Worries about bilingualism have now often been replaced by concerns over dual citizenship. Anxieties about additions to one side or the other of the 'colour line' now compete with questions as to whether the newcomers, especially Latinos, might pursue some third course between the straight line blending in of white Europeans and the path of permanent aggrievement of blacks. Even the debate about welfare has undergone mutation rather than die in the wake of reformist legislation. Whereas before 1996 the arguments primarily had to do with the nature and extent of alleged freeloading, now they tend to centre on whether present policy is creating a new underclass in America and all that that entails for assimilation efforts.[25] Add to this the likelihood of a future recession leading to calls for tighter restrictions and the fact that immigrants and their native born offspring already make up a sizeable and rapidly growing segment of the total U.S population, and it is not too much to conclude that the 'forgotten issue' of the 2000 presidential campaign will have to be directly addressed again.

Notes

1   G. Escobar, 'Immigrants' Ranks Tripled in Thirty Years', *Washington Post,* 9 January 1999, p. A1.

2   C. Clark, 'The New Immigrants: Do They Threaten the American Identity?', *CQ Researcher*, 24 January 1997, p. 51.
3   L.E. Purcell, *Immigration* (Phoenix: Oryx Press, 1995), pp. 103-4.
4   D. Masci, 'Assisting Refugees: Do Current Aid Policies Add to the Problems?', *CQ Researcher*, 7 February 1997, p. 112.
5   W. Booth, 'One Nation, Indivisible: Is It History?', *Washington Post*, 22 February 1998, p. A1.
6   See M. Lind, 'Legal Immigration Harms American Workers', in T.L. Roleff (ed.), *Immigration: Opposing Viewpoints* (San Diego: Greenhaven Press, 1998), p. 78.
7   D. Carney, 'Republicans Feeling the Heat As Policy Becomes Reality', *Congressional Quarterly Weekly Report*, 17 May 1997, p. 1133.
8   M. Valbrun, 'Border States, Clinton Feud on Immigration', *Wall Street Journal*, 26 February 1999, p. A16.
9   R. Suro, *Strangers Among Us* (New York: Alfred A. Knopf, 1998), p. 270. Contrary to popular impression, it was this daytripping that once accounted for the great bulk of illegal entry. In the early 1990s, more than 3 million undocumented people annually entered the U.S., but ninety per cent. of them did not stay permanently. The majority of these were 'sojourners' or temporary migrants, mainly seasonal labourers from Mexico, who crossed and recrossed the border every working day or week. See R.D. Griffin, 'Illegal Immigration: Does It Damage the Economy and Strain Social Services?', *CQ Researcher*, 24 April 1992, p. 374.
10   Purcell, p. 100.
11   J.W. Anderson, 'Mexico Gets a Big Boost from Exports', *Washington Post*, 30 January 1998, p. A15; also D. Masci, 'Mexico's Future: Is It on the Path to True Democracy?', *CQ Researcher*, 19 September 1997, p. 825.
12   R.J. Samuelson, 'Ignoring Immigration', *Washington Post*, 3 May 2000, p. A23.
13   See the leader article 'Middle Class Immigrants' in the *Wall Street Journal*, 10 July 1998, p. A14.
14   W. Branigin, 'Immigration Advocates to Seek Softening of Laws', *Washington Post*, 30 January 1998, p. A13.
15   W. Branigin, 'Immigrants Question Idea of Assimilation', *ibid.*, 25 May 1998, p. A13.
16   C.W. Dugger, 'Among Young of Immigrants, Outlook Rises', *New York Times*, 21 March 1998, p. A1.
17   C. Clark, pp.53-4. That said, 30% of all third generation Hispanics continue to speak the language of their forbears as well as English, compared to only 10% of equivalent Asian Americans. This, too, is put down to force of numbers sharing a common tongue. See P. Waldmeir, 'Great Wave on the No 7', *Financial Times*, 18/19 September 1999, Weekend Section, p. I.
18   A.E. Schwarz, 'Classical Case for Diversity', *Washington Post*, 2 April 1998, p. A25.
19   'Enter the Garcias' Own Party', *Economist*, 15 August 1998, p. 21.
20   See, for instance, G. Rodriguez, 'From Minority to Mainstream, Latinos Find Their Voice', *Washington Post*, 24 January 1999, p. B1, in which it is asserted that younger Hispanic state assemblymen and women and city and county officials more and more prefer a consensus- to an ethnic based approach to politics.
21   Clark, p. 54.
22   M. Ojito, 'INS Moving to Cut Citizenship Backlog', *New York Times*, 22 January 1999, p. A16.
23   The phrase belongs to journalist and author G.A. Geyer, quoted in Clark, p. 52. By contrast, some think INS application procedures too obstacle laden and strict and so the main reason rather than ineligibility or homesickness for four Hispanics in five still not

190 *Race and Ethnic Relations in Today's America*

becoming American citizens. See, for instance, P. Pan, 'Naturalisation: An Unnatural Process', *Washington Post*, 4 July 2000, p. A1.

24   S.G. Richter and D. Bachmann, 'How to Keep Growth Alive: Welcome More Immigrants', *Wall Street Journal*, 22 July 1999, p. A26. The Government appears to have accepted these labour pool arguments to the point of recently leaving alone most undocumented newcomers already in the U.S., if not those trying to cross the border. Whereas in 1997 twenty two thousand illegal immigrants were arrested for deportation, in 1999 barely a third of that number were so detained, most of them aliens who had committed a crime. See L. Uchitelle, 'INS Is Looking the Other Way As Illegal Immigrants Fill Jobs', *New York Times*, 9 March 2000, p. A1.

25   According to the reform minded Centre for Immigration Studies, there is a growing danger of 'foreignisation' of poverty in the United States. Already between 1979 and 1997 the fraction of newcomers living in poverty went from less than $1/6^{th}$ to more than $1/5^{th}$ while a steady one in eight of native born Americans fit this description. The Centre expects the gap between the two to widen as welfare changes take greater hold and indigenous Americans with their language advantage find it easier than less skilled immigrants to get jobs. See M.A. Fletcher, 'Immigrants' Growing Role in U.S. Poverty Cited', *Washington Post*, 2 September 1999, p. A2. The debate that has really been emerging, however, is whether poverty rates for immigrants decline significantly with time spent in the U.S. Advocates of the status quo say that they do, drawing upon analysis of 1996 census data revealing that within 15 years of arrival a typical immigrant has about the same poverty rate as U.S. born citizens and within 20 years less so. (See the letter of P.R. Yanni of the American Immigrant Lawyers Association to *ibid.*, 18 September 1999, p. A19.) But opponents point to a study released by the California Senate in 1999 that Hispanic workers in that state, at any rate, 'lag far behind all other groups in wages and educational attainment, even through the third generation' as evidence that economic progress is not being made. See Fletcher, *loc. cit.*

11 An Overview

The considerable attention that the media and others have devoted to race relations problems in the U.S. recently might well lead one to conclude things are as vexed as ever. Tensions undeniably exist, and blacks and members of other racial and ethnic minority groups continue to face many challenges. Yet many would contend that to say there has been no real improvement is arguably to exaggerate the difficulties. Amazing change has occurred since the inception of the modern day civil rights revolution in the 1950s, and there is no reason to believe similar progress cannot be achieved in the next half century too, given proper care and attention.

To all outward appearances, signs of improvement in virtually every measure of well being have abounded in the 1990s alone. Whereas at the start of the decade millions of U.S. blacks were caught up in one way or another in rising drug use, growing violence, disintegrating families and other undesirable conditions, before too long matters had started to turn round. Thus the black teenage birth rate fell by 9% in 1995 and had dropped by 17% since 1991. The percentage, if not the ratio, of black babies born out of wedlock fell in the mid-Nineties for the first time since the late 1960s and has continued falling since. For the first time since 1959, the poverty rate fell below 30% of all African Americans in 1995, and median income for black households rose faster that year than it did for whites. If African Americans have not been leaving welfare rolls as quickly as Caucasians, their dependency on state aid has been dropping noticeably. Meanwhile, the rate at which blacks were becoming victims of murder was dropping by at least 10% a year during the mid- to late 1990s, and the average life expectancy for black males was at last again increasing after years of decline.[1]

A number of people see the improvements as overstated. Just as some economists claim that the existence of a big disparity between whites and blacks in median household earnings is not necessarily indicative of racism because of extraneous factors like age, education and family structure, as we saw in Chapter 5, so others contend the closing of the racial gap in many of the above areas does not reveal progress so much as flawed statistical record keeping. Many of the surveys, for instance, count most

Americans of Hispanic origin as whites. The recent increases in the number of Latino immigrants, many of them poor, thus hold down overall Caucasian performance. Similarly, some say that the non-inclusion of three-quarters of a million black adults in various prisons when looking at such areas as unemployment or high school completion rates make African American improvements seem greater than they really are. Compounding matters is the issue of group differences. Black Americans are a fairly homogeneous group, whereas whites are not, and Asian and Hispanic Americans even less so. True statistical comparisons would have these latter groups broken down into separate ethnic categories such as Jewish-, Cuban- and Japanese Americans. The fact that they do not must in the opinion of some leave it open to doubt whether blacks are genuinely catching up. In reply, the optimists say much of the data show improvements in black-on-black rates that are unaffected by such considerations.

Others worry that even if there have been improvements, what is currently happening is as about as good as it gets. There is real concern that the recent gains may be reversed if the current boom falters. By February 2000, the U.S. economy was well into its ninth consecutive year of growth, the longest expansion of the past century, in either peace or war. However remarkable, this cannot go on forever, as even the most optimistic concede. African Americans, who as a group were generally among the last to feel the benefits of prosperity, could well be among the first to suffer during hard times. Recent welfare reform setting time limits to public assistance will not provide anyone, regardless of race, with much of a cushion in the event of a serious downturn. But African Americans with their much smaller accumulation of wealth than whites will be particularly vulnerable. For their part, civil rights advocates caution that significant hurdles need to be overcome and that the improvements should not be used to hide the very real social and economic problems that continue to confront the black population of the country.

Certainly, it is important to distinguish between the material benefits accrued by blacks in recent years and the progress made in addressing the underlying social and historical causes of inequality. There are two schools of thought about this. One is that the United States has come a long way over the years towards eliminating the stain of racism from the white American heart. According to this view, inequalities exist, but they are more a problem of poor education, weak skills and the prevalence of single parent families than of race. Individuals such as Colin Powell, Oprah Winfrey, Michael Jordan and Tiger Woods are idolised by whites, Asians and Hispanics as well as blacks. Surveys show that well over half of white people as well as blacks claim to have a 'good friend' of the other race. Only a small percentage of African Americans say they have no Caucasian neighbours. Even the taboo concerning interracial sex, long considered to be the greatest source of divide, has begun to break down. Black-white marriages are on the rise, though admittedly from a very low base. And 1998 claims of DNA findings that Thomas Jefferson, author of the Declaration of Independence and one the most revered presidents in the nation's history, fathered a child with his slave Sally Hemings have generally been greeted with equanimity.

The second school of thought comes to nearly the opposite conclusion. It holds that racism has not disappeared but merely gone underground. Hardcore bigotry might have become marginalised, as can be seen in the decline of KKK membership from about two million in the 1920s to a few thousand today. But subtle discrimination is widespread and plays a big role in perpetuating inequalities. Thus African Americans are 'steered' towards certain types of housing, which restricts their access to good schools, which in turn leads to the much discussed black-white skills differential and so the racial earnings gap. Which viewpoint is right and which wrong is difficult to say. Central to the issue is the fact that whites and blacks tend to define racism differently. The former generally see racism as a matter of personal attitudes and actions. The latter are more likely to describe it in institutional terms, as a matter of the racial group in power opposing another racial group. By the white definition progress has been made, even if 'hate crimes' sometimes make this seem otherwise; by the black definition it has not. It is perhaps possible to say that the two conclusions are correct at the same time. The proverbial glass is both half full and half empty.

Whether or not there has been a reduction in anti-black feeling in America in recent years, true racial harmony sometimes seems as elusive as ever. In retrospect, the view of the early civil rights campaigners that all that was basically needed to cure the nation of its racial ills was a few pieces of equal opportunities legislation now appears naïve. There is a sense among Caucasians that the time of large scale social remedies is past. Amongst the minorities, integration has not always made blacks happy, and many African Americans, while not implacably against it, do not particularly espouse it as a goal. They want the right to be able to mix with others but not necessarily to have to do so. It is an ambivalence that needless to say suits many whites but leaves others perplexed and resentful at perceived ingratitude just as the racial barriers were thought to be tumbling in earnest. The feeling of being rebuffed has induced some of the more liberal middle class whites to take up newer causes like the environment, whose beneficiaries such as spotted owls, dolphins and rainforests 'never grumble, or turn resentful or ungrateful'.[2]

Even when integration does take place it is often only in the obvious physical sense, not the emotional one. Because African Americans and Caucasians view both the nature and extent of racism in quite contrasting lights, they occupy what one black journalist for the *Washington Post* has called 'parallel universes' with regard to specific external events. Whites and blacks living next door to each other or working in a desegregated office might see the same images on their television sets and read the same details in their newspapers, but they sometimes reach widely varying conclusions about what has happened or experience the developments differently.[3] Thus delayed police questioning of parents of white teenage suburban school killers in Colorado is an act of decent sensitivity to the one group but an example of double standards to the other used to less patient treatment elsewhere. The spate of such killings in the late 1990s came about through a preventable 'culture of alienation' in the opinion of the one. But it was the inevitable result of ignoring the country's 'culture of violence' when it seemed to be confined to the inner cities in the view of the other. Both groups have difficulty in understanding that theirs is not the only reality.

How does one improve race relations when there is such disconnection and when for so many 'the era of big government is over'? President Clinton's solution was to have a national dialogue on the subject, which it was hoped would clear the air somewhat and stop blacks and whites talking past each other on matters like racism. But this initiative got bogged down in all sorts of technicalities and oversights and was overtaken by more pressing events like the President's very survival in office so that it had to be abandoned in the autumn of 1998 after only one year's existence. A few think that success is more likely to come if the goal is pursued indirectly. Blacks, whites, Asians and Hispanics should be brought together by having them work on some problem of mutual interest so long as it has nothing to do with skin colour. The U.S. Army does it, as do mixed race working crews and professional sports teams. The indirect approach can be quite effective, but only so long as it arises out of a genuine sense of national urgency. In this context, most common projects usually mentioned are either too parochial (*e.g.*, cleaning up neighbourhoods or guaranteeing safe streets) or as yet too vague and uncompelling (*e.g.*, a children's crusade) to work in a time of peace and runaway consumerism. But were life somehow to seem more threatening for all concerned, the 'common cause' idea might just work.

Despite the numerous doubts and misunderstandings, it is undeniable that the racial climate in America is more physically peaceful and muted than before. There are now no cities burning as a result of riots. 'Parallel universes' might well exist, but divisive events no longer seem to preoccupy blacks and whites in the way they did at the time of the O.J. Simpson trial a number of years ago. Daily experience, not political action, tends to define race relations nowadays. The black marches and demonstrations that do take place are as likely to be about self-improvement as about white misrule, and a *Wall Street Journal*/NBC News poll in early 2000 revealed that, while only a fraction of African Americans and Caucasians considered the state of race relations in the U.S. at the time to be 'very good', substantial numbers in both groups regarded them as being at least satisfactory.[4] Throughout this book a variety of explanations has been put forward for this phenomenon: the sustained period of prosperity in the 1990s that in time came to benefit ordinary black people as well as whites; the demoralised and disorganised state of the NAACP and other liberal civil rights groups, which have failed to rally opposition to a conservative controlled Congress; the personal interest of President Clinton in race relations; and the belief of many African Americans that he understands their plight. It is up to the reader to determine which of these is the most important, suffice it to say that some are at times more relevant than others and that none is guaranteed to last.

A more complicated picture comes to the fore when one considers America's other racial and ethnic minorities. Not only are there both Hispanics and Asians to take into account but subsets within these groups, each having fairly distinct cultural characteristics. Making generalisations that ring true is therefore quite hard and only to be attempted with care. Broadly speaking, one can say that the material well being of these groups has also for the most part been on an upward trend during the past decade and for largely the same reasons as those applying to African Americans. Native born minority members have on the whole done better than immigrants, and the improvements have usually been more noticeable in the later rather than the earlier part of the 1990s. One possible exception is Latinos, some of whom for a variety of reasons have been progressing less certainly than others for much of the past decade. But even here one needs to tread cautiously and acknowledge the fact that for all the U.S. born Mexican Americans who have lapsed into deeper poverty almost as many have joined the ranks of the middle class. Meanwhile, Cuban Americans, including many of the more recent arrivals, thrive economically.

Complications also emerge when trying to assess the impact of these other groups on the racial climate in the U.S. Here, too, there are two schools of thought. On the one hand is the view that the rapid growth in numbers of Asians and Latinos will render the task of achieving racial harmony much more difficult, turning a two-dimensional problem into one that exists on several planes as blacks and whites worry not only about each other but also about the newcomers. On the other is the opinion that the newcomers will ultimately have an essential role to play as neutral arbiters between whites and blacks. Hispanics in particular are seen as potentially useful here, 'both as the uncomplaining greasers of the wheels of the American economy' and as people who, because they are brown, black and white, have 'no racial axe to grind'.[5] Their coming from lands that have a more elastic view of race, with people of different skin colourings simply being put on a gradient or continuum, often at personal whim, rather than into formal categories, does not hurt matters in the opinion of many.[6]

Only time will tell which will be the more correct forecast, but there can be no denying that the worst fears of the anti-immigrationists a decade ago have hitherto proved to be without foundation. If the newcomers have been stealing jobs, they have not been taking that many to raise the unemployment figures of native born blacks and whites. Certain parts of the country where immigrants have been arriving in droves like California, New York City and the Washington, D.C., area now have labour shortages. Equally groundless so far are the predictions of restrictionists that the latest set of foreign arrivals, in contrast to previous waves of immigrant groups, would never blend in. Starting with the 1996 presidential election campaign and continuing with subsequent ballots, they have been participating in the political process as never before. Admittedly, at times this has been in response to the calls of their own activists, who do not always believe in assimilation. But on other occasions recently naturalised Americans have shown considerable independence of mind. Of course, none of this is to say that the USA will not revert to an earlier hostile climate, especially if the economy worsens. To date, however, the optimists have been largely right.

Whatever the future holds, the stakes are considerable. Success in the current multiethnic, if not necessarily multicultural, experiment could not only make for everlasting peace at home but a shining example to other countries like Brazil and South Africa with a similarly complex demographic composition. Failure could turn America into an oversized Bosnia, jeopardising domestic tranquillity and prosperity and hampering any attempt on the USA's part to play an effective role on the world stage. Perhaps it was these concerns that President Clinton had in mind in 1997 when he referred to solving the problems of race and ethnic relations as the country's 'millennial challenge'.

At the outset of this book it was stated that race relations is America's interminable problem. Other difficulties might come and go, but this one remains intransitory. Much that was written in subsequent chapters seemed to confirm this view. We have seen that the continuing desire of a number of blacks as well as whites to associate with their own race has in many areas kept schools, neighbourhoods and even television viewing habits differentiated and segregated. Arguments have taken place about the racial composition of all sorts of different bodies, ranging from juries to city police forces to membership of the Supreme Court. Disparities in income and unemployment rates have been the subject of at least as much debate. Yet for all the rancour, glimmers of hope have begun to appear as the twentieth century draws to a close. Older suburbs as well as workplaces are becoming integrated. Dating and marital habits are changing. Newcomers with different experiences and perspectives are arriving. Political parties are becoming more inclusive as minorities become more numerous. The South, once a bastion of white supremacy, has experienced some sense of reconciliation. A consensus seems to be emerging that affirmative action in its present form cannot continue. Whether these developments will proceed apace remains to be seen, but it is hard to imagine them all being passing phenomena. Optimists can therefore probably draw comfort knowing that, come what may, America will be taking at least a few more steps to try to stop the problem of the 21st century being one and the same as that of the 20th, the problem of the colour line.

Notes

1   S.A. Holmes, 'Quality of Life Is Up for Many Blacks, Data Says', *New York Times*, 18 November 1996, p. A1.

2   A. Hacker, *Two Nations* (New York: Chas. Scribner's Sons, 1992), p. 64.

3   C. Milloy, 'A Look at Tragedy in Black and White', *Washington Post*, 2 May 1999, p. C1.

4   A.R. Hunt, 'Blacks, Whites Find Common Ground on Attitudes Towards Race', *Wall Street Journal*, 9 March 2000, p. A19. The findings are in many ways remarkable because they came only a few days after a well publicised acquittal of four white New York City policemen accused of racism in their controversial gunning down of Amadou Diallo, an unarmed West African street peddler immigrant with no criminal record, outside his home in February 1999.

5   'A Minority Worth Cultivating', *Economist*, 25 April 1998, p. 21.

6   R.T. Schaefer, *Racial and Ethnic Groups* (New York: Addison Wesley Longman, 1998), p. 278; also E. Cose, *Colour-Blind* (New York: HarperCollins, 1997), p. 195. However, others, noting the tendency in many Caribbean and South American cultures to marry lighter as one moves up the social scale and the references to paler skin shadings on the part of some Hispanics of European origin to express personal flattery, doubt whether Latinos can act as true go-betweens in the U.S. See R. Estrada, 'Racism Among Hispanics', *Washington Post*, 5 October 1999, p. A17.

Bibliography

Bettelheim, A. (1998), 'AIDS Update: Are Researchers Closer to a Cure?', *CQ Researcher*, vol. 8, pp. 1049-72.

Bowen, W. G. and Bok, D. (1998), *The Shape of the River: Long-Term Consequences of Considering Race in College and University Admissions*, Princeton University Press, Princeton, N.J.

Clark, C. C. (1995), 'Housing Discrimination: Are Minorities Still Treated Unfairly?', *CQ Researcher*, vol.5, pp. 169-92.

Clark, C. C. (1997), 'The New Immigrants: Do They Threaten the American Identity?', *CQ Researcher*, vol. 7, pp. 49-72.

Coleman, J. (1997), *Long Way To Go: Black and White in America*, Atlantic Monthly Press, New York.

Cose, E. (1993), *The Rage of a Privileged Class*, HarperCollins, New York.

Cose, E. (1997), *Colour Blind: Seeing Beyond Race in a Race Obsessed World*, HarperCollins, New York.

D'Souza, D. (1995), *The End of Racism: Principles for a Multiracial Society*, The Free Press, New York.

Federal Bureau of Investigation (1997, 1998), *Uniform Crime Reports for the United States*, U.S. Department of Justice, Washington, D.C.

Foner, E. (1995), 'Discrimination in Favour of Minorities Is Necessary', in B. Szumski (ed.), *Interracial America: Opposing Viewpoints*, Greenhaven Press, San Diego.

Griffin, R.D. (1992), 'Hispanic Americans: Can They Find Prosperity and Political Power?', *CQ Researcher*, vol. 2, pp. 929-52.

Griffin, R. D. (1992), 'Illegal Immigration: Does It Damage the Economy and Strain Social Services?', *CQ Researcher*, vol. 2, pp. 361-84.

Gurwitt, R. (1993), 'Blacks and Latinos Are Competing for Political Power', in P. Winters (ed.), *Race Relations: Opposing Viewpoints*, Greenhaven Press, San Diego.

Hacker, A. (1992), *Two Nations: Black and White, Separate and Unequal*, Chas. Scribner's Sons, New York.

Jost, K. (1994), 'Talk Show Democracy: Are Call-In Programmes Good for the Political System?', *CQ Researcher*, vol. 4, pp. 361-84.

Jost, K. (1995), 'Rethinking Affirmative Action: Are Policies Based on Race and Gender Unfair?', *CQ Researcher*, vol. 5, pp. 369-92.

Jost, K. (1997), 'Diversity in the Workplace: Is It Good for Business?', *CQ Researcher*, vol. 7, pp. 889-912.

Langan, P.A. (1994), 'America's Justice System Does Not Discriminate Against Blacks', in P. Winters (ed.), *Race Relations: Opposing Viewpoints*, Greenhaven Press, San Diego.

Lind, M. (1996), 'Legal Immigration Harms American Workers', in T. Roleff (ed.), *Immigration: Opposing Viewpoints*, Greenhaven Press, San Diego.

Masci, D. (1997), 'Assisting Refugees: Do Current Aid Policies Add to the Problems?', *CQ Researcher*, vol. 7, pp. 97-120.

Masci, D. (1997), 'Mexico's Future: Is It on the Path to True Democracy?', *CQ Researcher*, vol. 7, pp. 817-40.

Masci, D. (1998), 'The Black Middle Class: Is Its Cup Half-Full or Half-Empty?', *CQ Researcher*, vol. 8, pp. 49-72.

Masci, D. (1998), 'Hispanic-Americans' New Clout: Will Hispanics Desert the Democratic Party?', *CQ Researcher*, vol. 8, pp. 809-32.

Miles, J. (1992), 'Immigrants Take Jobs from Blacks', in P. Winters (ed.), *Race Relations: Opposing Viewpoints*, Greenhaven Press, San Diego.

Milton S. Eisenhower Foundation and the Corporation for What Works (1998), *Millennium Breach: Richer and Poorer in America*, First and Second Editions and Printing, Washington, D.C.

Morgan, K.O. and S. (eds) (1999), *State Rankings 1999: A Statistical View of the 50 United States*, Morgan Quitno Press, Lawrence, Kansas.

Page, C. (1996), *Showing My Colour: Impolite Essays on Race and Identity*, HarperCollins, New York.

Purcell, L.E. (1995), *Immigration*, Oryx Press, Phoenix, Ariz.

Rymer, R. (1998), *American Beach: A Saga of Race, Wealth and Memory*, HarperCollins, New York.

Schaefer, R.T. (1998), *Racial and Ethnic Groups*, Addison Wesley and Longman, New York.

Shipler, D. K. (1997), *A Country of Strangers: Blacks and Whites in America*, Alfred A. Knopf, New York.

Steele, S. (1990), *The Content of Our Character: A New Vision of Race in America*, St. Martin's Press, New York.

Suro, R. (1998), *Strangers Among Us: How Latino Immigration Is Transforming America*, Alfred A. Knopf, New York.

Swain, C. M. (1993), *Black Faces, Black Interests*, Harvard University Press, Cambridge, Mass.

Taylor, J. (1992), *Paved With Good Intentions: The Failure of Race Relations in Contemporary America*, Carroll & Graf, New York.

Thernstrom, S. and A. (1997), *America in Black and White: One Nation, Indivisible*, Simon & Schuster, New York.

U.S. Census Bureau (1997, 1998), *Statistical Abstract of the United States*, 117th and 118th Editions, Washington, D.C.

Index

References from Notes indicated by 'n' after page reference

205

National Black Leadership Forum 118
National Centre for Health, U.S. 45
National Institute of Health 90
National Urban League 118-9
Native Americans (see also 'affirmative
    action') x-xii, 3-6, 13-5, 18, 20-1,
    24, 50n, 78, 142-5
nativism – see 'immigrants, immigration'
Nazi Germany 11, 21, 98
New Deal 10, 115
New England 54
New Hampshire 112
New Jersey 130, 134
New Mexico 26, 30, 134, 136
New York City (see also 'Harlem',
    'Manhattan' and 'Queens' borough)
    28, 30, 33n, 84, 109, 140, 174, 179,
    183, 196, 197n
New York State 112, 130, 134, 139, 141
New York Stock Exchange 39
Newark, N.J. 69
Nixon, Richard, Nixon administration
    12-3, 73, 127n, 150
North, the 7-12, 17, 29, 69, 109
North Carolina 109, 120-2, 127n
Northeast, the 28-30, 33n, 69, 134
Northwest, Pacific 53, 161
NYPD Blue (TV show) 96, 107n

octoroon 4
Ohio 29, 92, 112
'one-drop rule' 22, 162
Oprah Winfrey Show, The (TV show)
    100
Orlando, Fla. 28

Pacific Islanders – see 'Asian
    Americans' and 'Hawaii'
Page, Clarence 107n
Parks, Rosa 11
'passing' 4
Paying the Social Debt (America) 5
Pearl Harbour, Hawaii 13
Pentagon 169n
Pentecostalist churches 135
Pequod 144
Perot, Ross 113
Philadelphia, Pa. 33n, 57, 59
Philippinos 138, 140, 173, 184
Phoenix, Ariz. 28, 69

Plessy v. Ferguson 9, 11
poll tax 8
population – see 'blacks', 'census'
poverty line 35, 41-2, 49n-50n, 133,
    147n, 164
Powell, Colin 3, 112, 117, 192
Prince George's County, Md. 56
Proposition 187 (California, 1994) 134,
    175, 186
Proposition 209 (California, 1996) 135,
    159-62
Proposition 227 (California, 1998) 185
Puerto Ricans 23, 30, 130, 133-4, 146n

quadroon 4
Queens (New York City borough) 25

race, definitions of x-xi, 196
'race norming' 159
race riots (1960s) 12, 15, 31, 99
'racial profiling' 84
racism x, 2-3, 5, 14, 31-2, 43, 50n, 64n,
    67, 73, 79-80, 87-8, 92, 94, 127n,
    149-50, 152, 181, 191-4, 197n
    environmental 92
Rage of a Privileged Class, The (Cose)
    41
rap music 48
Reagan, Ronald/Reagan administration
    53, 61, 117, 122, 144, 159, 177
Reagonomics 115
reapportionment, congressional 17, 20
Reconstruction 8-9
Red Indians – see 'Native Americans'
redistricting, congressional 17, 20, 111,
    119-25, 126, 141, 150
Reed, Ishmael 98
Reform Party – see 'Buchanan, Pat' and
    'Perot, Ross'
reparations 5, 124, 161
Republican Party, Republicans 10, 12,
    19-20, 43, 46, 61, 79, 109, 112-3,
    117-9, 122, 125, 127n, 135-6, 142,
    144, 149, 159, 161, 164-5, 167, 175-
    7, 180, 186, 188
Rio Grande River 14, 178, 184
Robinson, Jackie 11
Rocky Mountain states 28, 54
Roman Catholic Church 133, 135, 146n
Roosevelt, Eleanor 10

206